HANDBOOK to the OLD TESTAMENT

CLAUS WESTERMANN

Translated and Edited by
Robert H. Boyd

AUGSBURG PUBLISHING HOUSE
Minneapolis   **Minnesota**

HANDBOOK TO THE OLD TESTAMENT

First paperback edition, 1976

Copyright © 1967 Augsburg Publishing House

All rights reserved

Library of Congress Catalog Card No. 67-25362

International Standard Book No. 0-8066-1529-X

This volume is a translation of the introduction and Old Testament sections of *Abriss Der Bibelkunde* published in 1962 by Verlagsgemeinschaft Burckhardthaus- und Kreuz-Verlag GmbH. (4th edition, 1966), Stuttgart/Gelnhausen, Germany.

Manufactured in the United States of America

HANDBOOK to the
OLD TESTAMENT

Translator's Preface

The abundance of books which flood the market on every aspect of the Bible may well lead one to echo the wearied complaint of the Preacher: "Of making many books there is no end, and much study is a weariness of the flesh" (Eccl. 12:12). What more can a biblical handbook such as this contribute to a market already overcrowded with books about the Bible? Does it have anything significant to offer that is not already adequately covered in other books of this type?

To anyone familiar with the German original of this translation and the pastoral concern that brought it into being, the answer will be obvious. Here is a handbook that performs a genuinely superb service in leading one into the content of Holy Scripture.

With a fine cognizance of the importance of biblical criticism and the manner in which it has contributed to our present understanding of the relevance and significance of the Bible, Professor Westermann has been able at the same time to point up the living and abiding value of the biblical message as God's Word to us today.

He does not lose himself in cumbersome and intricate detail but opens a clear pathway into the Scriptures themselves, exciting the reader's interest, whetting his appetite, and preparing him for the delight of pursuing Bible study on his own. In this little guide he succeeds in providing an overall view of the vast scope and significance of the biblical message. In doing this he does not offer a substitute for reading the Word of God itself, but rather demonstrates in an effective manner how to read it. The graphic and informative charts and outlines as well as interpretive comments enable one to grasp quickly the basic content of each biblical book and to understand it in relation to other parts of the Old and New Testaments.

In rendering this excellent guide into English, I have made a number of modifications as well as additions to the original text in order to increase its usefulness. These have been introduced with the understanding and approval of the original author, although their introduction is my own responsibility and any shortcomings and faults inherent in them is chargeable entirely to me.

For easier and more ready reference the outlines of the various biblical books as well as the accompanying interpretive comments have been set up according to the scheme of notation and indention recommended by *A Manual of Style* (The University of Chicago Press). As a result, letters and numbers occasionally used in the German original have had to be disregarded.

To bring the explanatory text into more exact conformity with the charts it has been found necessary at times to add further captions and also to modify slightly the original format of the charts themselves. Compare pp. 55 f. (Germ. ed., p. 49) with the explanatory text that follows (pp. 57-63; Germ. pp. 50-55). As a rule, however, the original format of the charts has been strictly observed. One new chart based on the descriptive material in the text has been added (cf. p. 18).

To preserve a greater overall consistency or conformity with the charts on the individual books, the text has been rearranged on the following pages: p. 36 (cf. Germ. ed., p. 32), 171 f. (Germ. 137 f.), 253 f., 257 f., (Germ. 200 f.), 262 ff. (Germ. 206 f.).

Considerable freedom has been exercised in rendering certain frequently repeated German words and phrases that are not used by the author in a technical sense. This has been done to avoid a monotonous and jejune effect in English. Thus *Heilswort* has been rendered variously as *good news, promise of welfare, words of good omen, redemptive word, promise of salvation.* Other examples are: *Heilsprophet, Lob, Klage.*

An attempt has been made to provide a complete documentation of Scripture references, all of which are noted in the index that has been prepared for the English edition. When Scripture is quoted, the Revised Standard Version has normally been followed, unless the author's comments are based on a German version that conveys a different meaning than that expressed in the R.S.V. In such cases, footnotes have been added to explain the difference between the English and German versions in relation to the original text.

It would have become very cumbersome and only added confusion to have placed brackets around all the above-noted editorial changes and additions in the main body of the text. They therefore have not been used. Editorial comments have been noted, however, in the footnotes.

The present translation is based on the introduction and Old Testament section of Claus Westermann's *Abriss der Bibelkunde (Handbücherei des Christen in der Welt, Band I).* The New Testament section will appear later in a companion volume.

I wish to express appreciation to many of my colleagues at Luther Theological Seminary for their encouragement and helpful suggestions during the course of the preparation of this translation, also to my wife for many long hours spent in typing, and to student David Langseth for assistance in compiling the indices.

ROBERT H. BOYD

Luther Theological Seminary
St. Paul, Minn.

From the Author's FOREWORD

The essential material for this project has grown out of a course in Bible content that I conducted at the Kirchliche Hochschule in Berlin in the years following 1950. In my association with the students in this course I came to realize how important a basic knowledge of the Bible is for theological study as well as all subsequent church work. This book is intended for all who are convinced that a survey of the entire Bible is a necessary prerequisite for a responsible transmission of the words of Scripture in preaching, teaching, and the practical ministry.* . . .

C. WESTERMANN

*Translator's Note: English sources that provide a bibliography for the individual biblical books, and that correspond to German sources, cited here by the author are *The New Schaff-Herzog Encyclopedia of Religious Knowledge* (Supplementary volumes) (Grand Rapids, Michigan: Baker Book House, 1955) and *The Interpreter's Dictionary of the Bible* (New York: Abingdon Press, 1962).

CONTENTS

xi

Part Three: THE PROPHETS

Part Four: THE WRITINGS

Charts and Tables

A Time Chart

OF SIGNIFICANT DATES IN THE HISTORY OF ISRAEL

After 1350 B.C.	Beginning of the occupation of Canaan by the tribes of Israel	
13th cent.	Oppression in Egypt Exodus	*Song of Miriam*
c. 1200	Assembly of the tribes at Shechem (Joshua)	*Traditions of the exodus and occupation*
c. 1100	End of the period of occupation	
12th-11th cent.	Period of the judges	*Sources lying behind J and E The Book of the Covenant*
c. 1005/4	Saul	
c. 1000-961*	David	*Beginning of psalmody Narrative of the ark of the covenant (I Sam. 4-6; II Sam. 6)*
c. 961-922	Solomon	*Formation of the Yahwistic source*
c. 922	Division of the kingdoms of Israel (922-721) and Judah (922-587)	

---

*Translator's note: The dates for the kings (David to Zedekiah) are based on the approximate chronology prepared by W. F. Albright in the *Bulletin of the American Schools of Oriental Research*, Dec. 1945, pp. 16-22. The remaining dates are based on the chronology in *Evangelisches Kirchenlexikon*, Göttingen. 1958, vol. II, pp. 418-422 as selected by C. Westermann.

	Kings of Israel		Kings of Judah	
c. 922-901	Jeroboam I	**c. 922-915**	Rehoboam	
9th cent.				*Origin of Elohistic source?*
c. 876-869	Omri (Founding of Samaria)			
c. 869-850	Ahab (Period of Elijah)	**c. 873-849**	Jehosha- phat	
c. 849-842	Jehoram	**c. 849-842**	Jehoram	
c. 842-815	Jehu (Revolu- tion)	**c. 837-800**	Jehoash	
c. 786-746	Jeroboam II (Amos)	**c. 783-742**	Uzziah	*Amos* *Hosea*
		c. 735-715	Ahaz	
735-734	Aramean-Israelite war Initial period of Isaiah's activity			
721	Fall of Samaria Assyrian exile			
c. 715-687	Hezekiah (Micah. Siege of Jeru- salem by Sennacherib in 701. Second period of Isaiah's activity)			*Micah* *Isaiah*
c. 640-609	Josiah			
c. 639-621				*Zephaniah* *Nahum*
c. 626-621	Initial period of Jere- miah's activity			
621	Deuteronomic Reform			*Deuteron- omy*

609-598	Jehoiakim (Second period of Jeremiah's activity)	*Habakkuk* *Jeremiah* *(original scroll)*
598	Jehoiachin (First captivity)	
597-587	Zedekiah (Third period of Jeremiah's activity	
593-571	Activity of Ezekiel	*Limited portion of Ezekiel*
587	Fall of Jerusalem	
587-538	Babylonian exile	*Lamentations*
546-539		*Deutero-Isaiah* *Priestly Document?*
Between 538 and 519		*Trito-Isaiah*
520	Activity of Haggai and Zechariah	*Haggai* *Zechariah 1-8*
515	Dedication of the temple	
c. 460		*Malachi*
c. 450-430	Activity of Ezra and Nehemiah	*Ezra, Nehemiah*
4th cent.		*Jonah, Job*
4th-3rd cent.		*Joel. Chronicler's history*
c. 332		*Zechariah 9-14*
3rd cent.		*Proverbs* (partial formation) *Song of Solomon* (final form)
c. 250		*Ecclesiastes*
Between 170 and 160		*Esther* *Daniel*
167-63	Period of the Maccabees	*Qumran texts*

INTRODUCTION

THE PURPOSE OF A HANDBOOK TO THE BIBLE

In the last few generations and above all the present one the disparity between our world and the world of the Bible has greatly increased. This is not due actually to the fact that so many words of Scripture are now but vaguely understood (if at all)* or that our sense for verbal distinctions has been impaired by the abundance of technical terms. It is rather due to the fact that our whole way of thinking and appreciation for life and existence in the last two generations has been drastically modified by the direct as well as the indirect effects of the natural sciences together with the great changes in the forms of community and individual life that they have occasioned.

That this disparity has increased cannot mean that the Word, which God directs to us in the Bible, is now of remote significance; for the promise that our Lord will be with us always even to the end of the world has not altered. The increasing alienation of the biblical world and its language from our world and its manner of speech should only be a challenge to seek ways to gain a new familiarity with the Scriptures.

This handbook of biblical information will be an aid in this. It is based on the Reformation principle: *Sacra Scriptura sui interpres.***

---

*Translator's Note: The author is referring here to the German Bible, translated by Martin Luther, which would roughly correspond to the King James Version in terms of its intelligibility to the modern reader. The comment which he makes about the vagueness of many of the words of the Bible would not pertain to modern versions such as the Revised Standard Version.

**Scripture is its own interpreter.

3

By this is meant: whoever would heed the words of the Bible will find that the more intently he listens to and becomes involved in and familiar with Scripture, the more clearly and directly the Bible will speak to him. A genuine and basic familiarity with the books of the Bible is the prerequisite for apprehending an individual expression, even as it is implied from the standpoint of the entire biblical context.

A handbook of information concerning the Bible can indeed perform only a modest service in helping one gain such a new intimacy with the Scriptures. It cannot, as its title seems to imply, provide a complete and thorough knowledge of the Bible. For this one must add exegesis and theological study in all its various ramifications.

A handbook such as this can only indicate a few ways that lead into the broad land of Scripture. Whenever one provides biblical information, exegesis is, of course, carried on. Information about the Bible that had nothing to do with exegesis would be an illusion. There is also concern for introduction into the biblical books, especially problems as to their origin. Exegesis and problems of introduction, however, must play an unobtrusive role, remaining as much as possible in the background.

It is characteristic of biblical exegesis in the last few decades not to follow simply the text of a biblical book word-for-word. In seeking to become acquainted with Scripture, we will therefore rather let the question concerning its message *as a whole* be our motivating concern in order that we thereby may become involved with the question as to the *focal point* of that entire message as it becomes apparent.

When one starts with the Bible in whole or in part and tries to get at its singular characteristic, one comes only to a conclusion which is already granted, namely, that in Scripture as a whole God's Word has been entrusted to the congregation. This is true whether one examines main groups of biblical books, individual books, or even sections within books. From beginning to end the Bible gives an account of a great history, diverse and manifold, focused in the account concerning Jesus of Nazareth. Individual biblical words can only be rightly perceived in connection with this whole account and in relation to its central message.

An essential aspect of biblical information must be almost entirely omitted here for lack of space, viz., the pointing up of relationships that cut across Scripture. It should be emphasized at once, however, that the task of biblical study should proceed farther along this line.

One should be directed, for example, from the creation account in Gen. 1-3 to the psalms of creation, to Job 38 ff., Deutero-Isaiah, and the New Testament statements concerning creation.

What Gen. 3-4 and 6-9 have to say concerning man's sin is continued along the dual line of individual and social sin in the historical books, in a number of the psalms, but above all in the prophetic indictments and ultimately in the New Testament (Galatians, Romans, and other books).

From the promise of blessing in Gen. 12:1-3 runs a line of benediction, proceeding through the patriarchal history, Deuteronomy, the psalms of benediction, even to the words of blessing in the New Testament.

The deliverance at the Sea of Reeds* introduces the chain of God's saving acts up to the final act of deliverance in Christ. At the same time the history of the Mediator begins in the opening part of Exodus, leading in various ways ultimately to the Songs of the Suffering Servant in Deutero-Isaiah, and then to Christ.

With the building of an altar (already in Gen. 4) and Abraham's sacrifice the history of sacrifical worship and the shrine begins. This likewise points throughout the entire Old Testament to the ultimate sacrifice of Christ (cf. Hebrews). In him the old sacrificial worship was once-for-all suspended.

From the establishment of the kingdom under Saul and David one looks beyond the dramatic royal history in the north and south and the collapse of both kingdoms and sees the connection with the expectation of another king who was to come. He perceives the messianic hope and its fulfillment in the title of Christ, given to Jesus of Nazareth.

In like manner, all the lines must be carefully traced, as one goes

---

*This is a more accurate rendering of the Hebrew *yôm sûf*, used in Exod. 13:18. Cf. *The Torah*. A new translation of the Holy Scriptures according to the Masoretic text. Philadelphia: Jewish Publication Society, 1962.

about getting a knowledge of both Old and New Testaments. These are the ones that present at times a single event within the context of the entire Bible, an individual portion of God's history with his people, or basic concepts, such as Spirit, faith, precept and law, grace and wrath, promise and fulfillment, man's response through worship, prayer, and confession. Thus a book-by-book presentation must be accompanied by one that cuts diagonally through the biblical writings, linking individual sections with the whole.

In this respect, and in many other ways, this handbook can only indicate the initial steps into the Bible. Once there is a familiarity with Scripture and a delight in carrying on study of one's own, the imparting of biblical information can recede into the background.

THE BIBLE AS A WHOLE

In a first over-all view of the entire Bible, the Old Testament appears as a great expanse alongside the smaller expanse of the New Testament. Both are composed of many smaller areas, which (as in a map) exhibit sometimes independent regions, merging into larger unities. All the writings of the Old and New Testaments were once independent books, before they were combined into the present collections.

Just as one can view a map as a historical presentation, exhibited on a flat surface, so a biblical handbook (which can deal but superficially with the biblical writings) directs one constantly to the history, to which there is only an allusion in this cursory presentation of the sections and outlines of the account. For the Bible in its totality is essentially a great history. It is only in reference to this history that one can read the writings and books and parts of the Bible in their true context. Only thus can one get at their significance.

In Luther's translation of the Bible, the same primary division is used for the table of contents of both Old and New Testaments, viz., Historical Books, Didactic Books, and Prophetic Books. This division, however, is but a superficial synopsis; for the books that appear under these headings have a much more diverse character. This is evident when one examines them more carefully.

There is a group of narrative or informative books in the Old and New Testaments, which are the origin as well as the matrix of the entire collection. These are the Pentateuch and the Gospels respectively. The reader of the Bible should take careful note of this fundamental material in both Testaments and never forget that it is the Bible's proper manner of speech—it tells a story. That the Old Testament and the New Testament agree in this is by no means accidental. It is essential to both. Besides this, however, they have much in common: both tell how God's history with his people in the old as well as in the new covenant turned out. At the heart of both is the account concerning the divine saving act whereby the covenant was established.

Neither is a historical account in the modern sense of the term but is rather a witness or testimony to that for which the faith and confession of those who here speak is basic. Closely connected with this is the fact that there are several witnesses narrating the individual events of which the history in almost all the Pentateuch and Gospels is composed. What is more, these two, three, or four accounts (as the case may be) do not agree literally—something quite characteristic of first-hand reports.

The only difference between the Pentateuch and the Gospels lies in the fact that the Gospel's first-hand reports exist side-by-side in separate books, whereas those in the Pentateuch have been woven together into one general account. Only Deuteronomy has remained as a separate account alongside the others. Here the correspondence with the New Testament is so close that Deuteronomy (like the fourth Gospel in relation to the other Synoptics) occupies also a special position. It consists especially of longer addresses.

From here on the differences are greater than the similarities. In the New Testament the Gospels are followed by the Acts of the Apostles, a history after the main event, telling how the apostles of Jesus Christ fared in the world. In the Old Testament the Pentateuch is succeeded by the account of Israel's history from the Book of Joshua to 2 Kings. The ancient designation for this section is "the Former Prophets," a title that gives decisive significance to the prophets, appearing in the course of this history or to the word of God, issuing through them. The work of the Chronicler (1 and 2 Chronicles, Ezra, and Nehemiah), which comes next, did not belong to the historical books according to the ancient arrangement but to "the Writings," hence to the third part of the canon. This is due to the character of its historical presentation, which is essentially different (see below, p. 253). The real historical books of the Old Testament conclude with the exile.

In the New Testament the Acts of the Apostles is followed by the epistles; in the Old Testament the "Former Prophets," by the prophetic writings. They correspond also to one another in this, that they are both concerned with a message and with the office of a messenger. It was only by the word they proclaimed that God's work on behalf of his people was accomplished in the ministry of the apostles as well as the prophets. This ministry was carried on with the one as well as the other amid opposition and trouble, and it was accepted only by small groups of people. The difference in the content of their message, however, immediately strikes the eye: the apostles were messengers of good news—the Gospel; the prophets, messengers of judgment, for the most part. When the latter, however, had good news to bring, they pointed to the future, whereas the apostles in their message pointed back to that which had taken place.

According to the arrangement in Luther's Bible the Revelation to John is the only prophetic book in the third part of the New Testament, and it has therefore been classified with the prophetic books of the Old Testament. This no longer agrees with present understanding of prophecy; for Revelation is an apocalypse—hence a book dealing with the "last things." In this respect it does not correspond with the prophetic books but with Daniel, the second part of which is also an apocalypse.

The third part of the Old Testament, which Luther called the books of instruction (the books of poetry in later Bibles), has nothing corresponding to it in the New Testament. Whereas a real as well as a formal correspondence is to be observed in the Old and New Testaments in the case of the first section (the books that are historical), and whereas the prophetic books and the epistles have a formal correspondence along with a content that is largely adverse in character, the third part (the Writings) has no section whatsoever corresponding to it in the New Testament.

The nucleus of this third section is the Book of Psalms, consisting of prayers and songs. In the New Testament, prayers and songs were never admitted as a collection but were handed down separately in addition to the New Testament. This third part of the Old Testament includes furthermore another body of material that has nothing resembling it in the New Testament, viz., wisdom, in the Book of Proverbs.

To these two fundamental collections in the third section were attached still other writings: first of all, the Book of Job, which stands somewhere in between Psalms and wisdom literature; then the five festival scrolls (the Megilloth). These latter are five short books that are quite diverse. They served as readings for the five Jewish festivals and are as follows:

1. The little Book of Ruth, which relates an episode from the time of the Judges and was later added therefore to the Book of Judges.

2. The Song of Songs, a collection of love songs or wedding ballads that got into the Bible simply because of their messianic interpretation.

3. Ecclesiastes, a late wisdom book.

4. Lamentations, which is closely related to the Psalms but was added to the book of Jeremiah because of its being ascribed to him.

5. The Book of Esther, a story which gives the basis for the Jewish festival of Purim.

There is finally the Daniel-apocalypse and the work of the Chronicler, consisting of the two Books of Chronicles and Ezra-Nehemiah.

The third section of the Old Testament is accordingly a very loose group of detached writings, which at different times and for various reasons were added to the body of sacred writings. Psalms and Wisdom (i.e. Proverbs) continued to be the really fundamental books of this third division.

Part One

THE PENTATEUCH

I. Its Structure and Development

II. The Primeval History

III. The Patriarchal History
    The Abraham Stories
    The Jacob-Esau Stories
    The Joseph Stories

IV. From Exodus to Numbers
    Exodus
    The Priestly Code
        The Legal Collections of
        the Pentateuch
        The Sections of the
        Priestly Code:
        Exodus 25-31, 35-40
        Leviticus
        Numbers 1-9
    Numbers 10-36

V. Deuteronomy

I

Structure and Development
of the Pentateuch

Pentateuch signifies "a compilation of five" (Gk. *pente* "five" + *teuchos* "tool"). The name was introduced in connection with scientific studies to indicate that in place of five books there was once a single holy book—the Torah, which comprehended all five within itself. Later it was then divided into five books. This, however, was but the last two stages of this compilation. Previously centuries had affected its development.

It is easy to make a quick survey of its contents by starting at the conclusion. The last chapter of Deuteronomy tells how God showed Moses the land he had promised his people before Moses' death.

> And the Lord showed him all the land, Gilead, as far as Dan, all Naphtali, the land of Ephraim and Manasseh, all the land of Judah as far as the Western Sea . . . .
> And the Lord said to him: "This is the land . . . !" (34:1-4).

In these words, spoken to Moses before his death, a transaction was consummated whose origin is revealed by the Book of Exodus at its beginning. Here too it is a divine word, addressed to Moses. At the time of his call (Ex. 3) Moses was told:

> "I have seen the affliction of my people who are in Egypt, and have heard their cry . . . .
> "I have come down to deliver them out of the hand of the Egyptians, and to bring them up out of that land to a good and broad land . . . " (vv. 7 f.).

13

The two references just cited (from the beginning of the second book of the Pentateuch and from the end of the fifth) mark the span that stretches from promise to fulfillment. In these words it becomes clear why the Pentateuch, this compilation of five books, must be understood as a unity.

The arch of promise does not take its rise at the beginning of the Pentateuch but at the beginning of the second book, at the time of the deliverance of the Israelites from Egypt. It becomes evident therefore that Genesis, the first book, has a special setting within the Pentateuch as a whole. It is a kind of prehistory to the happening, reported in the Pentateuch.

The passage cited from Deut. 34 continues as follows:

"This is the land, of which I swore to Abraham, to Isaac, and to Jacob, 'I will give it to your descendants'" (v. 4).

Here the arch of promise begins already with the patriarchs, whose entire history (Gen. 12-50) is pervaded by this promise, starting with the story of Abraham:

Now the Lord said to Abraham, "Go from your country and your kindred and your father's house, to the land that I will show you" (Gen. 12:1).

In the patriarchal history, however, which we have recognized to be prehistory, this promise is set within a much broader framework. The word to Abraham ends as follows:

"And in you all the families of the earth shall be blessed" (v. 3. Cf. R.S.V. marg.).

This far-reaching promise, however, is to be rightly heard only against the background of the first eleven chapters of the Book of Genesis, the so-called primeval history, in which divinely-created mankind, increasing under a peculiar tension and expanding far and wide, appears nevertheless to be standing under a curse and to be threatened on all sides.

In the midst of this human race God initiates a way by means of Abraham and this way is supposed to become a blessing someday for everyone. Here the first fundamental correspondence between the Old Testament and the New Testament appears. Even as God became flesh for everyone's salvation in the one man, Jesus of Nazareth, so he here calls forth this one family out of the nations in order to bless by it all families of the earth. The blessing beginning here points beyond the entire history of this family that became a nation even to the words of the New Testament, telling of the time of fulfillment. The opening part of Gen. 12 directs one to John 3:16:

> For God so loved the world that he gave his only son.

This résumé sums up the most important items that indicate the structure of the Pentateuch. It begins with a prehistory, embracing the primeval (Gen. 1-11) and patriarchal histories (Gen. 12-50). Next comes the account of the exodus from Egypt, extending until the time immediately preceding the entrance into the Land of Promise. This begins in Exodus and continues to the end of Deuteronomy.

As simple and easy to comprehend as this structure appears to be, it becomes complicated, when one attempts to penetrate more deeply into its structural plan. From what has been said thus far, one may gain the impression that the Pentateuch is a comprehensive and continuous account from the creation on— through the call of Abraham, the exodus from Egypt, up to the arrival at the border of the Promised Land.

In its final form the structure of the Pentateuch actually did become such a continuous account. The men who gave it this form, however, did so with utmost care and wise restraint, so as not to cover up or efface the fact that a great number of independent traditions were involved in it. These traditions have had their own independent existence and reflect many quite diverse sources.

This may be indicated by an example that should be at once apparent: Deuteronomy in its last four chapters contains the conclusion to the history of the wilderness wandering as recorded in Exodus through Numbers. To this history the Book of Deuteronomy (which is quite independent in itself) was added. This was done by placing it at the end, before the account of Moses' death, and the appointment of Joshua as his successor. To the pentateuchal conclusion that originated in this way a great psalm (the song of Moses, Deut. 32) and a collection of proverbs (Deut. 33, cf.

Gen. 49 as a parallel) were added. What is true of the concluding chapters of the Pentateuch applies to this great work as a whole. It was not written as a continuous account but grew out of living traditions and was gradually put together.

The building stones or primary elements of the Pentateuch are the individual stories that still can be perceived in the structure as a whole. They are almost as distinct as the uncut boulders in the walls of old village churches in Germany. These individual stories, whether they be those dealing with Abraham's journey to Egypt, the flight of Jacob to Laban, the deliverance at the Sea of Reeds, the appearance of God in the burning bush, or the miraculous feeding in the wilderness—all were narratives rather than written accounts. They were passed on orally for years, decades, and centuries before being put down in writing and then combined in the greater collections.

An oral as well as a written tradition probably existed alongside one another also for awhile, until ultimately the great collections arose, which in scientific research are termed the pentateuchal sources. (It is customary now to speak of the strata of tradition.) It is only from our own standpoint, however, as we look backward that they are sources—sources through which the Pentateuch came into being. If one sees them in their proper place, they are rather works comprising dissimilar sources and terminating a long period of growth.

The two older sources, the Yahwist (or J) and the Elohist (or E), so called from their use of the divine name, arose in about the ninth and eighth centuries* respectively. One distinguishes between them and the later Priestly source (or P), which was not completed until the exile or shortly thereafter. The latter contains the great Priestly Code. For all other details, refer to books in Old Testament introduction.**

---

*Translator's Note: Many recent scholars suggest a still earlier date—the tenth and ninth centuries respectively.

**Translator's Note: Eissfeldt, Otto, *The Old Testament: An Introduction.* Translated by P. R. Ackroyd, New York, 1965, pp. 158 f.

Kuhl, Curt, *The Old Testament: Its Origins and Composition.* Transl. by C. T. M. Herriott, Richmond, 1961, pp. 46 ff.

Weiser, Artur, *The Old Testament: Its Formation and Development.* Transl. by D. M. Barton, New York, 1961, pp. 74 ff.

The most important fact, however, concerning the origin of the Pentateuch has still not been mentioned, viz., that the impulse for bringing these sources into being was a confession that went back to the beginning of Israel's history. This was the historical Credo, which in a few sentences summarized the fundamental saving acts of God on behalf of his people (von Rad).* It is encountered, for example, in the description of the presentation of the first fruits by an Israelite farmer (Deut. 26:1-11), who utters this confession concerning the great acts of God, as he presents his offering. In it appear all the great themes from the time of the patriarchs to the entrance into the Promised Land. The nucleus of this great work, therefore, is a religious confession, which gathers about itself and within itself the ancient national traditions in all their abundance.

With these comments the first step toward a biblically-informed introduction to the Pentateuch has also been provided. The Pentateuch developed from a nucleus, the first part of Exodus with its account of the deliverance of the Israelites from Egypt. From this nucleus the whole may be simply presented as follows:

1. If the Pentateuch were to be depicted primarily in concentric circles, Ex. 1-15 would form the innermost circle. Closely associated with its account of the deliverance of the Israelites would be the story of their preservation (Ex. 16-18) and their journey through the wilderness (Num. 10-34).**

2. The second circle would be made up of the story that precedes the central event, viz., the account of the patriarchs (Gen. 12-50). By means of the Joseph story, in which the theater of action is shifted from Canaan to Egypt, the patriarchal history has been linked with the account of the deliverance at the Sea of Reeds.

3. Finally the primeval history (Gen. 1-11) would constitute the outermost circle. For it has only a loose connection with the central account. It is a prologue, setting the history of God's people within the broad expanse of human history.

---

*Gerhard von Rad, *The Problem of the Hexateuch and other Essays*. Transl. by E. W. T. Dicken, Edinburgh, 1966, pp. 1-78.

**Between these two accounts is the important Sinai pericope (Ex. 19—Num. 10), which for the moment will not be discussed.

The concentric circles that have been thus established indicate the growth of the Pentateuch around the nucleus. As we now begin with the primeval history, following the sequence of the biblical books, we must always bear in mind this picture of the concentric circles.

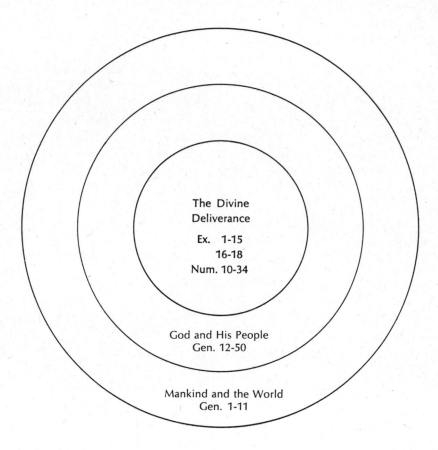

The Divine
Deliverance

Ex.   1-15
16-18
Num. 10-34

God and His People
Gen. 12-50

Mankind and the World
Gen. 1-11

II

The Primeval History

(Gen. 1-11)

These eleven chapters deal with mankind and the world, considered from the standpoint of the history of God with his people. They are therefore something like a prologue or overture, in which the one great and fundamental motif of the Bible is touched upon. All that the Bible states concerning this divine history has to do with human history as a whole. It concerns truth in its entirety as established by God.

The historical framework of the world and humanity rises before us in these eleven chapters. To this is then added, after Gen. 12, the story of God with his people. The primeval history (Gen. 1-11) directs one to the final history of the Bible, as found in the Revelation to John. Here the history of the people of God once more becomes a universal history of mankind.

The way which leads from the primeval beginning into history is presented in the form of three genealogies (chs. 5, 10, 11). Around it are organized the events of the primeval history, as indicated in the chart below.

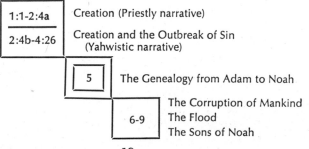

1:1-2:4a	Creation (Priestly narrative)
2:4b-4:26	Creation and the Outbreak of Sin (Yahwistic narrative)
5	The Genealogy from Adam to Noah
6-9	The Corruption of Mankind / The Flood / The Sons of Noah

Chart of Primeval History Events (cont.)

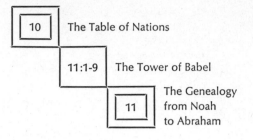

10	The Table of Nations
11:1-9	The Tower of Babel
11	The Genealogy from Noah to Abraham

A. THE CREATION NARRATIVES AND THE FALL OF MAN
(Gen. 1:1—4:26)

1. The Story of Creation (P's account): (1:1—2:4a)

The description of creation in the Priestly narrative has a distinct prose rhythm that sounds almost like a litany. The whole has the effect of a ballad concerning creation, a hymn that includes everything created within a seven-day period of work.

This may be illustrated as follows:

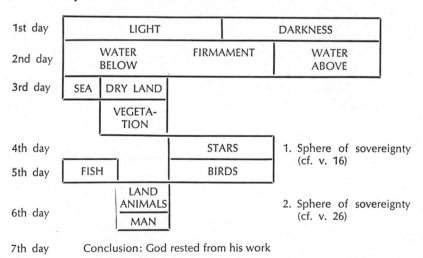

1st day	LIGHT		DARKNESS	
2nd day	WATER BELOW	FIRMAMENT	WATER ABOVE	
3rd day	SEA | DRY LAND			
	VEGETATION			
4th day		STARS	1. Sphere of sovereignty (cf. v. 16)	
5th day	FISH	BIRDS		
6th day	LAND ANIMALS		2. Sphere of sovereignty (cf. v. 26)	
	MAN			
7th day	Conclusion: God rested from his work			

Two series of statements extend throughout the entire account which define the rhythmic pattern of the creative acts. The one set simply describes the various aspects of a command that is being executed; the other depicts the diverse activity of the Creator:

The divine command	The Creator's activity
And God said . . .	God made, divided . . .
Let there be . . .	God called . . .
And it was so . . .	God blessed . . .
And God saw that . . .	God set . . .
And it was evening . . .	(to rule) . . .

The creative activity of God has its initial objective in man:

> God created man in his own image,
> in the image of God he created him (1:27).

The final objective of his creative activity is indicated by his rest on the seventh day, which refers remotely to the sabbath and thereby to the goal of creation.

2. Creation and the outbreak of sin (J's account) (2:4b—3:24)

At the beginning of the Yahwist's history there was once an independent account of creation. The obvious difference in its language can be recognized at once. It is a story that tells of a continuous episode from ch. 2:4b to the end of ch. 3.

In the Priestly narrative the creation account is motivated by the question: "What is the origin of everything that exists?" In chs. 2 and 3, on the other hand, the leading question is rather: "Why is man the way he is—an erring creature, moving on to his death?"

The story is constructed, as follows:

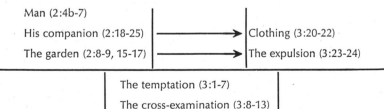

The question of God: "Adam, where are you?" is at the heart of this account. In this question God pursues man who has gone astray and would like to hide himself. In this pursuit two ideas are implied: (1) God arrests man in his disobedience (by an examination and punishment), (2) yet he gives life to condemned man (by graciously clothing him). The enigma as to how evil can emerge out of God's creation remains unsolved.

3. Cain and Abel. The continuing effect of evil (Gen. 4:1-16)

At the heart of the story is the warning that Cain receives (vv. 6-7). The increasing effect of evil consists of the way Cain becomes the murderer of his brother despite the warning given him. Iniquity is so overpowering that it no longer needs an inducement. It can even shrug off warning. The seriousness of the offense is correspondingly great, viz., fratricide (vv. 8-12). That Cain continues to live, although "a fugitive and a wanderer," signifies that God does not destroy a man who is even capable of his brother's death.

4. The descendants of Cain (Gen. 4:17-24)

    a. These were men capable of producing cultural works (4:17-22)

    b. The song of Lamech. The ultimate possibility of the sons of Cain (4:23-24)

5. The third son, Seth. The invocation of the name of Yahweh (4:25-26)

B. THE GENEALOGY FROM ADAM TO NOAH (P)
(Gen. 5:1-32)

In vv. 1-3 the Priestly narrative proceeds from the creation account to the history of mankind. The whole creation finds its goal in man as a counterpart to God. God creates mankind in his own image (5:1). Adam fathers a son (Seth) in his image (5:3); and so one generation follows another from Adam to Noah. The enumeration of bare statistics, making up a man's life, sounds monotonous to us: "He was born. He begat a son. He lived x number of years;

and begat sons and daughters. The length of his life was x number
of years; then he died." To ancient hearers of such data, however,
these words connoted the sheer abundance and colorful character of
life. Cold statistics constitute the inescapable substratum of all spiritual, political, and personal life. Up to the present time all the drama
of man's existence is based on these primary facts.

The great longevity of man (Methuselah lived 969 years!) indicates that there was an antiquity before recorded history, extending
far into the past. The stages of this remote era are intimated by the
life span of these patriarchs. At the heart of this account the story
of Enoch, the man who "walked with God" (v. 24), stands in a
strange and unexplained manner.

The fifth chapter follows immediately upon ch. 1 and like it belongs to the *Priestly narrative.* Here one can clearly perceive P's
characteristic method, extending from the story of creation to the
death of Moses. (Some parts of Joshua probably belong to it too.) It
has a whole series of distinctive characteristics, an extremely
monotonous mode of expression, betraying its obvious origin from
within priestly circles.

In the Book of Genesis it is characterized by a fixed pattern of
genealogies into which the primeval and patriarchal histories have
been woven. Each section begins: "These are the generations."*
They are as follows:

1. The history of the world (2:4a) and of man (5:1)

2. The history of Noah (6:9) and his sons (10:1, 32)

3. The history of Shem (11:10) and Terah (11:27)

4. The history of Ishmael (25:12) and Isaac (25:19)

5. The history of Esau (36:1, 9) and Jacob (37:2)

The following chart gives in particular detail the sequence of
generations from Adam to the sons of Jacob, that is the tribes of
Israel.

---

*In Hebrew: *'ellah tôledôth. Tôledôth* corresponds somewhat to the term
"genesis."

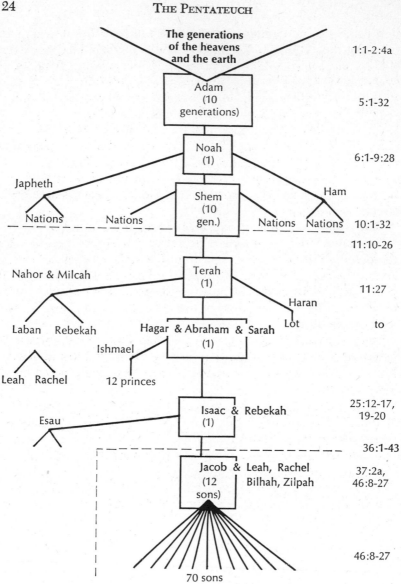

The generations
of the heavens
and the earth   1:1-2:4a

Adam
(10
generations)   5:1-32

Noah
(1)   6:1-9:28

Japheth   Ham

Shem
(10
gen.)

Nations   Nations   Nations   Nations   10:1-32

11:10-26

Nahor & Milcah

Terah
(1)   11:27

Haran

Laban   Rebekah   Hagar & Abraham & Sarah   Lot   to
     (1)

Ishmael

Leah   Rachel   12 princes

Isaac & Rebekah   25:12-17,
Esau   (1)   19-20

36:1-43

Jacob & Leah, Rachel   37:2a,
(12   Bilhah, Zilpah   46:8-27
sons)

46:8-27

70 sons

(Note the branching out and progressive narrowing-down in this chart of the generations in Genesis.)

The generations of the heavens and earth (cont.)

1. Heaven and earth
   (Gen. 1)
2. Mankind (Gen. 5-9)
3. The table of nations   1st branching out: the nations
   (Gen. 10)   of the earth
4. The sons of Shem   2nd branching out: the Semites
   (Gen. 11)
5. The sons of Terah
   (Gen. 11:27)
6. The sons of Abraham
   (Gen. 12-25)
7. The sons of Isaac
   (Gen. 25-36)
8. The sons of Jacob   3rd branching out: the Israelites
   (Gen. 37-50)

C. THE CORRUPTION OF MANKIND (J & P)
(Gen. 6:1—9:28)

1. The Flood (6-9)

The introduction (Gen. 6:1-4) indicates that the Flood was occasioned by the rise of giants in the earth, produced by the marriage of divine beings with the daughters of men. This is recorded as an example of human depravity.

This is one of the few passages in the Bible containing a myth or alluding to one and it is a hint concerning the mythical period of human history that preceded the history of God with his people. It is adopted here by J as an example of the trespassing of barriers (cf. chs. 3, 4, and 11), widening the gulf between God and man.

It is so evident that the Flood story (6:5—9:17) is a combination of two originally independent accounts that the interweaving of the two strands may be exhibited here for once as an example:

J	P
God's decision; Noah (6:5-8)	
	The story of Noah (6:9-12)
	God's covenant with Noah (the command to build an ark (6:13-22)
The Flood (7:1-23)*	The Flood (7:11-24)*

J	P
The end of the Flood (8:2-13)*	The end of the Flood (8:1-5, 13-19)*
Noah's offering and God's promise (8:20-22)	The benediction and the command (9:1-7)
	The covenant (9:8-17)
The sons of Noah (9:18-27)	
	The age of Noah and his death (9:28f)

Each reader as he observes the various inconsistencies will be able to note that two accounts have here been combined into one.

The interchange between the divine names (*Yahweh* "the Lord" and *Elohim* "God," cf. for example 6:22 with 7:5) is especially obvious in this story. There are also a great many repetitions (e.g., the command to enter the ark—6:18; 7:1), including discrepancies. Thus in the one account there is a reference to a pair of every animal (6:19 f.; 7:15 f.); in the other, a reference to seven pairs of every clean animal and two pairs of every unclean animal (7:2). The Flood lasted either 61 days (7:4) or a year and ten days (8:13).**

In regard to this juxtaposition of the two accounts, Walter Zimmerli says in the Swiss commentary, entitled *Prophezei:*

> There are two witnesses that give an account concerning the Flood, each having his own individuality. The action of God, however, in this world event is the same. This one divine act is meant to be heard through the mouth of two witnesses in its twofold version.***

One should perceive above all in this story that the majesty of God's wrath against the sins of mankind includes destruction by

---

*The asterisk denotes that the verses of the respective sections do not all refer to the source in question.

**Translator's Note: According to J the rain lasted 40 days and 40 nights (7:12). The water then subsided in 21 days (cf. 8:6-8, 10, 12). The Flood according to P, however, began "in the six hundredth year of Noah's life, in the second month, on the seventeenth day of the month" (7:11). The earth became dry again "in the six hundred and first year . . . in the second month, on the twenty-seventh day of the month" (8:13, 14), that is, a year and ten days.

***Schweizerisches Bibelwerk für die Gemeinde, Zurich, 1943, Vol. 2, p. 44.

tremendous catastrophes, also that the maintenance and preservation of our world is a miracle of his goodness. Both of these concepts find unique expression in the apparent contradiction between the introduction and the conclusion to the Yahwistic narrative. At the beginning (6:5) the inclination of man toward evil is cited as the reason for God's decision to destroy mankind. At the end (8:21) this becomes the basis for God's resolve never again to send a flood. There is here accordingly a profound comment concerning the manner in which human malice and divine goodness stand in incomprehensible opposition.

At the turning point of the periods depicted in the flood story a promise is given mankind, embracing all human history. It is as follows: "While the earth remains, seedtime and harvest, cold and heat, summer and winter, day and night, shall not cease" (8:22). At this place also is the first fundamental law for all human society: "Whoever sheds the blood of man, by man shall his blood be shed" (9:6).

D. THE TABLE OF NATIONS (P) & J
(Gen. 10:1-32)

Whereas ch. 5 described how man in his development became involved in history, as one generation succeeded another, the table of nations in ch. 10 deals with the way man spread out over the expanse of the then-known world. Two accounts have again been combined. The basic material is the table in P (vv. 1-7, 20, 22-23, 31-32), supplemented by J (vv. 8-19, 21, 24-30).

The table is organized into three great national groups, originating from the three sons of Noah: Shem, Ham, and Japheth. The modern designation of Semite and Hamite, which is borrowed from this table, coincides only in part with the respective national groups mentioned here.

For a knowledge of Scripture it is important to realize that the basis for its universalism is to be found in this chapter. When God chooses one nation out of many nations for himself (from ch. 12 and on), the promise given to that one nation refers nevertheless to "all the families of the earth" (12:3). God's ultimate purpose to save is directed thus to his entire creation. The view of the nations reappears again in the national oracles of the prophets (Isa. 13-21; Jer. 46-51, and in many other places), in the songs of the Suffering Servant (Is. 42, 49, 50, 52 f.), whom God appointed as a light to the nations, and in the mission of the apostle to the gentiles in the New Testament.

E. THE TOWER OF BABEL (Gen. 11:1-9)

In close conjunction with God's approval of earthly nations in their multiplicity and extensiveness stands this story concerning the building of a tower. It demonstrates the peril that threatened the nations in their struggle to increase their power by force. At this point a law of history is anticipated which is remarkably pertinent, viz., that such a forcible increase in power will lead inevitably to the ruination of society. The biblical antithesis to this narrative, immediately preceding the call of Abraham, is the story of Pentecost (Acts 2). Here again the theme concerning tongues recurs, this time in the sense that a mysterious power, making possible a new understanding among the languages of the nations, is inherent in the preaching concerning Christ.

F. THE GENEALOGY FROM NOAH TO ABRAHAM (P)
(Gen. 11:10-32)

This is an exact equivalent to ch. 5. In that passage the epoch before the Flood comprised ten generations or ten periods of time. Here again the epoch after the Flood up to the time of Abraham consists of ten generations or periods. The difference, however, is all the more remarkable, when one notes that the span of life in this later epoch is much more brief. In this way P intends to indicate the dissimilarity between the great historical epochs in the early period of mankind. The second epoch is closer to present-day man than the first.

The precise number of generations and the manner in which they are enumerated in a monotonously solemn style expresses rhythmically an arrangement which the Priestly narrative knows governs every happening. It is the way of God through history, which proceeds after the primeval period according to his plan.

III

The Patriarchal History

(Gen. 12-50)

The cycle of patriarchal stories is a little world in itself. In their present form they simply tell the story of a family, covering a period of three generations. Behind the account, however, is an era that stretches far back into the distant past, the era of nomadic, half-settled tribes. This epoch is preserved in the patriarchal stories and is added as a preface to the national history.

It is linked with the national history through the theme of promise, a theme that in Gen. 12:1-3 precedes the entire account and then continues to appear again and again throughout every section. This theological thematic link unites the complex group of patriarchal stories into a whole. In addition there is a biographical link that fits together each of the three cycles of patriarchal narratives into a biographical narrative. These are the Abraham cycle, the Jacob-Esau cycle, and the Joseph cycle.

This double manner of combining the stories has been accomplished with remarkable finesse. From the very first sentence one is captivated by the flow of an account that permits one to follow Abraham's journey from his homeland, then the fate of his son, grandchildren, and great-grandchildren. Finally one comes to that exquisite, solemn conclusion describing the funeral procession which brought the body of the patriarch Jacob back to the homeland, after he had rediscovered his beloved son amid the splendor of his high office in Egypt.

Individual stories constitute the building material of this continuous account. Until their insertion in the whole account, however, they were simply narrated as individual stories. These were passed on from generation to generation. Thus it happened also that many features of the stories changed during their journey through time and country. New features were added; old ones receded into the background. Even the chief characters changed. Thus the theme, telling how the patriarch's wife was compromised, appears three times. It is told twice in connection with Abraham (Gen. 12 and 20), once in connection with Isaac (Gen. 26).

As far as this part of the Bible is concerned it is necessary in a special way to become gradually involved *in the individual stories* if one would become really familiar with their texts. This is the only way one can come into closer contact with the mysterious vitality of these ancient tales. It would be a great help in this connection to try to retell them—that is as far as possible in the spoken word, in which they once had vitality.

A handbook of biblical information can for this reason render only a very modest service in connection with the patriarchal stories. If the present reader fails to follow the suggestion that he read the stories again and again, until they begin to speak themselves, the lines of thought that one can point up in a handbook will be of little help.

* * * * *

THE ABRAHAM STORIES (Gen. 12-25)

An introductory résumé

Beginning with the story of Abraham, there is a third source, the Elohist (E), that has been added to the sources (J and P) encountered in the primeval history. Whether it was once an independent document or only a later expansion and continuation of J cannot as yet be definitely said. At any rate, after Gen. 15 it appears alongside J as a source that is clearly and definitely exhibited in important details. E is much closer to J in time and subject matter than the much later Priestly narrative.

The basic theme concerning the promise to the patriarchs, which gives direction to the entire patriarchal history, is found in all three sources in the Abraham stories. It is even accentuated thematically at the beginning of chs. 12 (J), 15 (E), and 17 (P). It recurs still more often in J (12:6-7; 13:14-18; 15:7-18; 18:9-16).

The Yahwist in Gen. 15 expresses the promise in the form of a covenant, in the mode of an ancient rite (vv. 7-21) without using the term "covenant" in this connection. P refers to a covenant that was definitely and solemnly established (17). In E the comment concerning Abraham's faith occurs in place of this (15:6).

To begin with, Abraham was promised a son. All three sources agree that a son would be born to Abraham, and all have something to say concerning Isaac's birth (21:1-7). It is possible to arrange the stories of the Abraham cycle around the nativity account as the nucleus. Most of the earlier stories move toward it; those which follow proceed from it.

The promise of a child is contained by implication in the promise of a blessing (12:1-3). In 13:14-18 it is expressed as a promise of descendants. It is precisely stated in the account of the three men who visit Abraham (18:9-16), viz., Abraham shall have a son by Sarah. The above three references are all from J. In E there is in addition the promise of offspring (15:1-6) with the special pledge that Abraham will receive a son of his own. In P there is the general promise of posterity (17:5 f.) and the special promise that Abraham will receive a son through his wife Sarah (17:15-22).

The two stories concerning the way the mother was compromised occur between the general promise (12) and the specific announcement concerning a child by means of Sarah. The danger was of two types:

1. The danger to which she was exposed as a creature: she continued to be childless (15:2 f.; 16:1). The account of Abraham's concubine Hagar, who bore Ishmael to him, belongs here. It is found in J (Gen. 16, although vv. 1a, 3, 15 f., are from P) and in E (21:8-21).

2. The danger she encountered through men: the account of Sarah in Egypt (12:10-20 from J); and the same theme of Sarah in the presence of Abimelech (ch. 20 from E).

Land is promised along with posterity. God commanded Abraham to depart "to the land that I will show you" (12:1). After Abraham passed through Canaan, he promised him: "To your descendants I will give this land" (12:7).

The passages that have to do with land are those dealing with the stations along Abraham's route (12:6-9 and 13:14-18 from J), the separation from Lot (13:1-13 and 19:1-38 from J and P), the theme concerning the fight over the well (21:22-34 from E), and the purchase of a burial plot (23 from P).

Some of the stories coming after the birth of Isaac have already been mentioned. J relates only one important story after this, in which the line of promise is continued to the next generation, viz., the wooing of Rebekah (24). In the account concerning the purchase of a burial plot (23 from P) the Priestly narrative brings to a conclusion the theme concerning the promise of land. Abraham acquired in the land of his sojourn a little plot as his property, the place for his and Sarah's grave.

A quite independent development of the theme concerning the promise of a son is furnished by E in ch. 22. This is the account of how the heir and bearer of the promise was placed in jeopardy by God's command, requiring Abraham to offer his son. Here the fundamental theme of the Abraham stories is developed to a depth of profound theological penetration.

Ch. 25 has a list of genealogies and the account of Abraham's death and burial in the personally acquired cave of Macpelah.

Only ch. 14 falls entirely outside this relatively uniform cycle of Abraham stories. It is here alone that Abraham appears as a warrior. Only here do the patriarchal stories become involved in contemporary political history. Only here does a priest appear with a religious rite. Thus this chapter provides a mysterious foreign element at the heart of the patriarchal account. It has been handed down in a late form, reminiscent of P, although it indeed contains a nucleus of ancient traditions. These traditions refer to the patriarchs of Israel in a way quite different from that of other stories.

With this résumé the cycle of Abraham stories has been essentially covered. They tell of promise—the promise concerning a son, the promise concerning land. The birth of the son is at the heart of the Abraham cycle, in which the two poles are the promise concerning this son and his birth.

There is to be noted here a distant resemblance to the initial stories in the Gospels. The promise and birth of a child are also a fundamental theme there (Luke 1-2), albeit in a different context. In this account as well as that of Abraham it is a theme of the early history, an event that is placed at the beginning of the account concerning salvation.

THE ABRAHAM STORIES IN J, E, AND P

A. THE EMIGRATION (Gen. 12-14)		
J	E	P
1. The command and promise to Abraham (12:1-3)		(11:27, 31-32)
2. The migration of Abraham (12:6-9)		(12:4-5)
3. Sarah in Egypt (12:10-20; 13:1)		
4. Abraham and Lot a. The separation from Lot (13:2-13) b. The promise (13:14-18)		(13*)
		5. (The war of the kings 14:1-24)

B. THE COVENANT (Gen. 15-20)		
1. The establishment of the covenant (15*)	The promise to Abraham (15*)	The establishment of the covenant (17:1-27)
2. Hagar and Ishmael (16:1-16)	(Cf. The expulsion of Hagar—21)	(The birth of Ishmael 16*)
3. The visit to Abraham's home (18:1-33)		
4. Sodom (19:1-38)	5. Sarah at Abimelech's home (20:1-18)	

C. THE BIRTH OF THE SON (Gen. 21-24)		
1. The birth of Isaac (21:1a, 2a, 7)	(21:1b, 6) 2. Hagar and Ishmael The expulsion of Hagar (21:8-21) 3. The dispute over a well (21:22-34) 4. The sacrifice (22:1-24)	(21:2b-5)
6. The wooing of Rebekah (24:1-67)		5. Sarah's death and burial in the cave of Macpelah (23:1-20)

*Cf. note p. 26 concerning the use of an asterisk for the above chapters.

D. THE DEATH OF ABRAHAM		
1. The descendants of Abraham (25:1-6, 11)		2. Abraham's death and burial (25:7-10) 3. The descendants of Abraham (25:12-20)

A. THE EMIGRATION (Gen. 12-14)

1. The command and promise to Abraham (12:1-3)

In this introduction to the patriarchal stories the Yahwist has laid the theological foundation for the whole patriarchal history:

a. *The command:* "Go out of your land . . . " (v. 1) which corresponds to the beginning of the national history in Ex. 1 ff. This is the call of the deity who saves and preserves.

b. *The promise:* "I will bless you . . . " (vv. 2-3) combines the fundamental theological theme of the patriarchal history (blessing) with that of the national history (promise) and furnishes thereby the connecting link between the two.

c. *The blessing,* which Abraham is promised, is unfolded in three successive statements:

1. The blessing will make Abraham a great name (v. 2).
2. The fate of those who are near at hand will be determined by their attitude toward Abraham (v. 3a).
3. The fate of those who are far-off (i.e., all races of the earth) is the goal of the blessing Abraham is promised (v. 3b).

In the final sentence the promise points far beyond Abraham to the distant objectives of God's action on behalf of his creation (v. 3a). Gen. 12:1-3 is accordingly the connecting link between the primeval history and the special line concerning the story of salvation that begins with Abraham.

2.. The migration of Abraham (12:6-9)

3. Abraham and Sarah in Egypt (12:10-20; 13:1)

Into his composition that begins with the promise (12:1-3) J has inserted an older narrative. It tells how Abraham experienced a wonderful preservation, while surrounded by the peril of hunger and violence in a foreign land. At the same time, however, he was put to shame because of his little faith. This is indicated by the way he was willing to forfeit his wife who was to become the mother of the child that had been promised him.

The later versions in chs. 20 and 26 tend to excuse Abraham (or Isaac). They also indicate how this story portrays a test of faith, which was typical of Israel. It was continually reflected upon and conceived in a fresh way.

4. Abraham and Lot (13:1-18)

    a. The migration of Abraham from the Negeb to Bethel (13:1-4)
    b. The separation of Abraham from Lot (13:5-13)
    c. The promise of land and posterity (13:14-17)
    d. Settling by the oaks of Mamre near Hebron (13:18)

The theme of expansion lies at the basis of the account concerning Abraham's parting from Lot (vv. 5-13). The determining factor here is lack of pasture land; in 21:22 f. it is lack of water. Thus begins the controversy over land and food; and in this the efficacy of God's blessing is affirmed, viz., that this dispute in the patriarchal narratives is carried on peacefully. Abraham, certain that God would take care of his wants, permitted Lot to choose the better land.

5. The war of the kings. The rescue of Lot by Abraham (14:1-24)

    a. The war of the kings (14:1-11)
    b. Abraham's defeat of Chedorlaomer and his rescue of Lot (14:12-16)
    c. Melchizedek's blessing of Abraham (14:18-20)
    d. The king of Sodom regains his property from Abraham (14:17, 21-24)

As to vv. 18-20, Melchizedek was king of Salem (Jerusalem?) and at the same time a priest of *El Elyon* (God most high). By his blessing he received Abraham into his cult fellowship, and Abraham acknowledged this by his tribute. Here Melchizedek is viewed as the ancestor of Jerusalem's pre-Israelite priestly family. In Ps. 110:4 the tradition concerning Melchizedek is transferred to the Davidic king, and it was in this sense that Heb. 7 took it over.

B. THE COVENANT (Gen. 15-20)

1. The establishment of the covenant and the promise (15:1-21)

Here are two narratives that are independent of one another: vv. 1-6 and vv. 7-21. Both elaborate events which in their fundamental elements may still be perceived.

Gen. 15:1-6 contains a complaint, directed by Abraham against God (it is in two variants—vv. 2 and 3), a promise concerning welfare addressed by God to Abraham and introduced by "Fear not!" (v. 1), and a sign connected with this promise (v. 5). The comment concerning Abraham's faith that is to be reckoned to him for righteousness constitutes the conclusion. It was probably not added to the narrative until its final stage of development.

Gen. 15:7-21 has at its center a very old rite concerning the establishment of a covenant (vv. 9-12, 17), the individual details of which are no longer clear. The rite as a whole represents probably the administration of an oath, in which God obligated himself to give to Abraham's descendants the Land of Promise (vv. 7 and 18). The details of the interpretation (vv. 13-16) were added later.

P's account of the establishment of God's covenant with Abraham (17:1-27) is as follows:

    a. The covenant promise: aid, posterity, land (17:[1]3-8)
    b. The covenant command: circumcision (17:9-14)
    c. The blessing and promise of offspring to Sarah (17:15-16)
    d. Abraham's protest (17:17-18)
    e. The promise of a son Isaac by Sarah (17:19-22)
    f. The performance of circumcision (17:23-27)

2. Hagar and Ishmael (16:1-16)

    a. Hagar becomes Abraham's concubine (16:1-3)
    b. The quarrel of the wives and the flight of Hagar (16:4-6)
    c. The angel's appearance and promise at Lahai-roi (16:7-14)
    d. Hagar bears Ishmael to Abraham (16:15-16)

3. **The visit of the three men to Abraham's home** (18:1-33)
   a. Abraham invites the divine messengers into his home and entertains them (18:1-8)
   b. The promise of a child and Sarah's laughter (18:9-16)
   c. The announcement of Sodom's destruction and Abraham's intercession for the city (18:17-32)

4. **The fall of Sodom** (19:1-38)
   a. Lot invites the divine messengers into his home and entertains them (19:1-3)
   b. The wickedness of the people of Sodom (19:4-11)
   c. The messengers of God save Lot from destruction. His flight toward Zoar (19:12-23)
   d. Sulphur and fire rain down upon Sodom and Gomorrah. v. 26 Lot's wife (19:24-28)
   e. The origin of the Moabites and Ammonites through the daughters of Lot (19:29-38)

5. **Abraham and Abimelech** (20:1-18; cf. comments at 12:10-20)

C. THE BIRTH OF THE SON (Gen. 21-24)

1. **The birth of Isaac** (21:1-7)
2. **Hagar and Ishmael** (21:8-21)
   a. The expulsion of Hagar (21:8-14)
   b. The rescue of the child and the promise (21:15-19)
   c. "God was with Ishmael" (21:20-21)

In ch. 16 Hagar flees; in ch. 21 she is banished. In the first instance this took place before the birth of Ishmael; now he was already a lad. The special feature of this story is the wonderful rescue of the boy in the wilderness from death by thirst. In this connection a characteristic of God's manner of acting is revealed—he hears the cry of his suffering creatures and delivers them from the peril of death (21:17). This then becomes later a theme of Israel's psalms of praise. It can be said also of Ishmael: "God was with him" (21:20).

3. **The dispute over a well** (21:22-34)

4. The sacrifice (22:1-24) (E)
   a. "God tested Abraham" (22:1)
   b. God's command (22:2)
   c. The carrying out of the command by Abraham (22:3-11)
      (1) On the way (22:3-8)
          vv. 6-8 The conversation between father and son: "God will provide" (v. 8)
      (2) The sacrifice (22:9-11)
   d. The annulling of what had been commanded.
      Reason: "For now I know that you fear God . . . " (22:12)
   e. The substitute offering of a ram (22:13)
   f. The naming of the place: "The Lord will provide" (22:14)
   g. The return home (22:19)
   h. A later expansion: the renewal of the promise to Abraham (22:15-18)

The narrative was recited for many centuries before it acquired this final form. Underlying it is a story concerning the redemption of human sacrifice by an animal sacrifice. In its present form, however, there is hardly a trace of this concept. The story has now been fitted into a theological framework—the testing of Abraham by God (vv. 1a and 12b). The real heart of the account is the sentence that Abraham in his distress uttered to his son: "God will provide!" With this sentence he also later designated the place of this incident, as he heaved a sigh of relief and praised God. His eulogy of God is the object of the story.

5. The acquisition of the cave of Macpelah (23:1-20) (P)
   a. The death of Sarah (23:1-2)
   b. The acquisition of a burial plot containing the cave of Macpelah from the Hittites, the field of Ephron (23:3-18)
   c. Sarah's burial in the cave of Macpelah (23:19)
   d. The ratification of this one landed possession of Abraham (23:20)

To the extremely concise account of Sarah's death (vv. 1-2) and burial (v. 19), P has added the very extensive description of how the place for the grave was acquired. In this way it intends to demonstrate the importance of a "home" in this particular relation. At least the place where man is laid to rest at the end of his life should be his own.

At this point the Priestly narrative continues entirely in a genealogical vein, laying stress on the three most important aspects of man's existence, linking each with a transaction that does not as yet belong to the realm of worship but is nevertheless ritualistic in a ceremonial way.

(1) At birth: circumcision (23:17)
(2) At death: burial (23:23)
(3) At a wedding: the parental benediction (28:1-9)

In emphasizing these three events the Priestly narrative places the history of a family in the setting of divine history.

6. The wooing of Rebekah (21:1-67)
   a. Abraham's commission to his oldest servant (24:1-4)
   b. The servant's oath (24:5-9)
   c. The journey to the city of Nahor (24:10-11)
   d. The request for a sign (24:12-14)
   e. The meeting with Rebekah at the well (24:15-25)
   f. A prayer of thanksgiving (24:26-27)
   g. The invitation and lodging (24:28-33)
   h. The fulfillment of the commission (24:34-49)
   i. The grant (24:50-54)
   j. The dismissal and blessing of Rebekah (24:55-60)
   k. The departure with Rebekah (24:61)
   l. The arrival, the meeting with Isaac, the wedding (24:62-67)

A brief note that Isaac married Nahor's granddaughter, a woman distantly related to him, has been fashioned into a simple, beautiful story of the wooing of Rebekah by Abraham's steward. The story only intends to point up the obvious connection between the small as well as the great decisions in life and the rule and will of God. The decisive meeting at the well is couched in the language of prayer and praise. It is a charming picture of everyday human life in this sphere. Everything has been included that has to do with simple faith in the fact that God's rule extends even over ordinary, commonplace events. As Rebekah received permission to leave, her brothers gave her a blessing (v. 60). This is an example of a farewell benediction.

D. THE DEATH OF ABRAHAM (Gen. 25)

1. The descendants of Abraham (25:1-6)
2. Abraham's death and burial in the cave of Macpelah (25:7-11)
3. The descendants of Abraham (25:12-20)
   a. The genealogy of Ishmael (25:12-18)
   b. The descendants of Isaac (25:19-20)

* * * * *

THE JACOB-ESAU STORIES (Gen. 25-36)

An introductory resumé

A first glance at the Jacob-Esau cycle clearly reveals that this central group of patriarchal stories is fundamentally different from the Abraham cycle. Chs. 12-25 are essentially single narratives, held together quite loosely by the basic theme of the promise of posterity (or of a son and of land). Chs. 25-36, on the other hand, are a unit in a clearer and more distinctive sense. This unity has been achieved by presenting the conflict between Jacob and Esau in two scenes (chs. 25-27 and chs. 32-33). The first scene ends with the flight of Jacob; the second takes place at the time of his return. In between is the episode at the home of Laban (29-31) with its own peculiar tension and drama.

The theme of this second cycle of patriarchal stories is obvious. It is the conflict between brothers—a conflict over the blessing. According to the most ancient linguistic usage, blessing signified the power of fertility. Deuteronomy refers to a threefold blessing: that of the womb (children), that of herds (cattle), that of land. It was not until the period of settlement, however, that the blessing of land came. The patriarchal stories deal here, therefore, with the blessing of the womb and of herds.

The Abraham cycle deals simply with the blessing of the womb. A child after all was born, a child in whom the blessing on Abraham's part could continue. The emphasis therefore falls upon the parental-child relationship.

In the second cycle the blessing moves into an entirely new kind of problem, viz., how shall the blessing be passed on if there are several sons and heirs? The emphasis here falls accordingly on the relationship of brother to brother. It has to do with the problem of the first-born, the right of the elder brother. The problem as such is here already assumed, but it is called into question from the standpoint of its absolute validity.

It is the concept of blessing that explains the construction of the Jacob-Esau cycle. The beginning (chs. 25-28) and the end (chs. 32-35) are concerned with the way the blessing was attained; the central section (chs. 29-31), with its effect. The blessing of the womb in this connection is prominent at both the beginning and the end of the account. In the central section is the blessing of herds.

One ought not, however, overemphasize or isolate these elements of the construction. The parent-child relationship that occupied the foreground of the Abraham cycle is also continued quite distinctly in this cycle. The fraternal relationship plays a correspondingly important role in all three cycles of the patriarchal narrative, although at times clearly under different aspects:

Cycle 1—The wife's son vs. the son of the handmaid—the son
Cycle 2—Two sons on an equal footing—the elder brother
Cycle 3—Many sons on an equal footing—the youngest brother (i.e., Joseph)*

These different kinds of fraternal relationships are also concerned with the association that the Israelites had with one another and with the tribes and nations near them. In the account of Ishmael (Ishmaelites) there was total separation. Yet Ishmael remained a son of the first parent and was acknowledged by God. In the case of Esau (Edom) there was a continuing tension; and with the twelve brothers, a living together despite tension.

The relation of the sources to one another in Gen. 25-36 is also different from that in chs. 12-25. J and E are largely parallel, much

---

*Translator's Note: The author indicates that he has designated Joseph as the youngest brother, because Benjamin, who was actually younger than Joseph, does not figure prominently in the story of the brothers until after Joseph is in Egypt.

more so than in chs. 12-25. P, on the other hand, is definitely periph-
eral in importance. It does not furnish any complete narratives but
only isolated remarks and notations. The way it sets forth the relationship of Jacob to Esau is also different.

A. THE BIRTHRIGHT (Gen. 25-28)

Two stories lie at the heart of this section: Jacob's cheating of
Esau out of his birthright (27:1-40) and Jacob's flight from Esau
(27:41-45). At the very beginning of this first part there are two
narratives preliminary to the central account, viz., the birth of
Esau and Jacob (25:21-26, a J account) and the transmission of
Abraham's blessing to Isaac (26:2-5). Gen. 26:7-33 does not belong
to this set of passages. Its account of Isaac and Abimelech is parallel rather to Gen. 12:10-20 and ch. 20.*

The account of the dish of lentils (25:27-34) is a variant to that
of ch. 27. In both accounts Esau is outwitted by Jacob and loses
his right of primogeniture to him.

At the very end of this first section is the account of the wives
of Jacob and Esau (a P account) and Jacob's dream during his
flight, including the renewal of the promise (an E account).

1. The birth of Jacob and Esau (25:21-26)

This is a very peculiar birth narrative, concealing age-old customs. Thus the theme of childlessness again appears. Rebekah's
husband intercedes on her behalf before God (as do Moses and
the prophets on behalf of their people, Job on behalf of his friends).
And God grants his request (v. 21). During the pain of pregnancy
Rebekah utters the lament: "If it is thus, why do I live?"—a lament
that is found again in Job. Out of this lament issues an interroga-
tion of God. The response is a divine proverb concerning the children that Rebekah will bear, a passage of great future significance
(vv. 22-23).

2. The dish of lentils (25:27-34)

This is a narrative that once had an entirely different meaning;
for it plays off, so to say, the farmer against the shepherd. The

---

*See above p. 34.

Yahwist has introduced it in an artistic manner into the Jacob story and given it an entirely new sense. Now it indicates what apparently happens to blessing in the hands of men, when God's will is disregarded. The same is true later in ch. 27. The object of the story, however, is thereby furnished, as God in a hidden manner remains the lord of blessing.

3. Stories concerning Isaac (26:1-35)

At one time there must have been a cycle of Isaac stories that are now no longer preserved. Ch. 26 is a later greatly amplified variant of the theme concerning the way the patriarch's wife was compromised (as in chs. 12 and 20). It has been supplemented in many ways.

4. Jacob cheats Esau of his blessings as the first-born (27:1-45)

    a. Isaac desires to bless Esau (27:1-4)
    b. The plot of Rebekah (27:5-13)
    c. The deception (27:14-24)
    d. The act and word of blessing (27:25-29)
    e. Esau's disappointment (27:30-40)
    f. The plot of Esau and Rebekah's plan of escape (27:41-45)

5. The wives of Esau and Jacob (28:1-9; 26:34 f.; 27:46) (P)

The Priestly narrative has greatly modified the Jacob-Esau story by omitting the account of the deception and depicting the tension between the brothers as a result simply of Esau's having taken two Canaanite wives against the will of his parents. Jacob, on the other hand, is portrayed as having been obedient to his parents. He journeys to Laban with his father's blessing in order to secure a daughter from him as a wife. (He does not flee according to this account.) In the end Esau also takes another wife from within the relationship (28:9).

6. Jacob's dream (28:10-22) (E)

    a. Jacob spends the night at a holy place (28:10-11)
    b. The dream of the ladder stretching to heaven (28:12)
    c. God's promise to Jacob (28:13-15)

    d. Jacob establishes the Bethel shrine (28:16-19)
    e. Jacob makes a vow (28:20-22)

This is one of the fundamental encounters with God in the Bible. At its heart is Jacob's cry, as he discovers the sanctity of the place:

> "Surely the Lord is in this place; and I did not know it. . . . How awesome is this place! This is none other than the house of God, and this is the gate of heaven" (vv. 16-17).

It is important, however, in just such a story as this to make clear that it bears traces of a long development. Long before Israel came to Canaan, Bethel was a shrine (from about 2000 B.C. and on). During the reign of Jeroboam I it reached its zenith. (It was about this time that this story developed.) Josiah destroyed the shrine after 622 B.C. Gen. 28 demonstrates quite impressively how the history of a very ancient shrine came to be absorbed into the history of God with his people, in this case with the story of the patriarch Jacob.

B. JACOB AT THE HOME OF LABAN (Gen. 29-31)

Two stories lie again at the core: Jacob's marriage to Leah and Rachel (29:15-30) and the command to return (31:3). At the beginning is the account of Jacob's arrival and his service in the home of Laban (29:1-14), his being blessed with children (29:31—30:24) and flocks (30:25-34). At the end is the account of Jacob's flight from Laban and his treaty with him (31:1-55).

1. **Jacob at the home of Laban** (29:1-35)
    a. The meeting with Rachel at the well (29:1-11)
    b. The reception and employment at Laban's (29:12-14)
    c. The service for Rachel and Leah (29:15-30)
    d. Leah bears Reuben, Simeon, Levi, and Judah to Jacob (29:31-35)

2. **The sons of Jacob** (30:1-24)
    a. Bilhah, Rachel's maid, bears Dan and Naphtali (30:1-8)
    b. Zilpah, Leah's maid, bears Gad and Asher (30:9-13)

    c. Leah bears Issachar and Zebulun (30:14-21)
    d. Rachel bears Joseph (30:22-24)

3. The parting from Laban (30:25—31:55)

    a. Jacob requests Laban for permission to leave (30:25-26)
    b. The increase of Jacob's flocks. The outwitting of Laban (30:27-43)
    c. God's command: "Return!" (31:1-3)
    d. The conversation of Jacob with his wives (31:4-16)
    e. Jacob flees (31:17-21)
    f. Laban overtakes Jacob and reprimands him (31:22-30)
    g. Laban looks for his stolen teraphim, household gods (31:31-35)
    h. Jacob reproaches Laban (31:36-42)
    i. Jacob and Laban conclude a treaty (31:43-55)

4. The angelic encounter at Mahanaim (32:1-2)

These three chapters describe a portion of the life of the Israelite tribes in an earlier period, conceived here as a part of Jacob's experience in a foreign land. They ought not be looked upon as a biography, still less as an edifying description. They tell rather of the actual life of wandering tribes, for which our standards of judgment may not be used.

Two scenes should be especially noted: the scene at the well in the beginning (29:1-11) and the ratifying of a treaty at the end (31:41-55). The former is one of the finest examples of how the Bible attaches significance to the simple meeting of two people with one another. The latter preserves all the elements of the way a covenant was established in early times. Verse 53 shows that each of the parties swore by his own god and that the various gods of other nations in this early period were accordingly considered as actually existing.

C. THE MEETING OF THE BROTHERS (Gen. 32-33)

At the heart is the meeting of the two brothers (33). At the very beginning is the account of Jacob's preparation for the meeting and his prayer (32:1-21), also his struggle with God at Jabbok (32:22-

32). At the very end is the account of Jacob's settlement at Shechem (33:18-20), the pilgrimage from Shechem to Bethel, and the
renewal of the promise (35:1-15).

All the other stories belong outside this group of passages and
have been but loosely attached. These include the rape of Dinah
and the massacre at Shechem (34), the birth of Benjamin and the
death of Rachel (35:16-20), the outrage of Reuben (35:21-22),
the listing of Jacob's twelve sons, the account of Isaac's death
(35:23-29), and the listing of Esau's descendants, the Edomites (36).

1. The preparation for the meeting with Esau (32:3-21)

    a. Jacob sends messengers to Esau (32:3-6)
    b. He divides his people into two camps (32:7-8)
    c. The prayer (32:9-12)
    d. Jacob sends Esau a gift (32:13-21)

2. The struggle with God at Jabbok (32:22-32)

    a. The crossing of the river (32:22-23)
    b. The struggle and the blow on the thigh (32:24-25)
    c. The winning of the blessing. Jacob becomes Israel (32:26-31)
       The naming of the place—Peniel v. 30
    d. A rite derived from this event (32:32)

Underlying this account concerning the struggle with God at Jabbok is also a much older pre-Israelite saga about the struggle of a
man with a river demon that wanted to keep him from crossing the
stream. The Yahwist has adopted it into the patriarchal story in
order to point out that there is always the most remote and sinister
possibility of a struggle with God in man's relationship with him.
This was a struggle in which Israel did indeed conquer, although
as one who had been smitten.

Blessing is something that can only be granted by God as a gift.
That it can be turned into something gained through struggle, in
remote border-line situations, is permitted here to remain unexplained, as one of the incomprehensible realities of man's relationship over against God.

3. **The meeting with Esau** (33:1-20)

    a. An introduction to the meeting (33:1)
    b. The arrangement of the company (33:2)
    c. The submission (33:3, 6-7)
    d. The reconciliation (33:4)
    e. The pardon and its confirmation (33:8-11)
    f. The parting of the reconciled (33:12-17)
    g. Jacob settles in Shechem (33:18-20)

This narrative is meaningful only if one realizes that the kneeling of Jacob before Esau (the one who was blessed before the one who did not receive the blessing) signifies a real and complete submission.

The fragile character of blessing, which remains God's blessing in this very way, was experienced by Jacob in a life that was one of continual flight, although it abounded in children and flocks. It led him to become a servant in a foreign land and finally to submit to his brother who had not been blessed. In a wonderful way the narrative demonstrates how forgiveness and reconciliation can nevertheless ensue.

With this account the Jacob-Esau cycle is terminated.

D. SUPPLEMENTARY MATTER (Gen. 34-36)

1. The violation of Dinah and the slaughter at Shechem (34:1-31)

    a. The rape of Dinah, Jacob's daughter (34:1-7)
    b. Hamor seeks the hand of Dinah on behalf of his son Shechem (34:8-12)
    c. The demand concerning circumcision as a stipulation and its execution (34:13-24)
    d. The massacre of the helpless Shechemites (34:25-31)

The narrative in this chapter does not belong to the story of Jacob. It is akin in character rather to the Book of Judges, for it deals with the attempt of the Israelite tribes to maintain themselves among the Canaanites. In this warfare they here gain a victory over them in a cruel and deceitful manner.

2. The pilgrimage from Shechem to Bethel (35:1-7)

    a. The command to go to Bethel (35:1)
    b. The demand of Jacob on his household (35:2-3)
    c. The renunciation of the foreign gods (35:4)
    d. The road to Bethel (a terror from God) (35:5-6)
    e. The erection of an altar and the naming of the place (35:7)

According to Alt[*] there is a cultic act behind this account—a pilgrimage from the sanctuary of Shechem to that of Bethel. The preparatory act of the festival, the renunciation of foreign gods took place at Shechem; the principal act occurred at Bethel. Our narrative bases this custom on a solitary event, the journey of Jacob from Shechem to Bethel, commanded by God. All that was later connected with the celebration occurred at this time.

3. The death and burial of Deborah, Rebekah's nurse (35:8)

4. The divine appearance and promise at Bethel. Jacob becomes Israel (P) (35:9-15)

Here the Priestly narrative repeats once more the account of Gen. 28:10-22, at the same time removing all the archaic features. All that remains is the promise and the account of the erection of a stone that here is transformed into a monument. This narrative also chooses to tell how Bethel was founded.

5. The birth of Benjamin and the death of Rachel (35:16-20)

6. The outrage of Reuben (35:21-22)

7. A list of the sons of Jacob. The death and burial of Isaac (P) (35:23-29)

8. Esau and the Edomites (36:1-42)

    a. The descendants of Esau; his migration to Edom (P) (36:1-8)
    b. The sons of Esau (36:9-14)
    c. The Edomite chiefs (36:15-19)
    d. The sons of Seir, the Horite (36:20-30)
    e. The kings who reigned in Edom (36:31-39)
    f. The Edomite chiefs (36:40-43)

---

[*]Alt, Albrecht, "Die Wallfahrt von Sichem nach Bethel," *Kleine Schriften zur Geschichte des Volkes Israel,* I, Munchen, 1959, pp. 79-88.

The genealogy of Esau at the end of the Jacob-Esau narratives corresponds to that of Ishmael at the end of the Abraham stories (25:12-18). The chapter includes only lists and genealogies. Unusually valuable from a historical standpoint is the list of kings (36:31-39) with its information even as to the period when a dynasty began in Edom.

*   *   *   *   *

THE JOSEPH STORIES (Gen. 37-50)

As already noted, the Abraham cycle consists of single stories, closely knit together into a whole, whereas the Jacob-Esau cycle forms much more obviously a unit. This is achieved especially by the account of Jacob's flight and return, which unites the three parts of the cycle. The Joseph narrative, however, appears as one continuous account, flowing uninterruptedly from ch. 37 to 50. It leads like a chain of closely knit events from the conflict in ch. 37 to the final dissolution in ch. 50. The story of Joseph has therefore been called a novel, and rightly so, if one bears in mind the difference occasioned by the time interval.

It is the function of the Joseph story in the entire Pentateuch to link the sphere of action in Canaan, where the patriarchs wandered about and settled down, and connect it with that of the national history in Egypt, beginning with the account of the deliverance from Egypt. It answers the question: "How did the patriarchs come to Egypt?" The initial answer to this query is: "*Jacob moved to Egypt because of a famine.*" To the additional question: "*How* did Jacob come to Egypt?" the Joseph story replies: "The youngest son of Jacob was sold by his brothers into Egypt. There he became an important man and had Jacob come there later."

Out of this story of migration, telling only how Jacob came to Egypt, the ancient historians (J and E) have each produced an independent and comprehensive account with a character quite its own. No section of Genesis is closer to present experience than the

Joseph narrative. It starts with a conflict within a small group of people, the family of Jacob. The consequences of the increasing conflict among the persons and groups concerned are sketched in detail, and the episode is brought to a kind of initial climax in the lament of the aged father (37:31-35).

In the second act the narrative begins in a new setting with Joseph now in Egypt. His rise at court until he was elevated to the post as one of Pharaoh's ministers is once more depicted in a vivid, animated, and exciting way.

The third act picks up once more the theme of the initial act. Thus the brothers of Joseph were forced to journey to Egypt because of a famine. The story now moves abruptly to its climax— the reconciliation of Joseph with his brothers. Through the skill of the narrator the reconciliation here takes a turn that resembles quite closely the original state of conflict. Everything is thus brought to a genuine denouement that summarizes concisely what happened.

As a sequel the father's grief is transformed into thankful joy. The harmony in the circle of people where the drama was enacted is once more restored. At the same time the threat of famine in connection with Jacob's family is also removed. The aged father can therefore die in peace.

The narrative strands (J and E) may be traced more distinctly in the Joseph story than is usually possible. Much in the narrative becomes apparent only when one views the sources side by side:

J	E
A. THE CONFLICT (Gen. 37:3-35)	
1. Its basis (the coat) (37:3-4)	Its basis (the dreams) (37:5-11)
2. The errand for the father (37:12-17)	
3. The deed (37:18-30)*	The deed (37:18-30)*
4. The concealment of the deed (37:31-35)*	The concealment of the deed (37:31-35)*
B. JOSEPH IN EGYPT (39:1—41:57)	
1. The promotion and downfall of Joseph (39:1-23)	Joseph as a prison attendant (fragmentary) (39:1, 2, 4, 6)
a. Joseph among the Egyptians (39:2-5)	

*Cf. note p. 26.

b. Joseph's unmerited downfall
(39:6-20)
c. His promotion in prison
(39:21-23)

2. Joseph and the two officials in prison (fragmentary) (40:1b, 5b, 14b, 15b)	Joseph and the two officials in prison (40:2-23) a. The dreams of the two men (40:2-5) b. The interpretation (40:6-19) c. The fulfillment (40:20-23)
3. The promotion of Joseph (41:31-57)* a. The announcement of a famine (41:31) b. The advice given to Pharaoh (41:33-36)* c. The installation of Joseph (41:39-45)* d. Joseph in office (41:45-57)	The promotion of Joseph (41:1-44)* a. The dreams of Pharaoh (41:1-32) b. The advice given to Pharaoh (41:34-37 [38])* c. The installation of Joseph (41:41-44)*

C. THE RESTORATION OF HARMONY (Gen. 42-45)

1. The first journey of the brothers to Egypt (42)*	The first journey of the brothers to Egypt (predominantly E) (42:1-38)*
2. Second journey of the brothers (predominantly J) (43:1-34)	The second journey of the brothers to Egypt (only a few sentences) (43)*
3. The cup (44:1-34) a. Departure and the accusation en route (44:1-12) b. The trial in the house of Joseph (44:13-34) vv. 18-34 The speech of Judah	Joseph reveals his identity (45:1-27)* a. The denouement (45:2-15)* vv. 4-8 Joseph explains what has happened b. The brothers are dismissed and return home (45:16-27)*
4. Joseph reveals his identity (45:1-28)* a. The denouement (45:1-7)* b. The brothers are dismissed and return home (45:16-28)*	

D. THE CONCLUSION OF THE STORY OF JOSEPH AND THE PATRIARCHS (Gen. 46-50)

1. Jacob comes to Egypt (46:1—47:12)*	Jacob comes to Egypt (46:1—47:12)*
2. Joseph reduces the Egyptians to serfdom under the Pharaoh (47:13-26)	Jacob's benediction (48:1-22)*
3. Jacob's benediction and death (47:27—48:22*; 49:33)	

a. The increase of Israel in Goshen (47:27)	
b. The age of Jacob (47:28)	
c. The vow (47:29-31)	
d. Jacob blesses the sons of Joseph (48:1-22)*	Jacob blesses the sons of Joseph (48:1-22)*
e. The death of Jacob (49:33)	
4. The burial of Jacob (50:1-14)*	The burial of Jacob (50:3-10)*
	5. The final reconciliation of the brothers (50:15-21)
6. The death of Joseph (50:22-26)*	The death of Joseph (50:22-26)*

There are two chapters that did not belong originally in the Joseph story. The one is ch. 38 with its account of Judah and Tamar. This is a unit that is quite complete in itself. It is inserted at this point because Judah is the subject of ch. 37. The chapter in many respects may be compared with the tiny Book of Ruth. Both tell of a widow who found a new place again in the tribe.

The other chapter is Gen. 49, containing the blessing of Jacob. It is a very old collection of tribal sayings, conceived as a blessing of Jacob upon his twelve sons. (Cf. the blessing of Moses in Deut. 33 as a parallel.) They are depicted here as the forefathers of the twelve tribes. Characteristics of the different tribes have been singled out in these sayings. They thus provide us with a valuable insight into the life and history of the tribes before their coming together as the people of Israel.

In order to comprehend the entire account it is important that one view the two strands of the Joseph story side by side, because the central theme in J and E is not the same. They present the course of events in the following manner:

J	E
1. The father's partiality	1. Joseph's dreams
2. The deed of the brothers	2. The deed of the brothers
3. Among the Egyptians	
4. The unmerited downfall	
5. Joseph in prison	3. Joseph in prison
6. Joseph becomes an official	4. Joseph becomes an official

Whereas J works out in detail the incidental events, describing how they actually took place, E endeavors to indicate the primary tendencies *[linien]*. In E the central theme is accordingly viewed

in a way that is correspondingly different from that of J. E brings
the account to a conclusion in which everything is drawn together
by the comment:

> "As for you, you meant evil against me; but God meant it for
> good, to bring it about that many people should be kept alive,
> as they are today" (50:20)

Compare the similar passage in 45:5-7. In these two statements
divine and human behavior are contrasted, and the narrative as a
whole becomes a eulogy of God, who in such a remarkable manner
transforms that which man has corrupted.

J, on the other hand, does not differentiate between divine and
human behavior but rather sees something wonderful in the way
God's actions are accomplished through the actions of men. He does
not delineate the central theme of the whole story through a general
statement. He leaves it rather unexpressed through the climax itself, when Judah under the pressure of a false accusation declares
as the brother who was accountable, "God has found out the guilt
of your servants" (44:16). In his petition, addressed to Joseph, he
then draws the inference that he himself should assume the (unde-
served!) penalty (vv. 18-24). This acknowledgment of the old
offense is succeeded by the words of Joseph (45:4-13), leading to
reconciliation. Thus the harmony that has been disturbed within
Jacob's family is once more restored. It was in *this* way that God
had been wondrously active.

In the juxtaposition of these two accounts of the same events one
can perceive the sources that side-by-side bear witness to the acts
of God—even as in the Gospels. Both portrayals in essence point
beyond themselves into the future of God's dealings with his people.

IV

From Exodus to Numbers

In the Book of Exodus the primary theme of God's history with his people is developed. This history begins with an account of deliverance out of dire distress (chs. 1-14), to which there is a response of praise by those who experience that deliverance (ch. 15). The deliverance is followed by an account of preservation (Ex. 16-18; Num. 10-20). Corresponding to this preservation by God is men's continuing obedience to God's commandment and law. In the formation of the covenant the rescuing and safekeeping activity of God and the activity of men in keeping the commandments of God are united, the one following the other.

The covenant, however, is immediately broken by Israel (the story of the golden calf in Ex. 32), and so God's activity, concerned with giving direction and meting out punishment, supervenes (Ex. 32-33). That the history of God's people does not terminate at this point is due solely to his merciful goodness. He renews his covenant despite their transgression (Ex. 34).

In this sketch of Exodus all the fundamental elements are presented which from now on are to determine the history of God's people. In addition there is P's amplified account of how the law was given (chs. 19-23). It introduces at this point the entire legal code (Ex. 25-31, 35-40; Lev.; and Num. 1-10), a code which had actually developed gradually. The departure from Sinai and the resumption of the journey through the wilderness (Num. 10-20) do not come until after this important interpolation, continuing where Exodus left off. With Num. 20 a new section begins—the conquest of the land east of the Jordan (chs. 20-24, 32). There is only an allusion to this, however, in a few episodes. The interpolation by the Priestly Code is concluded at the end of the Book of Numbers with a series of supplements (chs. 25-31; 33-36).

The Books of Exodus, Leviticus, and Numbers constitute therefore a close-knit unity. Together with the Priestly Code's interpolated material these three books contain the history of the exodus up to the conquest of the east-Jordanic region in unbroken sequence.

With these comments it is now more evident that the Pentateuch contains three primary sections: the primeval and patriarchal history (Genesis), the account of the exodus (Ex., Lev., and Num.), and the address of Moses (Deut.).

THE BOOK OF EXODUS

A. GOD'S SAVING ACT:
DELIVERANCE OUT OF DISTRESS
(Ex. 1-14)

1. **The distress** (chs. 1-11)
    a. Oppression in Egypt (ch. 1)
    b. Moses' call and commission (chs. 2-6)
       The promise (ch. 3)
    c. Moses and Pharaoh (The miracles and plagues in Egypt) (chs. 7-11)
2. **The deliverance** (chs. 12-14)
    a. The Passover and the departure from Egypt (12:1—13:16)
    b. The march through the wilderness. The pursuit and deliverance (13:17—14:31)

B. MAN'S RESPONSE IN PRAISE
(Ex. 15:1-21)

The hymn of praise; the song of Miriam (15:1 = v. 21), expanded into a historical psalm (vv. 2-18)

C. GOD'S ACTION: PRESERVATION
(Ex. 15:22—18:27)

meeting elementary needs of human existence

1. **Thirst:** through water (15:22-27; 17:1-7)
2. **Hunger:** through quails and manna (ch. 16)
3. **Despair:**
   a. Because of enemies: victory over the Amalekites (17:8-16)
   b. Because of domestic problems: the visit of Jethro. The installation of judges (ch. 18)

D. MAN'S RESPONSE IN OBEDIENCE
(Ex. 19-31)

1. The Law and the Covenant (chs. 19-24)
   a. God's manifestation at Sinai (ch. 19)
   b. The Decalogue (ch. 20)
   c. The Book of the Covenant (chs. 21-23)
   d. The establishment of the covenant (ch. 24)
      The covenant meal and offering.
      The tables of stone. The divine glory.
2. Instructions concerning the Law (chs. 25-31)
   Preparation of the sanctuary and the sacred vessels

E. TRANSGRESSION AND RENEWAL
(chs. 32-40)

1. The molten image and its destruction.
   Moses' intercession (ch. 32)
2. The command to depart (33:1-6)
3. The tent of meeting (33:7-23)
4. The New Covenant: the replacement of the tables of the law. The cultic decalogue (ch. 34)
5. The Law (chs. 35-40)
   The fulfillment of the instructions given in chs. 25-31.
   (Continued in Lev. and Num.).

A. GOD'S SAVING ACT: DELIVERANCE OUT OF DISTRESS
(Ex. 1-14)

There is a pronounced upward movement in this first section of Exodus, proceeding from the bitter distress of the Israelites in Egypt and leading directly to their deliverance. Within this section occurs that which was announced at the outset (3:7-8). The original promise, determinative for the whole Bible, is found here. The announcement of deliverance, however, is not issued directly to the people. It is proclaimed rather through a mediator, viz., Moses, who was thus a necessary participant in that which transpired.

It is necessary therefore to furnish an account concerning the mediator, especially his call (chs. 3-4, including ch. 6, which is based on P). At the heart of this account is the announcement he had to bring to his people. The story of his call is included in the account of the obstacles the mediator encountered as he responded to the distress of the people. This involves his birth, flight from Egypt, return, and inner struggle (chs. 2-5). Next comes the strange and difficult episode concerning Moses' conflict with Pharaoh in connection with the miracles and plagues (chs. 7-11). In chs. 12-14 this section reaches it climax—the exodus and the rescue of the people from their pursuers.

Inasmuch as this account deals with primary events in God's activity on behalf of his people, the lines of each specific theme to be found here may be traced throughout the entire Bible, as follows:

1. The announcement of deliverance in 3:7-8 has a connection with the promise concerning land, beginning with Gen. 12:1-3 and continuing on throughout the patriarchal history. The promise of deliverance is fulfilled quite soon; for there is but a brief span of time between Ex. 3 and 14. The Book of Joshua records the fulfillment of the promise concerning land (11:23), but there is something still definitely lacking. For Israel continues to be threatened even in her own land. An entirely new promise is accordingly issued in 2 Sam. 7 on behalf of kingship. Then the announcement of judgment looms in the foreground, out of which arises ultimately the promise of salvation, transcending and pointing beyond the

history of Israel. This promise is proclaimed in the New Testament as fulfilled.

2. The announcement is issued through an intermediary. With this the history of the mediator begins, which extends from Moses to Christ in many varying forms (judges, kings, prophets, the Suffering Servant).

3. The call of Moses has its sequel in the stories of the way in which the prophets received their calls (Amos 3; Is. 6; Jer. 1; Ezek. 1-3; Is. 40).

1. The distress (chs. 1-11)

a. *The oppression in Egypt* (1:1-22)

All three sources (P: vv. 1-7; J: vv. 8-14; E: vv. 15-20) tell of the oppression in Egypt, each adding that Israel multiplied despite all the oppression. Here the theme of blessing (i.e. growth in population) has been adopted from the patriarchal narratives. That Israel never forgot the oppression in Egypt is indicated for example by the way in which many of the laws against social oppression have as their motivation Israel's own suffering.

b. *The call and commission of Moses* (2:1–6:29)

The divine manifestation, standing at the heart of the account in ch. 3, includes all the elements of the biblical concept of holiness (cf. Is. 6). Moses resisted the call, even as did Isaiah and Jeremiah. (There are four objections and four promises.) At the time of the initial conference with Pharaoh in ch. 5 the motif of complaint begins. It continues throughout the exodus story. Each new burden aroused grumbling, aimed continually at the mediator, Moses. He therefore would appeal to Yahweh, who would help him take the next step. In ch. 6 P gives another account concerning the call.

c. *The contest: Moses and Pharaoh (The miracles and plagues)* (chs. 7-11)

In Ex. 7-11 there is an account of nine plagues, increasing in severity. These finally led Pharaoh to release the Israelites. In ch. 11 the tenth plague is announced. It occurred for the first time in connection with the festival of the Passover (12), at which time the exodus began.

The plagues were intended to call attention to the power of God, which produced all the signs and wonders and alone brought about Israel's exodus from Egypt. This special form of the story of the plagues probably reaches so far back into the past, however, that a complete understanding of them is not possible. There are frequent references to the story later on (e.g., Deut. 4:34; Ps. 105:27; 135:9).

2. The deliverance (chs. 12-14)

a. *The Passover* (12:1–13:16)

This is the clearest example of the way the great festivals in Israel were linked with the history of God's people. The Passover was formerly an ancient pastoral festival that was later combined with the Feast of Unleavened Bread, a festival held at the beginning of the wheat harvest. Its customs and observances were merged quite closely with this event, so basic to Israel's history, and they were intended henceforth solemnly to safeguard it. Ex. 12:11 indicates this in an especially impressive manner with the comment: "You shall eat it in haste. It is the Lord's passover."

b. *The release of Israel. The crossing of the Sea of Reeds* (13:17–14:31)

The description is a combination of several accounts. This is especially evident in the way the oldest stratum of tradition presents the miracle as a natural event that brought deliverance at the exact moment of greatest need. In the later accounts the miraculous element has been enlarged upon. Even in the case of this peril the Israelites grumbled against Moses, who stood alone between the people and God (14:10-12).

B. MAN'S RESPONSE IN PRAISE: THE HYMN OF PRAISE
(Ex. 15:1-21)

The song of Miriam is the oldest hymn preserved in the Bible:

Sing to the Lord, for he has triumphed gloriously;
The horse and his rider he has thrown into the sea (v. 21)

This was the immediate response, a jubilant cry of relief on the part of those who had experienced deliverance. It is introduced in vv. 19-20 as the song that Miriam, the sister of Aaron, began to sing after the event. Because this was such a decisive moment in the history of Israel, however, the song was later expanded into a great historical psalm (vv. 2-18), and the song of Miriam was again placed at the beginning (v. 1).

Response through praise belongs so definitely to the experience of the acts of God in the Old Testament that psalms have often been inserted throughout the historical books along with the account as here (e.g., Judges 5, a song of victory; 1 Sam. 2; 2 Sam. 22; Is. 38).

C. GOD'S ACTION: PRESERVATION
(Ex. 15:22—18:27)

Here a new theme begins—preservation, which is now included along with deliverance. It is not preservation, however, that is due to the sustenance that continually comes from the soil or is the result of stable and orderly institutions. It is rather preservation due to a series of miracles concerned with elementary needs of human existence: hunger, thirst, despair.

1. Thirst: Marah (15:22-27). The Israelites wandered into the wilderness for three days, only to come across "bitter" water unexpectedly. Once more grumbling broke out. Moses again cried to God, and he granted aid. The story of the water that issued from the rock belongs here (Ex. 17:1-7 and Num. 20:1-13).

2. Hunger (16:1-36). This chapter tells how they were delivered from famine in the Wilderness of Sin. It indicates how deeply this event was impressed on the people's mind. Although originally a simple brief account, it has been greatly amplified and filled with miracle stories that are actually more an interpretation of the event than a simple presentation. The same theme recurs again in Num. 11:4-35 and in Jesus' miracles of feeding.

3. Despair (chs. 17-18)

a. *The threat of enemies: the battle with the Amalekites*
   (17:8-16)

This is the first account of conflict involving Israel. From now on to the end of the period of the kings it is evident that Israel will have to fight its own battles as the people of God. In this first battle the intercession of Moses before God on behalf of the people was determinative. "Whenever he held up his hands, Israel prevailed . . ." (v. 11). In v. 16 is preserved an ancient song of war.

b. Domestic problems (18:1-27)

(1) The visit of Jethro (18:1-12). This is an especially fine and graphic narrative—this meeting between Moses and his father-in-law Jethro who was a Midianite priest. It is intended to echo God's magnificent achievement through the mouth of a non-Israelite. Jethro says: "Blessed be the Lord, who has delivered you out of the hand of the Egyptians " (v. 10).*

(2) The appointment of judges (18:13-27). At the advice of Jethro, Moses appoints judges to help him keep order. This narrative indicates that Israel in early times learned from other nations and adopted much from them.

D. MAN'S RESPONSE IN OBEDIENCE (Ex. 19-31)
1. The Law and the Covenant (chs. 19-24)

a. *God's manifestation at Sinai* (19:1-25)

Matching the introductory words to the First Commandment: "I am the Lord your God, . . . " is the legal section of the Pentateuch, introduced by a theophany (ch. 19), representing the statement: "I am the Lord your God." God in his majesty appears before his people in order to make known to them his will. This is the sense of ch. 19 as an introduction to the legal section.

The portrayal of the divine encounter has, moreover, a direct bearing on public worship (19:10-15). Here Moses has a different mediatorial function than hitherto. He stands between the divine holiness and the people, who shrink from it. He is the mediator of that which is holy. He is the one who receives and transmits God's imperative direction (the Torah). This in essence is also the function of a divine service.

---

*Cf. the similar eulogy of the queen of Sheba in 1 Kings 10:9.

b. *The Decalogue* (20:1-17)

Originally the Decalogue (or ten commandments) alone belonged to the theophany at Sinai. As a series of commandments complete in itself, belonging to the oldest stratum of commandments and laws in Israel, it serves as a foundation for them all. It has the function of a "primary law"—here as well as in Deut. 5, where it appears again in a slightly varied form. The fact that it is associated with the theophany at Sinai indicates that its actual setting *[Sitz im Leben]* in earlier times was the public worship, as indicated also by its language of direct address.

c. The Book of the Covenant (chs. 21-23)

This code of laws originated during the early period of settlement in Canaan—at any rate sometime before the period of the monarchy. This comprehensive collection demonstrates clearly how the ancient and genuine Israelite laws, expressed as commands of God (just as the Ten Commandments) were combined with the legal institutions of the native population in Canaan and united into a whole.*

d. The establishment of the covenant (ch. 24).

This is reported in quite different ways by the three sources. J has a very archaic account (vv. 1, 9-11), telling of a covenant meal that Moses ate on the mountain top with seventy elders in the presence of God. E gives a detailed description of how the covenant sacrifice was celebrated. Blood was strewn partially on the altar and partially on the people (vv. 3-8). In P the divine glory appears in a cloud upon the mountain (vv. 15-18).

e. Instructions concerning the Law (chs. 25-31). (See p. 66.)

E. THE BREAKING OF THE COVENANT AND THE RENEWAL OF THE TABLES OF LAW (Ex. 32-34)

1. The molten image and its destruction. Moses' intercession (ch. 32)

At this point a feature that will hereafter determine the history of Israel begins, viz., the breaking of the covenant by the people. In fashioning an idol (32:1-6) they transgressed one of the funda-

---

*Cf. Albrecht Alt's discussion of apodictic and casuistic law in *Essays on Old Testament History and Religion*, Oxford, 1966, pp. 81-132.

mental commandments. Ch. 32:7-35 tells what happened after this violation of the covenant.

In this connection something typical of the Old Testament is revealed, viz., divine "inconsistency." God was determined to annihilate the people; yet he did not carry out this intention. The reason in the end is not given. An essential factor, however, was the intervention of the Mediator on behalf of those who were guilty. This trend of thought after many stages leads ultimately to the office of Christ.

2. The command to depart (33:1-6)

3. The tent of meeting (33:7-23)

There is an allusion in ch. 33 to a sanctuary that belonged to the period of the wandering. This was "the tent of meeting," in which God met Moses and answered the questions the Israelites submitted to him (vv. 7-11). The chapter terminates with the unusual and obscure narrative, telling how Moses asked to see the face of God (vv. 18-23).

4. The New Covenant: the replacement of the tables of the law. The cultic decalogue (34:1-28).

This chapter is closely related to ch. 19. There the revelation at Sinai was followed by the Decalogue (ch. 20). Here the so-called "cultic Decalogue" has been substituted in ch. 34 (vv. 12-26), which is closely related to the one in ch. 20 in its fundamental commandments. It includes, however, also some commandments pertaining to public worship.

According to P (vv. 29-35) Moses' face still reflected God's glory. He therefore had to hide his face with a veil when he came forth from the tent (cf. 2 Cor. 3:12-18).

The remaking of the tables of the law, as described in ch. 34, did not signify a new covenant but only a resumption of the one established in ch. 24 *despite* the apostasy. The *new* covenant is not referred to in the Old Testament until the end of the epoch that here has its beginning (Jer. 31:31-34). At that time these words about a new and different covenant transcend and point beyond the Old Testament.

THE PRIESTLY CODE
The Legal Collections in the Pentateuch

After Ex. 24 and 34 the great Priestly Code is introduced, with its own newly arranged divisions, extending from this point to Num. 10. Thus it includes Lev. 17-26, which was once an independent legal corpus and introduced later into the great Priestly Code. The collection of laws in Lev. 1-7 and the laws of purity in Lev. 11-15 were also at one time independent.

A. THE SEQUENCE OF THE COLLECTIONS

The following chart indicates the sequence of the legal collections in the Pentateuch:

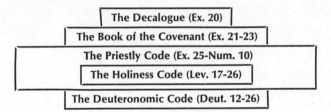

From a chronological standpoint the order is somewhat different:

1. *The Decalogue* (Ex. 20)—the early period (the similar series as noted below belong here also)
2. *The Book of the Covenant* (Ex. 21-23)—the period of the judges.
3. *The Deuteronomic Code* (Deut. 12-26—the seventh century (before the reign of Josiah).
4. *The Holiness Code* (Lev. 17-26)—the sixth century.
5. *The Priestly Code* (Ex. 25—Num. 10)—the sixth to the fifth centuries.

The most significant observations are as follows:

a. The Decalogue is included also in Deut. 5. Some of its commandments are found in Ex. 34 (the so-called cultic decalogue) and in Lev. 19.
b. The Deuteronomic Code in many of its parts resembles the Book of the Covenant.

B. SPECIMENS OF THE PRINCIPAL TYPES OF LAWS

1. *A command:* "You shall not revile God" (Ex. 22:28).

2. *A statute:* "When a man strikes his slave, male or female, with a rod and the slave dies under his hand, he shall be punished" (Ex. 21:20).

3. *A statute, expanded in a hortatory manner:* "When you reap your harvest in your field, and have forgotten a sheaf in the field, you shall not go back to get it; it shall be for the sojourner, the fatherless, and the widow; that the Lord your God may bless you in all the work of your hands" (Deut. 24:19).

4. *A cultic ordinance:* "If any one sins, doing any of the things which the Lord has commanded not to be done, though he does not know it . . . he shall bring to the priest a ram without blemish out of the flock, valued by you at the price for a guilt offering, and the priest shall make atonement for him for the error which he committed unwittingly" (Lev. 5:17 ff.).

C. THE MOST IMPORTANT DIFFERENCES IN THE CODES

1. The Decalogue, the Book of the Covenant, and the Deuteronomic Code are concerned with all forms of national community life.

2. The Holiness and Priestly Codes deal almost entirely with the cult community.

3. The Decalogue consists only of commandments. The Book of the Covenant contains only commandments and laws: the Deuteronomic Code, laws and commandments that have been expanded in a hortatory manner; the Priestly Code, cultic ordinances.

4. The Holiness Code stands at the center between the Deuteronomic and Priestly Codes.

The Sections of the Priestly Code

A. THE FIRST PART OF THE PRIESTLY CODE
(Ex. 25-31, 35-40)

1. The sanctuary, priests, and holy vessels (chs. 25-31)

  a. The ark, table, and lampstand (25:1-40)
  b. The sacred tent (the tabernacle) (26:1-37)
  c. The altar of burnt offering and the forecourt (27:1-21)
  d. The investiture of the priests (Aaron and his sons) (28:1-43)
  e. Rites for the ordination of the priests (29:1-46)

    f. Supplementary matter: the incense altar, anointing oil,
       etc. (30:1—31:11)

    g. The sabbath (31:12-17)

2. The fulfillment of the commands given in Ex. 25-31 (35:1—40:33)

3. The cloud descends upon the sacred tent (40:34-38).

Chs. 25-31 are formulated as a divine mandate addressed personally to Moses. Each of these commands has a corresponding fulfillment in Ex. 35-40 as follows:

The Lord said to Moses, "Speak to the people of Israel, that they take for me an offering" (25:1)	Moses said to all the congregation of the people of Israel, "This is the thing which the Lord has commanded. Take from among you an offering to the Lord" (35:4, 5)

Here the fundamental pattern of the Priestly narrative is indicated, beginning with the Creation account, viz., every happening is founded upon a command of God that is to be carried out. The formulation, "The Lord said to Moses," is not to be understood in the sense of God's dictating as it were all the divine instructions to Moses. The wording rather expresses the fact that the public worship as performed by Israel may be traced back in all its details to God's initial purpose. Nor should one suppose that all these detailed institutions originated already in the Wilderness of Sinai; for they presuppose instead life in an established community. The meaning is the same, viz., all the abundance of forms and institutions for public worship, as they came into being during the course of history, were initially founded in this way on God's covenant with his people at Sinai.

B. THE SECOND PART OF THE PRIESTLY CODE (LEVITICUS)

1. Laws of sacrifice (1:1—7:38)

    a. Instructions concerning the burnt offering (1:1-17)
       (1) Introduction: God's charge to Moses (1:1-2)
       (2) Instruction concerning the sacrifice of an ox (1:3-9)
       (3) The sacrifice of other animals: sheep, goats, doves
          (1:10-17)

b. Instructions concerning the cereal offering (2:1-16)
c. The peace offering (3:1-17)
d. The sin offering (4:1-35)
e. The guilt offering (5:1-19)
f. Supplementary matter (6:1—7:38)

Lev. 1-7 was once an independent collection of sacrificial regulations, inserted later into the Priestly document. It includes, in addition to the directions for the priests, instructions for the laity. Its distinctive style is apparent, affected by its long period of oral transmission. It was not until the latest stage that all the sacrifices gained an atoning significance (e.g., Lev. 1:4). Prior to this the various kinds of sacrifices dealt with quite varied situations. The closing, oft-repeated sentence, "It is a burnt offering, an offering by fire, a pleasing odor to the Lord," is to be understood as a spiritualization of the sacrificial event. In other words, the sacrificial material itself was not the essential thing (as if it had somewhat the sense of food for God). It was rather the veneration manifest in the sacrifice.

2. The consecration of the priests (8:1—10:20)

a. The consecration of Aaron and his sons (8:1-36)
b. The first offering presented by Aaron and his sons (9:1-24)
c. The sacrilege of Nadab and Abihu. Directions for the priests (10:1-20)

At the end of Ex. 40 is the account of the completion of the sanctuary, after which the consecration of the priests (Lev. 8-10) immediately follows. Lev. 1-7 was inserted at this point because it seemed proper to introduce the stipulations concerning sacrifice before the initial sacrifice was described.

The consecration of Aaron (8) includes a lavish abundance of rites, the offering of nearly every kind of sacrifice (9). Aaron was the one who did the actual sacrificing, whereas his sons provided only assistance. This therefore already anticipated a structuring of the priesthood into higher and lower offices. The sacrificial service closed with the blessing (9:22). The sacrilege and punishment of Nadab and Abihu reflect a struggle within the priestly family about which we otherwise know nothing.

3. The laws of purification (11:1—15:33)

Originally this also was an independent collection that was inserted into the Priestly Code. In the everyday life of the Israelites directions concerning purification had a profound significance, as is indicated even in the New Testament, where the violation of these laws (Acts 10) acquired particular significance in connection with the separation of the Christian and Jewish communities.

- a. Pure and impure animals (11:1-47)
- b. Women in confinement after childbirth (Cf. Luke 2:24 in connection with vv. 6-8) (12:1-8)
- c. Leprosy in human beings, clothing, and houses (13:1—14:57)
- d. Impurity due to secretions (15:1-33)

The limitation of these laws concerning purification is evident above all in the fact that purification of women after childbirth was understood as an act of expiation, even as an atoning sacrifice (12:7).

4. The great Day of Atonement (16:1-34)

This chapter is a supplement. The Day of Atonement was introduced very late, after the time of Ezra. It belongs in the same context as that of quite dissimilar sacrifices arranged under the work of atonement. In that late period of time there was a growing conviction that sacrifice, despite everything, could not avail before God —hence the intent of the Day of Atonement: "From all your sins you shall be clean before the Lord" (16:30). The Book of Hebrews (ch. 9) sees an allusion to the sacrificial death of Christ in this concentration on a "once for all."

The driving out of a goat for Azazel (vv. 8-10) is a very ancient animistic rite that originally applied to the bringing of an offering to a wilderness demon. In the context of the Day of Atonement this act became a sign, typifying the abolishing of the sins of the people.

5. The Holiness Code (17:1—26:46)

- a. The slaughter of every animal must take place at a holy site (17:3-9)
- b. Prohibition of eating meat with blood (17:10-16)
- c. Marriage laws (18:1-30)
- d. Commandments and laws of various kinds (19:1-37)

(1) Introduction: "You shall be holy, for I the Lord your God am holy." (19:1-2)

(2) Commandments corresponding to the first four commandments of the Decalogue (19:3-4)

(3) Regulation concerning the peace offering (19:5-8)

(4) Commandments relating to the community (19:9-18) "You shall love your neighbor as yourself" (v. 18)

(5) Various commandments (19:19-37. Cf. Ex. 34) "You shall rise up before the hoary head" (v. 32).

e. Idolatry (20:1-8)

f. Forbidden sexual relations (20:10-21)

g. An admonition (20:22-26; v. 26 = 19:2)

h. Priests and sacrifices (21:1—22:33)

i. Festival laws (23:1-44)

   (1) Sabbath (23:1-3)

   (2) Passover (23:4-8)

   (3) Harvest festivals (23:9-44)

j. Miscellaneous laws (24:1-23; 26:1-2)

   (1) Lamps (24:1-4)

   (2) Shewbread (24:5-9)

   (3) Blasphemy and retaliation (24:10-23)

   (4) Idolatry (26:1-2)

k. The sabbatical year and the year of jubilee (25:1-55)

l. A conditional announcement relating to welfare (26:3-13) and calamity (26:14-39)

m. A concluding promise of God's mercy (26:40-45)

The Holiness Code gets its name from the admonition in the introduction to ch. 19, repeated several times (20:7, 26; 21:6; cf. 22:31-33). Like the Book of the Covenant, it is a collection of laws that existed independently before being inserted into the Priestly document. It came into being gradually out of many individual elements.

There are two parts to it: commandments and ordinances for the community (19-20 plus ch. 18) and those for public worship, and the festival year (21-25 plus ch. 17). Its language is that of divine discourse in common with the Priestly Code and like Deuteronomy the commandments are situated in part within a hortatory framework, e.g., a general admonition to keep the commandments (18:2-5), marriage laws (18:6-23), an urgent admonition concerning that which has been commanded.

Such a hortatory conclusion is found also in 20:22-24. The final chapter (26) calls to mind especially Deuteronomy with its blessings and curses that developed into conditional announcements of welfare and disaster. Chronologically the Holiness Code belongs between Deuteronomy and the Priestly Code as noted above.

C. THE THIRD PART OF THE PRIESTLY CODE
(NUMBERS)

1. **Supplementary material** (Lev. 27; Num. 1:1-6)
   a. Instructions concerning oaths and tithes (27:1-34)
   b. The numbering and arrangement of the tribes (1:1—2:34)
   c. The mustering of the priestly and Levitical families (3:1—4:49)
   d. Procedure in special cases (5:1—6:21)
   e. The priestly blessing (6:22-27)

2. **Appendices** (Num. 7:1—10:10)
   a. The offerings of the tribal leaders (7:1-89)
   b. The consecration of the Levites and their service (8:1-26)
   c. A supplement to the Passover law (9:1-14)
   d. The fiery cloud (9:15-23)
   e. The two silver trumpets for signaling (10:1-10)

At the heart of this third section is Num. 1-4 with its catalog of the entire nation. The great gulf between the people (chs. 1-2) and the priests (chs. 3-4), in distinction from the register of families at the beginning, thus becomes apparent.

The priests are again divided into the genuine priests and the Levites. The latter are thereby also provided with their own ordination service and sphere of activity—at first in supplement (ch. 8). The list of the contributions made by the tribal leaders at the time of the dedication of the altar is also a part of the records (ch. 7).

Some stipulations concerning special cases have been added—in this connection a typical ordeal (or divine judgment) that was to be used, when there was suspicion of adultery (Num. 5).

The two concluding sections concerning the fiery cloud and the signaling trumpets (9:15—10:10) lead directly over to the account of the departure from Sinai. The priestly blessing concludes the entire section. (That which follows it is a later supplement.)

From this so-called Mosaic benediction: "The Lord bless you and keep you . . . " one should refer back to the benedictions in the primeval and patriarchal histories (Gen. 1; 12:1-3; 27; 49) and look ahead to those in the Psalms (esp. Ps. 67 and 121) and to the post-scripts in the New Testament epistles. Blessing thus extends throughout the entire Bible in both Old and New Testaments.

3. **Further supplementary material** (Num. 15, 19, 25-31, 34-36)
   a. Miscellaneous stipulations (15:1-41)
      (1) Cereal and drink offerings (15:1-31)
      (2) The stoning of a sabbathbreaker (15:32-36)
      (3) Tassels on clothing (15:37-41)
   b. Purification with the ashes of a red heifer (19:1-22)
   c. Establishment of the priestly right of Phinehas (25:6-13)
   d. The adjustment of the rights of female inheritance (27:1-11)
   e. Further stipulations concerning sacrifices and festivals (28:1—29:40)
   f. The validity of vows (30:1-16)
   g. The Midianite campaign and instructions about the division of the spoil (31:1-54)
   h. A list of stations along the wilderness route (33:1—34:29)
   i. The establishment of the Levitical cities and the cities of refuge (35:1-34)
   j. A supplement to the regulations concerning the rights of female inheritance (36:1-13)

It is apparent from these supplements to the Priestly Code, after Num. 10 (the departure from Sinai), that the abundance of regulations in it originated during a long process of development. This alone can explain why so much has been added after the end of the Priestly Code in Num. 6, material that is far removed from the event of the law-giving at Sinai. Now it has been placed in the midst of a report about the latter half of the wilderness wandering and close to the account of the conquest of the east-Jordanic region. A characteristic of these later additions to the law is the way in which the regulations have been based on a story, recalling the circumstances that led to the regulation (Num. 15:32-36; 25:6-13. Cf. Lev. 24:1-16).

The procurement of a remedy for cultic purification through the ashes of a red heifer (Num. 19) refers to an ancient rite, reminiscent of the one used for the Day of Atonement. In Heb. 9 this kind of purification has been adopted as an antitype of the purification made possible by Christ's sacrifice.

*　*　*　*　*

CONTINUATION OF NARRATIVE
(Numbers 10-36)
A. THE PATH THROUGH THE WILDERNESS (Num. 10-20)

Num. 10-20 is connected directly with Ex. 16-18, the account of the preservation following the deliverance (cf. Ex. 19:1 with Num. 10:11.) Both sections describe the journey through the wilderness and contain largely the same themes. These are again as follows:

1. Introduction: Departure from Sinai (10:11-36)

The brief note concerning departure (corresponding to Ex. 16:1) has been expanded by means of a list that gives the order of march (vv. 13-28). There is also a comment concerning the guidance given by Moses' father-in-law, who is here called Hobab rather than Jethro (vv. 29-32), and concerning the direction given by the ark. Here are included sayings about the ark (vv. 33-36), which belong to Israel's oldest traditions.

2. Preservation

a. *Thirst* (Num. 20:2-13). This story is parallel to that of Ex. 17:1-7 and like it is characterized by the grumbling of the people and the miracle that God performed through the Mediator.

b. *Hunger* (Num. 11:1-35). This story also corresponds to one in Ex. 16 about the miracle of feeding. Here too a short account has been greatly expanded. Of special importance is the detailed complaint of Moses, who cries out to God under the burden of his office as a leader.

c. *Domestic problems:* These stand out much more numerously and abruptly in Num. 10-20 in comparison to Ex. 16-18.

(1) The installation of the elders (11:24-30 matching Ex. 18)

This account has been combined with the miracle of feeding. God responded in two ways to Moses' complaint in the face of a hungry and rebellious people:

(a) by performing the miracle of feeding,

(b) by bestowing the spirit upon seventy elders who were to assist Moses in bearing the burden of leading the people. Striking in this connection is the way in which the bestowal of the spirit is described as a kind of prophetic spirit, something like that of Elijah and Elisha.

(2) The opposition of Miriam and Aaron (Num. 12)

This narrative is based on the rivalries between the prophetic and priestly leadership of the people, details of which are no longer to be ascertained. A divine decision was once again expected and provided. After the punishment was administered Moses acted as an intercessor.

(3) The spies (Num. 13-14)

Here an entirely new epoch begins: the crossing over into civilized country. The story of the spies points up the weak faith and inconstancy manifested by the people. They are punished by having the fulfillment of the promise postponed.

(4) The rebellion of Korah, Dathan, and Abiram (Num. 16-17)

Accounts of two different revolts have here been fused. The older sources (J and E) tell of an uprising on the part of the Reubenities Dathan and Abiram against Moses. This had to do with their scornful denial of the promise pertaining to land. The revolt of the Korahite band, on the other hand, involved the claim of priestly authority, which they did not want to ascribe solely to Moses and Aaron but wanted also for themselves. The hand of P is evident at this point; for it uses the narrative as the basis for setting up a distinction between the priestly and Levitical orders (Num. 18).

The emphasis in this latter half of the wilderness wandering is placed on the domestic problems. The description indicates how new perils threatened the people of God as the time of fulfillment drew near, developing within the nation itself.

The next important historical section with its account of how the land was settled will deal with the organization and leadership of

the people of God. At the same time, however, the fourth theme of
Ex. 16-18 now appears:

d. *The external peril.*[*] It occupies at first the foreground in the
final part of Numbers and then passes over directly into the books
of Joshua and Judges.

B. CONQUEST OF THE LAND EAST OF THE JORDAN
(Num. 20:14—36:13)

1. The Edomites refuse a peaceful passage through their country (20:14-21)
2. The death of Aaron (P) (20:22-29)
3. The victory over the Canaanites at Hormah (21:1-3)
4. The bronze serpent (21:4-9)
5. The list of stations (21:10-20)
   A song to a well (vv. 17-18)
6. The Amorites refuse to let them go through (21:21-32)
7. Victory over Og of Bashan (21:33-35)
8. The arrival opposite Jericho (22:1)
9. *The story of Balaam* (the subduing of Moab) (22:2—24:25)
   a. The Moabite king's commission to Balaam the seer (22:2—23:6)
   b. Balaam's first obstacle: "Who can count the myriads of Israel?" (23:7-10)
   c. A renewal of the commission (22:11-17)
   d. Balaam's second oracle: "I received a command to bless!" (23:18-24)
   e. Balak's third attempt (23:25-30)
   f. Balaam's third oracle: "Blessed be everyone who blesses you!" (24:1-9)
   g. Balak denounces Balaam (24:10-14)
   h. Balaam's fourth oracle: "A star shall come forth out of Jacob" (24:15-19)
   i. Supplementary matter and conclusion (24:20-25)
10. Israel attaches herself to Baal of Peor (25:1-5)
11. Phinehas kills an Israelite with a Midianite woman (P) (25:6-15)
12. Victory over the Midianites (P) (31:1-54)
13. Reuben, Gad, and the half-tribe of Manasseh settle in the country east of the Jordan, promising to take part in the conquest of the country west of the Jordan (32:1-42)

---

[*]Translator's Note: In Exodus the external peril (17:9-16) precedes the reference to domestic problems (Ex. 18).

Aside from the legal sections of Num. 20-36 and the Balaam pericope (22-24), there remain only about two chapters that furnish the actual account of the conquest of the east-Jordanic territory (the end of Num. 20, 21, 31). In addition there is a chapter telling how two and a half eastern tribes occupied this region. It is surely evident from this that only a few fragmentary details concerning the conquest of this area have been transmitted rather than a continuous account.

The heart of this section must be the two quite similar narratives about the struggle with the Edomites (20:14-21) and Amorites (21:21-31), necessitated by their refusal to permit Israel to pass through their countries peacefully. The account here accordingly emphasizes that the most important battles were *not* campaigns of conquest, when at least the east-Jordanic region was occupied. The Israelites would have preferred to pass through a country peacefully before coming to the territories promised them.

The narrative of the bronze serpent (21:4-9) is the last manifestation of the motif concerning the complaint of the people under the exigencies of the wilderness period. In contrast to the previous stories having this theme, God did not simply put an end to the serpent plague but had a symbol set up, which brought deliverance only to those who looked at it. Here for the first time faith is connected with God's saving action.

The Balaam pericope (Num. 22-24)

The Balaam story is a comprehensive pericope that was transmitted at one time by itself. It is the only rather extensive section in the Old Testament, in which a detailed account of soothsaying appears, a practice that later merged into prophecy. The whole account is permeated by a jubilant and grateful exultation over the blessing that God has granted his people, surrounded as they are by the superior might of other nations.

Blessing, which is really a nonhistorical concept, has been introduced here into the story of God's dealing with his people (even as in Gen. 12:1-3). Balaam, who is not an Israelite seer, is ordered by the Moabite king to weaken Israel with his curses. Instead he has to bless this people, because Yahweh, their God, who alone is the Lord of blessing and cursing, wants him to do so.

The introductory verses describe the reception of the oracle:

> The oracle of Balaam, the son of Beor,
> the oracle of the man whose eye is opened,
> the oracle of him who hears the words of God,
> who sees the vision of the Almighty,
> falling down, but having his eyes uncovered (24:3 f., 15 f.)

The oracles of Balaam also indicate how promise proceeds out of blessing. The seer beholds the yet hidden development of the blessing that has been pronounced upon a community. In the seer's oracle lies one of the sources of the promise concerning salvation. This combination of benediction and promise is found likewise in the benedictions of Jacob and Moses (Gen. 49 and Deut. 33).

V

Deuteronomy

The entire Book of Deuteronomy is couched in the style of an oration that Moses delivered in the plains of Moab at the conclusion of the wilderness wandering prior to the crossing of the Jordan (1:1-5). Most scholars have connected it with the book of the law that was the basis for Josiah's reforms in 621 B.C. (2 Kings 22) and is assumed to have originated in the preceding decade. The Deuteronomic Code (chs. 12-26) forms the heart of the book. At the beginning are two introductory speeches (chs. 1-4 and 5-11); at the end, concluding speeches (chs. 27-30) and the final part of the Pentateuch (chs. 31-34).

As compared with the other legal documents, Deuteronomy is interwoven throughout with hortatory material. There are sometimes comments that come at the beginning and at the end of a section. At other times such comments occur within the laws themselves. The most important characteristic of this hortatory type of discourse is the way in which law is founded upon historical recollection.

The admonition to keep the commandments is based on the proclamation of God's mighty deeds. Even as the past had been determined by the saving acts of God, so the future would be determined by his blessing, or by his curse if the people were disobedient. A central theological concept in Deuteronomy is benediction.

The way the individual sections fit together may be indicated as follows:

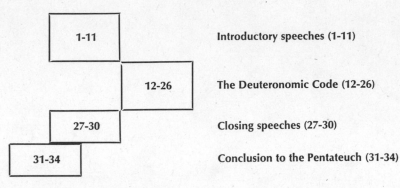

1-11	Introductory speeches (1-11)
12-26	The Deuteronomic Code (12-26)
27-30	Closing speeches (27-30)
31-34	Conclusion to the Pentateuch (31-34)

A. THE INTRODUCTORY SPEECHES (Deut. 1-11)

At the heart is ch. 6, which is a fundamental confession and command (vv. 4-5), linked with the disclosing of the fundamental commandment of the Decalogue (i.e. the first commandment). This central section is preceded and followed by a graphic review of recent as well as more remote history (chs. 7-10), from the exodus out of Egypt to the moment preceding the crossing of the Jordan.

1. **Looking back from Horeb to the conquest of the east-Jordanic region** (1:1—3:29)
   a. From Horeb to Kadesh (corresponding to Num. 10-20) (1:1-46)
   b. Migration through the territories of the east-Jordanic nations (corresponding to Num. 21) (2:1-25)
   c. The conquest and settlement of the east-Jordanic region (corresponding to Num. 21, 32-35) (2:26—3:20)
   d. The designation of Joshua as Moses' successor (3:21-29)

2. **The introduction of the law** (4:1-43)
   a. Admonition to hearken and obey (4:1-14)
   b. Warning against idolatry and astral worship (4:15-24)
   c. Announcement of exile and return (4:25-31)
   d. A eulogy of God, who chose Israel (4:32-40)
   e. Appendix: The cities of refuge (4:41-43)

3. **The Decalogue** (4:44–5:23)
   a. Introductory sentences (4:44—5:5)
   b. The Decalogue (5:6-21)
   c. The mediatorship of Moses (5:22-23)

4. **Confession and command** (6:1-25)
   a. The object of the law (6:1-3)
   b. The *one* God and *complete* obedience (6:4-5)
   c. The instilling of the commandment (6:6-19)
      The gift of the land (vv. 10-11)
   d. The historical credo in answer to the inquiry of the children (6:20-25)

5. **A preview of the conquest of the west-Jordanic region** (7:1—10:22)
   a. Prohibition of paganism (7:1-11)
   b. The reward of fidelity (7:12-15)
   c. "You shall not be afraid of them." The promise concerning land (7:16-26)
      Recollection concerning the deliverance from Egypt (corresponding to Ex. 1-15) (7:18-19)
   d. Admonition and warning (8:1—10:22)
      (1) In view of God's preservation (corresponding to Ex. 16-18) (8:1-20)
      (2) In view of Israel's stubbornness (corresponding to Ex. 32-34) (9:1—10:22)

6. **General admonitions and warnings** (11:1-32)

At the heart of the account is the confession concerning *one* God, who as the *one* God demands *complete* obedience (6:4-5).

> Hear, O Israel: The LORD our God is one LORD:
> and you shall love the LORD your God with all your heart,
> and with all your soul, and with all your might.

This fundamental commandment that was supposed to determine the entire life of the Israelites (6:6-9) is then impressed upon their minds. They were never to forget that everything they had was given to them by God's goodness (6:10-13).

The confession concerning the one God is developed into a historical credo* that sums up God's saving acts in history on behalf of Israel (6:20-25). This primary element in Israel's tradition is to be transmitted by the parents to the children in answer to their questions.

Moses' retrospective (chs. 1-3) and forward-looking (chs. 7-10) speech in the valley over against Baal-Peor then includes the entire sequence of events from the oppression in Egypt to the conquest of the land east of the Jordan. It proceeds from the moment of the new beginning provided by God. Because of this new beginning the speech is both reminiscent and persuasive at the same time. It associates the history before the departure of Israel from Horeb with the preview of what is to take place, linking events which are to follow with a review of the past.

If one bears in mind in this connection the fact that P was not yet available to the community in which Deuteronomy arose but instead only the oldest sources, the summary in general coincides with Exodus-Numbers as follows:

Deut. 1 = Num. 10-20	Deut. 7 = (Ex. 1-15)
Deut. 2 = Num. 21	Deut. 8 = Ex. 16-18
Deut. 3 = Num. 21, 32-35	Deut. 9-11 = Ex. 32-34

According to the thesis of Martin Noth** the introductions to the great Deuteronomic historical work (= Joshua-Kings) and the introduction to the Deuteronomic law have been interwoven with one another in Deut. 1-11. He considers chs. 1-3 as belonging to the former work. Inasmuch as Deut. 7-10, however, is closely associated with chs. 1-3, the introduction to the historical work may even be chs. 1-3 and 7-10. The fourth and fifth chapters stand out from these chapters as later additions, both probably added during the exile. Ch. 4 is a grand, comprehensive exposition of God's historical election of Israel, at the heart of which is a warning against astral worship and idolatry. In many details it calls to mind Deutero-Isaiah. As for ch. 11, it includes an abundance of general admonitions and warnings.

---

*von Rad, G., *op. cit.*, pp. 1-78.

**Noth, Martin, *Überlieferungsgeschichtliche Studien*, Tübingen, 1957, pp. 12 ff.

B. THE DEUTERONOMIC CODE (Deut. 12-26)

There are rather extensive sections at the beginning and end of the Deuteronomic Code, setting forth clearly the specific purpose of this law, as follows:

1. The law of centralization: "the place which the Lord will choose." (12:1-28)

    a. God will choose one place for all sacrificial worship (12:1-12)
    b. The distinction between sacrifice and slaughter, which is based on this choice (12:13-27)

With this demand concerning centralization are associated stipulations concerning tithes (14:23-29), first fruits (15:19-23), and festivals (16:1-17).

2. The temptation to serve other gods (12:29—13:18)

3. The offering of the first fruits, including a confession (26:1-11)

4. The offering of the tithe, including a prayer (26:12-15)

Chs. 14-25 contain an abundance of quite varied commandments and laws. Characteristic of the Deuteronomic Code is the way admonition is combined with historical reminiscence. The most important legal groups are as follows:

1. The laws for the people of God. These have a strikingly humane and social character, transcending in this respect that which is merely judicial.

    a. Poor people and slaves (15:1-18)
    b. Laws of protection (22:1-4, 6-8)
    c. Commandments on behalf of the needy (24:6—25:3)

2. Laws concerning rank:

    a. The judge (16:18-20; 17:8-13)
    b. The king (17:14-20)
    c. The priest (18:1-8)
    d. The prophet (18:14-22)

3. Martial laws (20:1-20; 21:10-14; 23:9-14)

4. Prohibitions concerning food (14:3-21)

5. Prohibitions against unnatural combinations (22:5, 9-11)

6. Sexual prohibitions (22:13-29; 24:1-4; 25:5-12)

7. Prohibitions pertaining to the assembly (23:1-8) and the camp (23:9-14)

The Deuteronomic Code is the last legal corpus to include all aspects of national life. After the Holiness Code (cf. pp. 68 ff.) legal matter is limited to the worshiping community. The Deuteronomic Code is especially important for the way in which it associates every sphere of life with the basic commandment concerning unquestioning obedience toward God. Also significant is its passionate concern for social righteousness.

C. CLOSING SPEECHES (Deut. 27-30)

1. Instructions concerning entrance into the land (27:1-13)
    a. The erection of an altar or two stones, inscribed with the laws (27:1-8 [10])
    b. Blessings and curses from Gerizim and Ebal (27:11-13)

2. A table of curses ("The people shall say: 'Amen.'") (27:14-26)

3. Blessings and curses (28:1-68)

4. The Moabite covenant (An addition made during the exile) (29:1–30:10)

5. The conclusion to the Deuteronomic Code (30:11-20)
    a. The nearness of the commandment (30:11-14)
    b. The decision: "Therefore choose life!" (30:15-20)

The original conclusion of the Deuteronomic Code was perhaps only 30:11-20, an especially important passage for the understanding of law in the Old Testament, because it demonstrates to what extent law could be understood as a genuine offer of God's grace.*
Here law is clearly described as something that can be performed, as something both near and comprehensible to man. Whoever chooses it, chooses life.

---

*von Rad, G., Old Testament Theology, Vol. 1, New York, 1962, p. 195.

Ch. 28 with its blessings and curses is the other section of closing passages that likewise belonged originally to the Deuteronomic Code. This affirmation of the law by means of such blessings and curses was for a long time a feature of legal ratification. Ch. 28, however, has been greatly amplified. In place of the simple formulas of blessing and cursing there appears here a definite announcement concerning prosperity (28:1-14) and calamity (28:15-68), the latter of which is one of the most unnerving documents in the Old Testament. It is shocking to note what threats of disaster have here been accumulated. Behind them rests a profound faith in God's directive holiness.

The Table of Curses in 27:14-26 has been attached rather loosely. It is an old apodictic set from the early period of Israel's existence, matching the Decalogue and other comparable series. It demonstrates that these old sets of laws once had a part in public worship; for the congregation was supposed to say "Amen" to each of them.

The charge given in 27:11-13 includes a third formulation of curses and blessings that Israel was commanded to pronounce upon the land from mounts Ebal and Gerizim. Lying behind them was surely an ancient rite that can now be but dimly perceived. Two injunctions concerning entrance into the land have been added at the beginning (27:1-8).

A later description of the covenant renewal service is the so-called Moab covenant (29:1–30:10), which gets its name from the superscription (29:1). Its elements for the most part consist of slightly altered restatements from the introductory and concluding words of Deuteronomy.

D. CONCLUSION TO THE PENTATEUCH (Deut. 31-34)

1. The appointment of Joshua (31:1-8, 14, 15, 23)

2. The tradition concerning the law (31:9-13, 24-27, 45-47)

3. The Song of Moses (31:16-22, 28-30; 32:1-43)
    a. The introduction to the Song (31:16-22, 28-30)
    b. The Song—a historical psalm (32:1-43)

4. The blessing of Moses (tribal sayings) (33:1-29. Cf. Gen. 49)

5. The death of Moses (32:48-52; 34:1-12)

The Pentateuch concludes with the installation of Joshua as the successor of Moses, together with the account of Moses' death. These two closing accounts, however, have been greatly revised and amplified. The description of Joshua's appointment begins in 31:1-3, and is continued in 31:14-15 in connection with the divine appearance at the Tent of Meeting, then once more in 31:23.

In 31:9-13 a section establishing the legal tradition has been added. It is continued in 31:24-26 and 32:45-47. The instruction to read the law aloud every seven years at the Feast of Booths is significant. Here it is distinctly stated that the proper place for the proclamation of the law is the divine service.

The account of Moses' death is introduced by the command of God that he ascend Mt. Nebo to view from there the Land of Promise, a place he was not permitted himself to enter (32:48-52 from P). The concluding words (34:10-12) emphasize the uniqueness of Moses in his office as mediator. What is more the brief remark, "But no man knows the place of his burial to this day" (34:6) is in accord with the nature of the Moses tradition.

Two poems have been inserted in this closing section. In the first place, there is the Song of Moses, a magnificent historical psalm, incorporating the entire dramatic history of God with his disobedient people. In it is the sentence:

> See now that I, even I, am he,
> and there is no god beside me;
> I kill and I make alive;
> I wound and I heal (32:39).

Ch. 33, the Blessing of Moses, is a comprehensive collection of tribal sayings, closely related to those of Gen. 39. Clothed in the language of a divine epiphany (vv. 2, 26, 27), it ends with a promise of salvation for Israel (vv. 28-29). The benediction concerning Joseph (vv. 13-17) is especially rich and detailed.

Part Two

THE FORMER PROPHETS

VI

Distinctive Character of
the Former Prophets

In its original arrangement this group of historical books was correctly considered to be a unit by itself. The historical books (Joshua to 2 Kings) deal with the period of occupation—from the entrance into the land (Joshua 1 ff.) until the departure from it (the Babylonian exile). At the same time the designation "Former Prophets" is not to be understood as an all-inclusive statement concerning the contents of these books but is rather an indication that Israel's sojourn in the land was to be determined by her obedience or disobedience in relation to the prophetic word.

According to a thesis of Martin Noth,[*] which is shared by many scholars, Joshua to 2 Kings is to be considered as one complete historical work—the so-called Deuteronomic history. All these books fit within a descriptive framework that may be recognized throughout by the same distinctive character. The language of this group of writings originating in the school of Deuteronomy is especially evident in Joshua 1, Judges 2:6 ff., and 1 Kings 8.

The heart of the entire historical work is the account in 1 and 2 Samuel concerning the origin and beginnings of the monarchy. This story from Samuel to Solomon is the only one that is told in detail. At the center is the kingship of David. In Joshua and Judges prior to the account of the establishment of the monarchy is the story about the turmoils and struggles that led up to the period when Israel became established in the land. Following this account are the historical events from the time the kingdom was divided into

---

[*]Noth, Martin, *op. cit.*, pp. 4 ff.

the states of Israel and Judah (1 Kings 12) up to the collapse of first the one kingdom (2 Kings 17) and then the other (2 Kings 22), sketched but briefly, however.

The purpose of the entire account becomes more apparent in the above sketch, viz., that Israel in her long history of disobedience and apostasy wasted the great opportunity entrusted to her in the gift of kingship.

VII

The Book of Joshua

The book of Joshua has a very simple arrangement. Chs. 1-12 tell about the conquest of the west-Jordanic territory. The central section (13-21) has to do with the partition of the land among the tribes. Both conclude with the account of the return of the eastern tribes to their homes (22), the address of Joshua which culminates his work (23), and the assembly of the tribes at Shechem (24).

Ch. 1	The command to break camp	(1)
	The spies	(2)
	The passage over the Jordan	(3-4)
	Preparations	(5)
Chs. 2-12	*The conquest of Jericho*	(6)
	The conquest of Ai (Achan's theft, ch. 7)	(7-8)
	The treaty with the Gibeonites	(9)
	Victory over the kings of the South (Conquest of the South, vv. 28-43)	(10)
	Victory over the kings of the North (Conquest of the entire land, vv. 16-23)	(11)
	List of the conquered kings	(12)
Chs. 13-21	Distribution of the land among the tribes	(13-21)
Ch. 22	Return of the eastern tribes Building of the altar at the Jordan	(22)
Chs. 23-24	Joshua's farewell address	(23)
	The assembly of the tribes at Shechem	(24)

A. DISTRIBUTION OF THE LAND (Joshua 13-21)

The central section contains the account of how the land was divided, starting with the territory east of the Jordan (13). There is then an account of the partition west of the Jordan: from the south (Caleb in ch. 14; Judah in ch. 15), to the central area (Joseph tribes, chs. 16-17) and northward (the northern tribes, chs. 18-19). At the close is an enumeration of the six cities of refuge (20) and the Levitical cities (21).

This simple enumeration of details about the distribution of land, which seems so tedious to us, is actually the heart of the Book of Joshua; for it brings about the fulfillment of the promise, first issued to the patriarchs and then to the Israelites who had suffered bondage in Egypt, as noted in such passages as:

Gen. 12:7 — "To your descendants I will give this land."

28:13— "The land on which you lie I will give to you and your descendants."

Ex. 3:6 — " . . . To a good and broad land, a land flowing with milk and honey."

The fulfillment of this promise is solemnly affirmed at the end of the central section of Joshua, as follows:

Joshua 21:43— "Thus the Lord gave to Israel all the land which he swore to give to their fathers."

21:45— "Not one of all the good promises which the Lord had made to the house of Israel had failed; all came to pass."

It is a basic trait of Israelite manner of thinking that the land distribution even to the minutest detail belongs to the promise. This is especially evident in Deuteronomy. *All* who belong to Israel have as sons of Abraham or sons of Jacob a share in the blessing and hence the gift of land as well. It is for *everyone* that God has given it. Therefore it must be carefully noted that all the tribes, clans, and families were considered in the partition.

B. CHAPTERS AT THE BEGINNING AND END WHICH SERVE AS BRACKETS TO THE BOOK (Joshua 1, 23, 24)

Matching this central section of Joshua are the initial and closing chapters that provide a theological interpretation concerning the fulfillment of the promise about land. The gift of land rests solely upon God's promise, which is developed once more in an exhortation to Joshua: "Only be strong and of good courage!" (1:6, 7, 9, 18). This is supported by the command to break camp.

At the same time Joshua is admonished to observe the commandments that God has given the people. Joshua transmits the command for departure to his subordinate chiefs. They accept God's promise and in turn pledge their allegiance to Joshua. The book ends with an assembly of the people at Shechem and with the establishment of the covenant. At this time Joshua bids farewell to the people and confronts them again with the question as to whether or not they will remain faithful to the God who has delivered them from Egypt and led them to this place. As a witness to the assent promised by the people Joshua erects a stone, ratifying the covenant between God and the nation. In answer to the divine promise, in which God pledges himself to his people (1), is the promise of the people who in response to Joshua's question obligate themselves by a free choice to this God (24). The essential character of the covenant is clearly set forth in this chapter.

Ch. 23 parallels ch. 24. It is Joshua's farewell address to the people, confronting them even more urgently than in ch. 24 with the admonition to remain faithful to God and his law. Here the characteristic language of Deuteronomy is especially evident. Joshua once more solemnly emphasizes that God's promises have come true (23:14 = 21:45).

C. CONQUEST OF THE WEST-JORDANIC REGION*
(Joshua 2-11)

There is but a small part of the book, comparatively speaking, that deals with the actual account of the conquest of the west-Jordanic region, viz., chs. 2-11. The heart of this section is ch. 6, the conquest of Jericho. The first five chapters lead up to the account of the conquest—from the command to depart (1), the spying out of Jericho (2), the crossing of the Jordan (3-4), up to the final preparations for conquest (5).

The second point taken by the Israelites is Ai (7-8). Before its capture, however, there was a setback, because one of the Israelites violated the law pertaining to property devoted to Yahweh (7).

The next city, Gibeon, was subjugated in peaceful fashion, because the Gibeonites by a clever ruse concluded a treaty (9). Up to this stage the conquered or occupied territory was limited to the single tiny tribe of Benjamin. The military camp (as indicated in 10:6) remained at Gilgal near the Jordan. In other words Josh. 2-6 and 7-9 contain only the description of the conquest of the tribal region of Benjamin. What inferences are to be drawn from this cannot be dealt with here.* For this biblical survey it is enough to establish the fact that eight of the ten chapters of Joshua, telling of the conquest, are limited to the territory of Benjamin.

In the two chapters following this section (10-11) there is at the outset an unusually schematic account of the victories over the southern kings (10:1-27) and the northern kings (11:1-9), followed in each case by an enumeration of the conquests in the south (10:28-43) and in the north (11:10-15). To this is attached the story of the conquest of the entire land (11:16-23).

1. The conquest of the territory around Gilgal (2-9)

The conquest of the narrow stretch of land around Gilgal, west of the Jordan, is not recorded in these chapters as one continuous happening with one event succeeding the other. The account is rather composed of individual stories, each of which could have been and actually was told individually before being combined into the whole account. At the conclusion of most of these narratives is the phrase "to this day," alluding each time to the distinctive feature of the site. These stories are as follows:

    a. The twelve stones along the Jordan at Gilgal (4:9, 20 ff.)
    b. The site of Gilgal (5:9)

---

*Cf. Noth, *Das Buch Joshua*, Tübingen, 1938.

Translator's Note: For a discussion in English see *The Interpreter's Dictionary of the Bible*, New York, Vol. 2, pp. 541 ff.

c. The membership of Rahab's kindred in Israel (6:25)
d. A heap of stones in the valley of Achor near Jericho (7:26)
e. The ruins of Ai (8:28)
f. A heap of stones at the gate in Ai (8:29)
g. Canaanite servants at an Israelite sanctuary (9:27)
h. Stones in front of a cave entrance at Makkedah (10:27)

The formula "to this day" is the characteristic designation of a so-called "etiological" legend, connected with the name of a place, i.e., a legend that explains a special local peculiarity. By "legend" is not meant a story that has been *invented* in contrast with one that is *true*, but rather (as the term literally implies) one that originated orally to explain the history of a site and then was transmitted by word of mouth.* It is probable that these traditions have their focal point in a sanctuary at Gilgal. They were combined much later into a complete account and then became significant to Israel as a whole.

The *story of the spies* (2) intends to demonstrate how the divine promise (1) preceded the army of Israel and prepared the way for them. The *passage through the Jordan* (3-4) is depicted as a solemn procession. Behind the formation of this story there must have been at one time a celebration in Israel, at which time the ark of covenant was carried in procession. The evidence is quite clear that several sources lie behind this account. In Joshua 4:21-22 is a fine example of a simple traditional event. The monument erected by the ancestors became a means of furthering the praise of God, whenever children would inquire about its meaning and the parents would tell why these twelve stones were once erected.

The first step toward conquering the land was prepared in cultic fashion by *circumcision* (5:1-9) and a *passover meal* at Gilgal (vv. 10-12). The gift of manna now ceased. Once the people entered the land they began to receive nourishment from its fruits.

In 5:13-15 is the *story of an angel* who appeared before Joshua with a sword. This is a fragment that once concluded with a promise concerning the occupation of Jericho (6:2?).

*Translator's Note: "Legend" is etymologically related to the Greek word *legein*, meaning "to speak." The author here uses the German term *Sage* (Cf. Eng. "saga") which is related to *sagen*, i.e., "say." Compare also "tale" and "tell."

The *conquest of Jericho* (6) is portrayed as a divine miracle, in which the Israelites had only to march around the city in religious procession. (It is analogous to chs. 3-4.) The walls collapsed and the city was thereby captured. One ought not view this as a historical account, nor is this its purpose. The story is supposed to bear witness to the truth that the essential feature in the conquest of Canaan was the action of God.

The story of *Achan's theft* (7) exhibits a characteristic feature of the "holy war." The entire army was damaged by the misdeed of one man, and the damaging effect set aside only by atonement. The guilty party was ascertained by drawing lots. As an atonement he had to acknowledge his guilt and thereby glorify God (7:19).

The *clever ruse of the Gibeonites* (9) provides an example of what happened at a good many places, viz., the subjugation of Canaanite groups by peaceful assimilation.

2. The conquest of the south (10)

Ch. 10 tells about a defensive struggle against a coalition of Canaanite kings who had formed an alliance against the invading Israelites (vv. 1-4). They besieged Gibeon, which had turned to Joshua for help (vv. 5-6). Joshua approached by night and routed the five kings (vv. 7-15), capturing them and putting them to death (vv. 16-27). Thus this battle also was fought within Benjamite territory. A summary of conquests in the South follows in 10:28-43.

3. The conquest of the north (11)

Ch. 11 clearly parallels ch. 10, presenting in similar fashion a summary concerning the northern conquest. At the outset there is again a coalition of Canaanite kings (this time northern kings) who unite against Israel and attack her by the waters of Merom in Galilee (vv. 1-15). The Israelites defeat them decisively (vv. 6-9), and with this victory the northern conquest, of which there is only a résumé, concludes. In this connection, only the cities around Hazor, a site that has just recently been excavated, are mentioned.[*]

---

[*]Translator's Note: For an account of the results of this excavation see: *The Biblical Archaeologist,* New Haven, Feb. 1956, Vol. XIX, pp. 1-11; May 1957, XX, 34-37; May 1958, Vol. XXI, pp. 30-47; Feb. 1959, XXII, pp. 2-20.

4. The conquest of the entire country (11:16—12:24)

A description of how the entire country was conquered follows in 11:16-23, and the first section of Joshua concludes in ch. 12 with a list of the vanquished kings.

D. THE FINAL SECTION (Joshua 22)

The final section, in addition to Joshua's two speeches (23, 24), includes only information concerning the return home of the east-Jordanic tribes, which had participated in the conquest of the west-Jordanic region (22). On this occasion there arose a dispute over the erection of an altar along the Jordan (v. 10). This was considered a breach of faith by the other Israelites as well as a movement toward religious exclusivism on the part of the eastern tribes (vv. 11-20). The latter, however, explained their action as evidence of their continuing bond of fellowship (vv. 21-29). The tension was thereby allayed (vv. 30-34).

VIII

The Book of Judges

The Book of Judges has a different tripartite division from that
of Joshua. In Joshua the three sections form an organic unity. In
Judges, however, the first and third sections, viz. chs. 1:1—2:5 and
17-21, must be treated separately. The actual Book of Judges has
2:6—3:6 as its introduction and 3:7—16:31 (the story of the judges)
as the main body, forming in this way an unbroken unity. Chs. 17-18
and 19-21 are two independent supplements, linked with Judges
merely because they tell of events relating to the same epoch. 1:1—
2:5 was added to the beginning of Judges at a later time. It is the
summary of a different description concerning the way the Israelites
gained possession of the land.

In the stories of the judges (chs. 3-16) two series are to be differentiated, the so-called major and minor judges. In the account of
Jephthah two sets of narratives have been joined together, one
dealing with tribal heroes who became saviors in a time of grave
peril, the other telling about men who held the office of judge consecutively over all Israel. The latter series, found in 10:1—12:15, has
been interrupted, however, by the account concerning Jephthah, a
major judge (10:6—12:7).

Martin Noth[*] explains the interruption, as follows: Jephthah
belonged to both sets of judges, combining them both in his person.
It is even possible that the term "judge" was transferred from the
list of actual judges in chs. 10-12 to the tribal heroes.

---

[*]Noth, M., *Überlieferungsgeschichtliche Studien*, pp. 47 ff.

The plan of Judges is as follows:

1:1—2:5	The piecemeal conquest of Canaan	(1:1—2:5)
2:6—3:6	Introduction: The period of the Judges (Deut. account)	(2:6—3:6)
3:7—9:57	Othniel, Ehud, Shamgar	(3:7-31)
	Deborah and Barak	(4:1—5:31)
	Gideon of Manasseh	(6:1—8:35)
	Abimelech	(9:1-57)
10:1-5	Tola, Jair	(10:1-5)
10:6—12:7	Jephthah	(10:6—12:7)
12:8-15	Ibzan, Elan, Abdon	(12:8-15)
13—16	Samson of Dan	(13:1—16:31)
17-18	The migration of the tribe of Dan	(17:1—18:31)
19-21	The punishment of Benjamin	(19:1—21:26)

A. THE PIECEMEAL CONQUEST OF CANAAN (1:1—2:5)

1. Southern and central Canaan (partial conquest) (1:18, 22-26)

2. Unconquered regions (1:19-21, 27-36)

3. The angel at Bochim (2:1-5)

The first chapter of Judges should actually be regarded as a complete biblical book. In subject matter it is parallel to the Book of Joshua; for it deals with the conquest of Canaan as a whole. But it is obviously an extremely condensed summary. Moreover, it is fragmentary and disconnected as well.

The editorial transitional phrase "after the death of Joshua" has transformed what was a parallel account into a sequel. A description complete in itself has thus become an introduction to the Book of Judges.

The significance of this prefatory addition is easy to perceive. One who has just finished reading the Book of Joshua would have difficulty comprehending the severe struggles of the individual tribes during the period of the judges. Against the background of Judges 1, however, they become more intelligible. There the sentence, "the tribe . . . did not drive out," recurs almost as a refrain. One cannot overlook the fact that the description of how Canaan was conquered is different in Judges 1 from that of Joshua. The latter account was written from a late point of view in which the details concerning the result of the conquest have been simplified. Joshua represents Israel as having conquered the entire land in one continuous campaign with all the tribes participating. All was quickly accomplished from the time of the crossing of the Jordan and on. In Judges 1, on the other hand, the tribes advance individually against different places and are able to gain a footing only in a few places.

Judges 2:1-5 is a real old story that has been later retouched. It tells of an angelic appearance. Originally it was probably intended to explain the name Bochim (= weepers).

B. INTRODUCTION: THE PERIOD OF THE JUDGES
(Judges 2:6—3:6)

The sentence in 2:6, "When Joshua dismissed the people . . . " is clearly a sequel to the concluding words of the Book of Joshua in ch. 24 (cf. v. 28) that tell of the people's assembling at Shechem. Ch. 2 corresponds to the chapters that serve as brackets around Joshua. Here also is a theological summary, interpreting the epoch when the judges lived. The story unfolds in a four-part cycle:

1. **Apostasy** (" . . . and served the Baals . . . and went after other gods," 2:11 f.)

2. **Oppression by the enemy** (2:13-15)

3. **Cry for help to God** (Cf. 3:9)

4. **Liberation through the raising up of a "judge"** (2:16)

The effect of the liberation continued indeed only as long as the generation experiencing it was alive. Nevertheless Israel had a forty-year period of rest, before the apostasy would set in anew.

C. THE STORY OF THE JUDGES (Judges 3:7–16:31)

The stories themselves do not always conform to the pattern provided for them in ch. 2. It is clearly evident that each of the judges served only within one tribe or a small group of tribes. Their office as judge was also not a continuous one which they held for life, but it went into effect during a period of special oppression.

1. Othniel, Ehud, and Shamgar (3:7-31)

There are not many concrete details in the account concerning Othniel, nor can the period of his activity be determined with historical precision. A concept, however, that is of the greatest theological importance, as far as the story of the judges is concerned, becomes apparent already at this point. This is the statement, "The Spirit of the Lord came upon him" (3:10). The concept "Spirit of God" appears frequently in the story of the judges.

In addition to this reference, there are two other important associations linked with this concept—those connected with the early prophets, Elijah and Elisha, and with a group of later prophecies of salvation.

In 3:12-30 Ehud rescues Benjamin by an assault on the Moabite king, Eglon. Only a brief note has been preserved pertaining to Shamgar (3:31).

2. Deborah and Barak (4:1–5:31)

Here is a prose account (4) and a song of triumph (5), both dealing with the same event. They are in essential agreement. The *Song of Deborah* is the only detailed song of victory preserved in the Old Testament. It is one of the most ancient compositions of the Old Testament, a song of exceptional beauty and freshness, derived indeed from its having been composed under the first flush of victory. The plan of the song is as follows:

    a. Introduction (5:3)
    b. The divine epiphany (God comes to aid his people) (5:4-5)
    c. The description of need (5:6-8)

    d. The summons and response of Deborah and Barak (5:9-12)
    e. The tribes are praised as well as rebuked (5:13-18)
    f. A description, suggestive of victory (5:19-22)
    g. A curse and a blessing (5:23-27)
       (1) A curse upon Meroz (5:23)
       (2) A blessing upon Jael, who killed Sisera (5:24-27)
    h. The futile wait of Sisera's mother (5:28-30)
    i. Conclusion: "So perish all thine enemies, O Lord! But thy friends be like the sun as he rises in his might." (5:31)

3. Gideon (6:1—9:57)

It is the Gideon stories that best demonstrate the distinctive feature of "charismatic leadership." The Midianite oppression (6:1-6) provides the point of departure. A divine messenger then comes to the son of a farmer and calls this individual, who at first offers resistance (6:11-24), to be a liberator. In the presence of the enemy encampment the Spirit of God takes possession of Gideon, who by his summons to battle rallies the men of his own and neighboring tribes (6:33-35). He asks God for a sign that he will deliver the enemy into his hands (6:36-40). Then follows the battle for liberation (7), waged with only 300 men, according to God's direction (7:1-8).

There are other activities mentioned concerning Gideon (8:4-21). He declined the office of king that had been extended to him (8:22-23). He had an ephod, however, fashioned out of the gold that had been taken as booty and with it the Israelites carried on idolatry (8:24-27).

Ch. 9 depicts vividly and clearly how Abimelech, the son of Gideon, attempted to make himself king but failed. This chapter is the earliest Old Testament example of historical composition in the narrower sense. Two political views come into conflict with one another at this point: the Canaanite type of city king, upon which Abimelech's attempt was based, and the old Israelite tribal concept, arrayed against it, which refused to acknowledge a sovereign alongside the tribal regulations and prerogatives. *Jotham's fable* (9:7-15) about the trees that wanted to anoint a king over themselves expresses this tension vividly.

4. Jephthah (10:6–12:7)

The charismatic leaders were called to be deliverers in quite different ways. Jephthah was the head of a band of adventurers (like David later on after his flight from Saul). The elders of Gilead procured him as leader in the battle against the Ammonites (11:1-11). He dealt first with the Ammonites by negotiation but without success (11:12-28). Then the Spirit of the Lord came upon him (11:29), and the battle for liberation began. At this juncture Jephthah made the vow that his only daughter assumed for him (11:30-40). This is a narrative that is comprehensible only against the setting of that period. It has to do with the unqualified validity of a vow.

5. Samson (13:1–16.31)

   a. The birth of Samson (13:1-24)
   b. He is moved by the Spirit (13:25)
   c. The marriage of Samson. His deeds of might and his riddle (14:1-26)
   d. His revenge on the Philistines (15:1-8)
   e. Samson slays 1,000 with the jawbone of an ass (15:9-17)
   f. In dire thirst he complains and experiences a miracle (15:18-19)
   g. Samson toys with the city gates (16:1-3)
   h. Delilah worms Samson's secret out of him (16:4-21)
   i. Samson in death avenges himself on the Philistines (16:22-31)

The Samson stories in their unrestrained bravado and openly profane motifs are also an integral part of God's history with his people. The life of Samson (as with few men in the Bible) is described from birth to death. He was a Nazirite (i.e., a man who had been consecrated*). He performed many feats of strength that did not indeed lead to victory over the Philistines but were a sign during the period of Philistine domination that divine miracles could still occur among oppressed peoples. In his death Samson gained a prominence far exceeding that which he had during his lifetime.

6. The "Minor Judges" (10:1-5; 12:8-15)

All that has been preserved concerning these judges is a list that gives some uniform notations pertaining to them. The list has to

---

*Translator's Note: The term "Nazirite" is based on the Hebrew term *nazir*, which means "one who is consecrated or devoted."

do with the office of an Israelite judge of an earlier period. The office was probably of use especially in the legal tradition and was of life duration. From the arrangement in Judges it is evident that at least one of the charismatic leaders was also at the same time a judge over Israel. This was Jephthah. He was perhaps not the only one. What the functions of this office may have been can only be surmised. It probably devolved later upon the king.

D. FIRST SUPPLEMENT: THE DANITES STEAL MICAH'S IDOL (Judges 17-18)

This is a very early narrative, coming from an environment in which the prohibition against idolatry was not yet in effect. An Ephraimite farmer erected his own domestic chapel with a graven image and installed an itinerant Levite as a priest for it. The Danites, who had been displaced by the Philistines, sought a new dwelling place and along the way stole the sanctuary together with the priest. The sanctuary was given a new location at the point captured by the Danites.

E. SECOND SUPPLEMENT: THE OUTRAGE OF THE BENJAMITES AND ITS EXPIATION (Judges 19-21)

The crime by the men at Gibeah was a serious violation of the law of hospitality and was accompanied by sexual excess (19). A situation now occurred in which the tribal league had to take responsibility in making amends for the outrage (20:1-10). Because the Benjamites refused to surrender the culprits, it became necessary to carry on a campaign against the whole tribe (vv. 11-48). After being disastrously defeated the remaining members of the tribe were able to continue their existence only by stealing wives (21).

Throughout both supplementary accounts there runs, as a refrain, the statement: "In those days there was no king in Israel; every man did what was right in his own eyes" (21:25).

IX

The Four Books Concerning Kings

The four books concerning kings (1 Sam.–2 Kings) embrace the history of kingship. This is the epoch in which Israel was an independent state (or actually two states after Solomon)—from the origin of the monarchy until the Babylonian exile.

The main events of this historical segment, however, have been distributed in quite unequal fashion throughout the four books pertaining to the kings. Thus 1 Samuel gives the account of Samuel (1-25), Saul (9-31), and the initial experiences of David (16-31); 2 Samuel deals only with David; 1 Kings 1-11, with Solomon; 1 Kings 12–2 Kings 17, with a history of both Israel and Judah; 2 Kings 18-25, with Judah alone. Half the books accordingly have to do with but two rulers; the other half, with all the rest (42 altogether).

The chart below indicates graphically how the material is distributed in the various books:

1 Sam. 1		Samuel			25
	9		Saul		31
		16		David	31
2 Sam. 1		David			24
1 Kings 1	Solomon	11			
1 Kings 12		History of both kingdoms			2 Kings 17
2 Kings 18		History of Judah		25	

PROPHECY AND KINGSHIP

For an informative presentation of the biblical facts of these four books it is necessary to limit oneself to the primary themes and areas of thought. The precise compilation of factual data is the concern of a history of Israel.

Two lines run alongside one another throughout these four books and to some extent become involved with one another—one that is historic in relation to monarchy and one that is prophetic. The books belong indeed to the "Former Prophets," and in point of time the history of kingship and the history of prophecy do coincide to a great extent.

PROPHETIC TRADITIONS

The material belonging to the prophetic line is much more complex. It includes the following topics:

1. The story of Samuel's childhood (1 Sam. 1-3).
2. Prophetic traditions relating to Samuel (1 Sam. 7; 8; 10:17-27; 12; 13:8-15; 15).
3. Nathan and Gad (2 Sam. 7; 12; 24).
4. Ahijah, the man of God in Bethel (1 Kings 13:1—14:18).
5. Elijah, Elisha (1 Kings 17-22; 2 Kings 1-9; 13:14-21).
6. Individual prophetic words (2 Kings 19-21).

The two focal points are to be found in the origin of kingship (about eight chapters in 1 Sam.) and in the climax to the history of the Northern Kingdom (about fifteen chapters between 1 Kings 17 and 2 Kings 9). The two topics together would be comparable to one large biblical book. The prophetic traditions accordingly constitute a really important part of the books dealing with the kings.

HISTORIC—KINGLY TRADITIONS
KINDS OF HISTORICAL MATERIAL

There is in addition a second important distinction to be noted— between the more extensive literary compositions and the chronological summary of brief reports and memoranda. The former furnish a coherent account of a historical period; the latter have simply been fitted into a chronological pattern.

1. The extensive literary compositions. These are to be found only in 1 and 2 Samuel and are, as follows:

a. The story of the ark (1 Sam. 4-6; 2 Sam. 6)

b. The history of the rise of Saul (1 Sam. 9-14)

c. The history of the rise of David (1 Sam. 16—2 Sam. 5)

d. The history of the succession to the throne of David (2 Sam. 9-20; 1 Kings 1-2)

2. The chronological summary. This begins after Solomon. In it the following literary strands may be perceived:*

a. A *synchronistic chronicle* that included the dates of the kings of Judah and Israel from Solomon to Hezekiah, along with a brief account of some important events relating to the royal house. It accordingly must have been an official chronicle kept at court. It was synchronistic in that it was based on a principle that related the length of reign of each of the kings of Israel and Judah, the one to the other.

b. Sections from a more extensive *annalistic work,* mentioned frequently in the Books of Kings, augment this chronicle. It has not been preserved, however, in its entirety. The description of Solomon's building activity for example is a part of it.

c. An *evaluation of the individual kings* based on the principles of Deuteronomy has been introduced by the Deuteronomic editors along with the corresponding prophetic traditions in order to demonstrate how God's will had been continually thwarted by the kings, although it had been proclaimed to them again and again. It intends to remind the remnant of Israel after the collapse of the kingdoms that God had to deal with them in this way because of the disobedience of the kings and the people. There would be a future for the remnant only if they obeyed God's will.

---

*This is the suggestion of A. Jepsen, in his *Die Quellen des Königsbuches,* 1953.

LITERARY STRUCTURE

The structure of the four books concerning the kings may be represented as follows:

The prophetic line	The political and historic line
1 Sam. 1-3	
	1 Sam. 4-6 (+ 2 Sam. 6)
1 Sam. 7, 8, 10, 12	
	1 Sam. 9-11, 13-14
1 Sam. 15	
	1 Sam. 16—2 Sam. 5
2 Sam. 7	
	2 Sam. 8
	2 Sam. 9-20; 1 Kings 1-2
	1 Kings 3-11
	1 Kings 12
1 Kings 13:1—14:18	
	1 Kings 14:19—16:34
1 Kings 17-19	
1 Kings 20-22	1 Kings 20, 22
2 Kings 1-9	
	2 Kings 8:16—17:6
2 Kings 17:7-41	
2 Kings 19-21	2 Kings 18-25

CLIMACTIC POINTS IN HISTORY

If one were to look for a central principle around which to orient oneself in biblical study, amid the length and diversity of the books about the kings, he could not do so, because so much material has been included in these four books. It is, however, perhaps possible to find such a center for the individual parts. These are the three climactic points toward which the action in each section moves:

1. The promise of Nathan to David and his descendants

From the very outset 1 Samuel points toward 2 Sam. 7, the *promise of Nathan to David*. The setting for the story of Samuel's youth (1-3) is Shiloh, the place where the ark was located. The story of the ark that begins in 1 Sam. 4-6, is not concluded until 2 Sam. 6. It leads directly over to the *promise of Nathan* (7) and encloses in a kind of parentheses the two groups of stories concerning the rise of Saul (9-14) and David (1 Sam. 16–2 Sam. 5). The arrangement here already reveals that Nathan's promise was the ultimate objective of the composition, as is fully attested by the contents. The entire account concerning the origin of kingship culminates in the divine pledge to the Davidic royal family that it shall continue to endure as God's gift on behalf of his people.

2. The dedicatory prayer of Solomon

Shortly thereafter the history of the succession to the throne of David begins (2 Sam. 9-20; 1 Kings 1-2). The goal toward which it tends is the comment at the end of 1 Kings 2: "So the kingdom was established in Solomon's hand." In the story of Solomon that now ensues (1 Kings 3-11) there is stress on the erection of the temple as the most important feature of his reign (chs. 5-8), and the climax is *Solomon's prayer at the dedication of the temple* (ch. 8). In his prayer there is a comprehensive exposition concerning the significance of the temple and its worship for the entire nation and its history. The temple together with the Davidic throne (2 Sam. 7) is the most important factor in this story. Here the royal history accordingly has its second climax and interlude.

3. The words concerning the fall of Israel

The history of the two kingdoms that began shortly thereafter in 1 Kings 12 has a significant focal point in the accompanying prophetic stories. The terminus, however, is clearly the account of the collapse first of the Northern Kingdom and then of the Southern Kingdom. In the account concerning the destruction of the Northern Kingdom the narrator again introduces a kind of interlude as a marginal comment to this history, explaining why it had to turn out that way. What he says at this point was equally valid for Judah's downfall. Such an observation, however, is not made in that account. In these comments that interpret the significance of the destruction (2 Kings 17:7-23) one can see the climax toward which the third part of the royal history is moving.

With the aid of these three directional points: (1) Nathan's promise, (2) the dedicatory prayer of Solomon, (3) and the words concerning the fall of Northern Israel, one can easily gain a simple over-all view of the entire royal history, which is so far-reaching and so complicated. These passages should offer a meaningful explanation concerning the sequence and decline of these historical epochs. In these three stages of the account, fundamental aspects concerning the entire concept of the royal history also become evident.

*　　*　　*　　*　　*

THE HISTORY OF KINGSHIP

A. SAMUEL, SAUL, AND DAVID (1 Sam. 1–2 Sam. 5)

1. **Samuel in Shiloh** (1:1—3:21)
   a. Hannah's vow (1:1-18)
   b. The birth of Samuel and his dedication to the sanctuary at Shiloh (1:19-28)
   c. The song of Hannah (2:1-10)
   d. Samuel in the service of Eli; the sons of Eli (2:11-26)
   e. A man of God notifies Eli of disaster (2:27-36)
   f. God's call to Samuel; the word of judgment against Eli (3:1-18)
   g. Samuel established as a prophet (3:19-21)

(1)

Of the few existing birth narratives in the Bible, one each may be found at the beginning of the patriarchal, national, and royal histories, viz., the births of Isaac, Moses, and Samuel respectively. In each case the story concerns either a marvelous birth or the safeguarding of a child. Samuel's birth belongs to the group of stories in which a woman is granted a child after a long period of childlessness. This theme runs throughout the Bible from the Abraham stories to Luke 1.*

(2)

History, prophecy, and psalmody are closely associated in a remarkable way in this prelude to the books pertaining to the kings. It is on the whole an account which initiates the royal history by introducing Samuel, the anointer of the first two kings. Samuel stood at the end of an epoch to the extent that he had to proclaim the end of the house of Eli, who was priest of the tabernacle in Shiloh. He thus performed the function of the later prophets of doom. In 3:1-18 there is an allusion to a prophetic call. Thus there is tacit indication concerning the manner in which also prophecy began, when kingship originated.

This introduction includes at the same time the principal elements of the Psalms: the *lament* of Hannah, her *vow*, and her *psalm of praise*. The priest Eli assured the weeping woman of a favorable hearing: "Go in peace!" he said, "And the God of Israel grant your petition which you have made to him" (1 Sam. 1:17). This is the clearest example in the Old Testament of a priestly assurance of answer to prayer *(Heilzusage)*.** Hannah's hymn now follows her prayer just as in Ex. 15 the hymn of the people who were rescued follows their cry for help and their deliverance from trouble. In this case, however, it is an individual's distress and hymn of praise. The song of Hannah could well stand in the Psalter. It is a descriptive psalm of praise, extolling God's wonderful transforming activity. "The Lord kills and brings to life; he brings down to Sheol and raises up"(2:6).

(3)

The basis for the declaration of judgment against Eli is the abuse of sacrifice by his sons. Here one is reminded also of a theme that is to have dominant significance in the period to follow, viz., the corruption of public worship. This was one of the primary indictments of the later prophets.

---

*Cf. Claus Westermann, *Gottes Engel brauchen keine Flügel*. Berlin, 1957, pp. 95 ff.

**Translator's Note: Cf. Westermann, C., "The Way of the Promise Through the Old Testament," in B. W. Anderson, *The Old Testament and Christian Faith*. New York, 1963, pp. 200 ff.

2. The history of the ark (1 Sam. 4-6. Cf. 2 Sam. 6)

 a. The Philistine victory over Israel at Aphek. The loss of the ark (4:1-11)

 b. The tidings of disaster and Eli's death. The birth of Ichabod (4:12-22)

 c. The ark among the Philistines, in the temple of Dagon, and moving from city to city (5:1-12)

 d. Back to Bethshemesh and Kiriath-jearim (6:1-21)

(1)

Before there was a king the external circumstances of Israel were determined by the predominance of the Philistines. At the beginning (4:1-11) as well as at the end (ch. 31) of 1 Sam. there is an account of a great defeat. This peril provided the main reason why a supreme central authority was needed. This explains the desire for a king. The peril became especially evident in the way the very presence of the ark was unable to forestall an overwhelming defeat (4:3-11).

(2)

The ark, captured by the Philistines, however, now demonstrated its power in spite of the defeat, and it caused serious damage among the Philistines. Here for the first time was a reminder of the theme that God accomplishes his wonders even though his people may suffer crushing defeat.

(3)

The ark was sent back by the Philistines voluntarily. Its uncanny power, however, was able to create life and bring about death. In 2 Sam. 6:7 it killed the man who touched it, even though he only wanted to keep it from falling. In this story of the ark are to be encountered traces of the ancient belief concerning the power of mana. According to this superstition, which was in existence long before the time of the Israelites, an object contains power to destroy as well as produce life. It is to be found in many religions at very early levels and is not a specific Israelite or biblical phenomenon.

These stories about the ark, however, include a factor that is significant and fundamental also for the Old Testament faith in God, viz., God's actions remain incomprehensible. It is never possible for men completely to comprehend why God brings blessing in one instance and death in another.

3. The origin of kingship (1 Sam. 7-12)

PASSAGES THAT WELCOME IT

PASSAGES THAT WARN AGAINST IT

a. *Samuel's activity as judge.*
   The victory of the Philistines at Ebenezer (7:1-15)

b. *Israel demands a king* (8:1-22)

a. *Saul is anointed king*
   (9:1—10:16)
   (1) Saul's parental home
       The she-asses (9:1-10)
   (2) The meeting with Samuel
       The sacrificial meal (9:11-25)
   (3) Samuel anoints Saul
       (9:26—10:1)
   (4) The signs. Saul among the prophets (10:2-13)
   (5) The anointing remains a secret (10:14-16)

c. *Israel gets a king* (10:17-27)
   (1) "You have today rejected your God" (10:17-19)
   (2) The casting of lots (10:20-24a)
   (3) Exultation and rejection)
       (10:24b-27)

b. *Saul's victory and elevation to the throne* (11:1-15)
   (1) The messengers from Jabesh-Gilead (11:1-4)
   (2) The Spirit of God and the conscription (11:5-10)
   (3) Victory over the Ammonites (11:11)
   (4) Saul is elevated to kingship at Gilgal (11:12-15)

d. *Samuel's farewell* (12:1-25)
   (1) Samuel gives an account of himself (12:1-5)
   (2) The desire for a king brings to an end the period of the judges (12:6-13)
   (3) Signs to demonstrate their wrongdoing (12:14-18)
   (4) Encouragement and warning (12:19-25)

(1)

It is evident, as noted in the two columns above, that chs. 8-12 have given two different accounts of how kingship in Israel began. According to one, it was joyously and gratefully welcomed as a gift of God to his people, helping them recover from a desperate affliction. According to the other, the divine approval of kingship was indeed acknowledged but the desire for a king on the part of the people is depicted as a "great wickedness," a repudiation of God. This second account is clearly a later one, written from the standpoint of Deuteronomy. Some of its sources are indeed early, but it pronounces its judgment from the standpoint of the final period after the bitter experiences of history. Its judgment concerning the guilt of the rulers corresponds to that of Deuteronomy.

What at first appears as a gross contradiction, however, preserves upon closer examination a truth that is historically significant, viz., that Israel's kingship throughout its entire history stood under both judgments, set side by side so strangely in the two accounts depicting its origin.

(2)

1 Sam. 11 is probably closest to the historical course of events. In this passage Saul is portrayed exactly like one of the charismatic leaders (cf. Judges). He is raised to kingship on the basis of his having proved himself (probably in view of the Philistine menace). 1 Sam. 11:1-11 along with Judges 6-7 is the clearest description of a charismatic leader who, faced by a deadly threat to an Israelite community, was seized by the power (i.e., the spirit) of God, issued a general summons, and averted the menace. The threat in this case was the siege of the city of Jabesh by the Ammonites.

Inasmuch as Saul now is proclaimed king, the period of the judges comes to an end (11:11-15).* In his address Samuel, from a negative point of view, confirms explicitly the conclusion of the period of the judges.

(3)

The fine account in 9:1—10:16 includes a wealth of significant features, drawn from the early period of Israel's existence. Samuel is represented as both a priest and a seer. The ancient mode of the

---

*A group hostile to the throne emerges at this point too (11:12-13).

sacrificial meal appears as a meal of communion. Prophetic bands, similar to the prophetic groups around Elisha, appear here for the first time.

(4)

The "right of the king," proclaimed by Samuel in 8:10-18, resembles closely the fable of Jotham (Judges 9), where the economic side of the new monarchal order is also depicted from a negative point of view. This is a significant criticism from a cultural and historical standpoint, going back perhaps to a very early period.

(5)

The same is true of the account Samuel gives of himself in 12:1-5. It is a public and orderly relinquishing of his office as judge and corresponds to the deep social sensitivity of the laws in the Book of the Covenant and Deuteronomy.

4. The kingship of Saul (1 Sam. 13-31)
- a. The Philistine battles (13:1—14:52)
  - (1) Conscription and dispersal (13:1-7)
  - (2) The first rejection announced by Samuel (the premature sacrifice) (13:8-15a)
  - (3) The army's encampment near Michmash (13:15b-22) ("There was no smith to be found throughout all the land of Israel," vv. 19-22)
  - (4) Jonathan's deed of heroism (14:1-15)
  - (5) Victory in the hill country of Ephraim (14:16-23, 31)
  - (6) The command concerning abstinence from food (14:24-30)
  - (7) The spoil and the sacrifice (14:32-35)
  - (8) The pursuit. Jonathan breaks the command concerning abstinence (14:36-46)
  - (9) A concluding account: Saul's military exploits. The family of Saul (14:47-52)
- b. The second rejection of Saul by Samuel (15:1-35)
- c. An evil spirit torments Saul. David's playing on the lyre (16:14-23)
- d. David becomes Saul's rival. He wins his daughter (18:1-30)
- e. Saul pursues David (19:1—27:12)
- f. Saul and the witch at Endor (28:1-25)
- g. The defeat and death of Saul on Mt. Gilboa (31:1-13)

(1)

The account concerning the rise of Saul continues only as far as
1 Sam. 14. It includes simply an extensive and extremely vivid
description of his first decisive victory over the Philistines (chs.
13-14), a victory in which Jonathan actively participated. At the
strategic moment he made a surprise attack on the camp of the
vastly superior Philistine forces and thus turned the tide of battle.
The comment in 13:19-22 indicates what significance this victory had.

The Philistines maintained their superiority over Israel by corner-
ing the iron market.* It was therefore necessary to wage battle
against a technically superior foe.

(2)

The story of Saul in 14:47-52 concludes with a brief summary
that assesses his reign in a quite positive manner: "He did valiantly
. . . and delivered Israel out of the hands of those who plundered
them" (v. 48). That which is mentioned later concerning Saul in
ch. 16 and following is part of the story of David's rise to power and
assumes as a matter of course the negative point of view regarding Saul.

According to the brief summary in 14:47-52, there existed at one
time a much more positive tradition concerning Saul, only fragments
of which still remain. Even the deeds for which he was rejected by
Samuel (13:8-15; 15:1-35) were performed for the purpose of serving
Yahweh and his people. What has been transmitted about Saul,
however, still indicates that his reign was beset by stark tragedy.
The conflict with David was likewise tragic. Even the story of the
rise of David exhibits this. The end of Saul's life (chs. 28 and 31)
belongs to the most shocking moments in the history of Israel.

5. The accession of David (1 Sam. 16-31; 2 Sam. 1-5)

  a. *Part 1: David at Saul's court* (16:1—20:42)
    (1) Samuel anoints David to be king (16:1-13)
    (2) David comes as a youth to the court of Saul (16:14-23)
    (3) David and Goliath (17:1-58)
    (4) David's covenant with Jonathan. Saul's rival (18:1-16)

---

*This was the beginning of the Iron Age in the Near East.

(5) David wins Michal, the daughter of Saul (18:17-30)
(6) Jonathan reconciles Saul and David (19:1-7)
(7) The flight of David and his sojourn with Samuel (19:8-24)
(8) David's final flight. Jonathan's friendship (20:1-42)

b. *Part 2: David as an outlaw* (21:1—31:13)
   (1) David with Ahimelech in Nob. The sword of Goliath (21:1-10)
   (2) With Achish, king of Gath (21:11-16)
   (3) He gathers a volunteer band in the cave of Adullam and continues on his way (22:1-5)
   (4) The revenge of Saul on the priests of Nob. Abiathar escapes to David (22:6-23)
   (5) David rescues Keilah from the Philistines (23:1-6)
   (6) Flight into the Wilderness of Ziph. Inquiring of God (23:7-14)
   (7) The visit of Jonathan (23:15-18)
   (8) The Ziphites want to surrender David. He continues to flee (23:19-28)
   (9) David spares Saul at Engedi (24:1-22)
   (10) Samuel dies. Nabal and Abigail (25:1-44)
   (11) David spares Saul in the Wilderness of Ziph (26:1-25)
   (12) David dwells with Achish of Gath. Plundering raids (27:1-12)
   (13) David is dismissed from the Philistine army (29:1-11)
   (14) David avenges the raid on Ziklag (30:1-31)
   (15) The end of Saul's life (28, 31)
       (a) Saul visits the witch of Endor (28:1-25)
       (b) Battle on Mt. Gilboa. The death of Saul and his sons (31:1-13)

c. *Part 3: David becomes king in Hebron* (2 Sam. 1-5)
   (1) A report concerning the death of Saul and his sons (1:1-16) •
   (2) David's elegy over Saul and Jonathan (1:17-27)
   (3) David is proclaimed king of Judah in Hebron (2:1-7)
   (4) Battles between David and Eshbaal° (2:8-32)
   (5) Abner deserts to David and is killed by Joab (3:6-39)
   (6) Eshbaal is assassinated. David puts the assassins to death (4:1-12)
   (7) David becomes king over the Israelite tribes (5:1-5)

°Translator's Note: The author uses here the original name of Ish-bosheth as found in 1 Chr. 8:33; 9:39. Names compounded with Baal were common in the early monarchal period. Because of the prophetic attack on Baal worship (cf. Hos. 2:16), later generations hesitated to pronounce the name Baal and substituted *bosheth* "shame" instead. Ish-bosheth thus means "man of shame." Eshbaal = "man of Baal" or "Baal exists."

(8) David captures Jerusalem and makes it his residence
     (5:6-12)
(9) The sons of David (5:13-16)
(10) Victories over the Philistines (5:17-25)

In this description of David's ascent to the throne one is able to
perceive the climax of the history that is recounted in the Old Testament. One must add at once, however, that it is a climax whose
height can be seen only from the depths that followed upon it.
Only in this ascent of David (and only here) was Israel what it
had longed to be, from the time of the patriarchs and on, and what
for centuries after David it expected from a future, in which there
would be a transformation.

In this rise there was no interruption. In radiant strength the
young king met one threat after the other and prevailed heroically
over them. With discerning shrewdness he knew how to get the
upper hand in the most difficult predicaments and how to gain the
friendship even of his opponents. In addition to his strength and
shrewdness, however, there was something more—for David had
luck to a remarkable degree. Again and again, at the opportune
time, the most fortunate things would take place on his behalf. In
his strength, in his sagacity, and in his good luck, he was blessed.
And it is easy to see that this king was God's splendid gift to his
people. In him Israel was granted a moment filled with growing
prestige, good fortune, and success. Never again did such a brilliant
era come.

The account in this section from 1 Sam. 16 to 2 Sam. 5 is so concise, so direct and clear, that it does not require any special biblical
aids for interpretation. The captions given above are sufficient. It is
up to the reader of this biblical guide whether or not he is ready to
read this account on the basis of the suggestions and lines of thought
here provided. It should offer no further difficulties whatsoever.

If the reader would like to do something in addition, he might
write out the entire narrative from beginning to end in a notebook
of his own. Only then will it become so familiar to him that he will
know David the king, who became for Israel the epitome of kingship and the symbol of the future king who was expected to bring
salvation.

For an understanding of the later history it need only be pointed out that the kingship to which David ascended in this account was a complex entity, a many-sided sovereignty. In 2:1-7 the southern tribes, of which Judah was the most significant, chose David as their king. He was thus essentially and primarily *king of the southern group of tribes,* later the southern kingdom of Judah. In 2 Sam. 5:1-5, after the death of Saul and Eshbaal, the northern tribes entrusted him with the kingship of North Israel. This took place, however, on the basis of a covenant (5:3) that could be dissolved again under certain circumstances. David was thus *king over Israel* on the basis of a personal agreement. There was in addition a third kind of sovereignty of a different sort that David exercised by virtue of his conquest of Jerusalem (5:6-12), a city that hitherto had been of Jebusite, i.e., Canaanite origin. It became his personal property, "the city of David," and he became *king of Jerusalem.* Since Jerusalem lies on the border between the Northern and Southern tribes, it was ideally suited as a residence; and its later dominant significance is understandable from this standpoint.

B. THE SUCCESSION TO DAVID'S THRONE
(2 Sam. 6—1 Kings 2)

There is a comprehensive account also in this section of the books concerning the kings. It has a terminus that is clearly evident in the concluding statement: "So the kingdom was established in the hand of Solomon" (1 Kings 2:46b). The author tells how this happened in his history concerning the succession to David's throne. Someone at court must have been an eyewitness of the events, indeed participated in them himself. Otherwise one can hardly explain his knowledge of so many precise details. This man has produced a genuine historical account of outstanding worth.*

The account begins with the final part of the ark narrative (1 Sam. 4-6; 2 Sam. 6). After the ark was retrieved by David, its

---

*Two important monographs dealing with this literary source should be noted: L. Rost, *Die Überlieferung von der Thronnachfolge* (Beiträge zur Wissenschaft vom Alten und Neuen Testament, III, 6. Stuttgart, 1926). G. von Rad, "The Beginnings of Historical Writing in Ancient Israel" in *The Problem of the Pentateuch and Other Essays,* Edinburgh and London, 1966, pp. 166-204.

transfer was celebrated by a solemn procession in which the king danced about in front of it. Here the narrator has inserted a little episode that actually belongs to the ark narrative. Michal, the daughter of Saul and the wife of David, had ridiculed his dancing. Then is included the comment: "Michal the daughter of Saul had no child to the day of her death" (2 Sam. 6:23). She was destined to be the mother of the heir apparent. Who would now become the heir to the throne? "This is a beginning which leaves us with gloomy forboding." * But over against this account stands in clear light the promise of Nathan on behalf of David's family and king- dom (2 Sam. 7). With it the subject matter now to be developed is given, even up to the answer to the above question at the end of 1 Kings 2.

1. Why Michal remained childless (2 Sam. 6**)
2. The promise of Nathan (7:1-29)
3. A summary account: the wars of David and his officials (8:1-18)
4. David receives Meribbaal*** (9:1-13)
5. An account concerning the Ammonite campaign (10:1-19; 12:26-31)
6. David's adultery and Nathan's reproof (11:1—12:25)
7. The outrage of Amnon. The revenge and flight of Absalom (13:1-39)
8. Joab appeases David on behalf of Absalom (14:1-33)
9. The rebellion of Absalom and the flight of David (15:1-37)
10. Friends and enemies (Ziba and Shimei) (16:1-14)
11. The two counselors (16:15—17:14)
12. David flees from his son (17:15-29)
13. The defeat and death of Absalom (18:1-33)
14. David's grief and unhappy return (19:1-43)
15. The revolt of Sheba (20:1-26)
16. How Solomon became king (1 Kings 1:1—2:46)

---

*Ibid., p. 177.

**Cf. footnote p. 25.

***Translator's Note: Meribbaal = "hero of Baal" or "beloved of Baal" was the original name of Mephibosheth = "from the mouth of shame." (Cf. 1 Chr. 8:34; 9:40.) See footnote above, p. 115.

At the heart of this section is the account of David's transgression against his captain Uriah and Uriah's wife during the Ammonite campaign (2 Sam. 10-12). This account reaches its climax again in the words of Nathan to David, "You are the man!" with which he indicts David. Preceding it is the above-mentioned transitional passage from the ark narrative (6) and the promise of Nathan (7).

There follows at this point a summary of David's wars and men. It has no fundamental connection with the history concerning the succession to the throne. In addition, there is a story which picks up themes from David's accession. One man from Saul's family still remained, a crippled son of Jonathan. David received him at court in compliance with his one-time promise (9).

Following the central event of this account (chs. 10-12) is an involved group of chapters (13-19) dealing with Absalom's revolt. In the subsequent period of David's reign the narrator has only one further rebellion to describe (20). Then while David was still alive, violent and ruthless struggles for the throne set in (2 Kings 1-2). In this latter period of his life there is no longer any of the brilliance of his accession to be discerned.

Solomon, the son of Bathsheba, emerged from these struggles as victor. But what a victory! Solomon held the sovereignty firm in his hand. The question raised at the beginning of the account, "Who will sit on David's throne?" receives an answer, but the answer does not indicate what the story about the succession to David's throne really has to say. It is not put into words at all but is expressed in the shocking way everything turns out, indicating with rare artistry what is most important by what is left unmentioned.

David was at the pinnacle of his dominion, when he received from Nathan, in God's name, the assurance that his house would endure (2 Sam. 7). The king, however, could not stand the security that was given him with this promise and destroyed the home of one of the men in his service. That he did not silence the divine voice, speaking through the prophet Nathan, who arrested him in his transgression, but instead humbled himself before this voice, says more plainly than anything else mentioned about David that this king was really being confronted by God.

He now has to adjust himself to whatever takes place in his own house, in his own family. One son after the other wrecks his life because of guilt. Amnon falls passionately in love with his half-sister Tamar. Absalom, her full brother, avenges himself on Amnon. The shocking drama that now takes place begins thus with betrayal, hatred, and feeble affection (chs. 13-19). Absalom ultimately is dead and David broken in spirit. The final struggle for the throne exacts the death of another of the brothers, Adonijah (1 Kings 2:13-25) and still more blood.

At the end of this drama the real message for the reader continues to be the contrast between the high promise, given to David (2 Sam. 7) and the actual guilt and agony this highly exalted king experienced in his life. It points from the stage of this drama to the Lord of history in his hidden majesty. If the story of David's accession has provided the messianic hope with its bright and radiant hues, then the story of the succession to his throne has added to that expectation the longing for a complete transformation.

Supplementary material (2 Sam. 8, 21-24)

The history of the succession to David's throne should not be regarded as a complete account of his reign. The summary reports in chs. 8, 21, 22 reveal many more facts about this period, above all his wars, in which he established an empire that extended from Damascus in the north to the vicinity of Egypt in the south, from the Mediterranean sea to the Arabian desert. Only brief notices and concise reviews concerning the majority of these wars have been preserved for us.

There are actually more events of political importance in 8:1-15 than in the entire history of the succession to the throne. Chs. 8, 21, and 23 indicate that there was once a rich tradition concerning David's military exploits. The shadow of Saul appears suddenly in a gruesome story about the Gibeonite revenge on Saul's descendants (21:1-14).

Ch. 24 tells of another prophetic encounter that is difficult for us to understand. It was occasioned by a census which David had been forbidden to take and for which he himself had to choose a punishment. The pestilence was checked by the building of an altar on the threshing floor of Arauna, where the temple was later to be erected.

C. THE KINGSHIP OF SOLOMON (1 Kings 3-11)

There was once a "Book of the Acts of Solomon" (1 Kings 11:41) that presented a coherent account of his reign. Only a very limited extract from it, however, has been preserved in the Bible. We know but little about Solomon.

1. **Solomon, the builder of the temple** (1 Kings 3:1-15; 5; 6:1—9:9)
    a. Introduction (3:1-15)
        (1) Solomon marries a daughter of Pharaoh (3:1)
        (2) Sacrificial worship persisted at the high places up to this time (3:2-3)
        (3) The divine manifestation at Gibeon. The king's request (3:4-15)
    b. Preparation for the building of the temple. Treaty with Hiram (5:1-18)
    c. The building of the temple (6:1-38)
    d. The palace buildings (7:1-12)
    e. The temple equipment (7:13-51)
    f. The dedication of the temple (8:1-66)
        (1) The ark is brought into the temple (8:1-9)
        (2) The glory of the Lord fills the temple. Solomon's temple address. ("He would dwell in thick darkness") (8:10-13)
        (3) Solomon blesses the congregation and gives reasons for the building of the temple (8:14-21)
        (4) Solomon's prayer and benediction (8:22-53)
        (5) Summary (8:54-61)
        (6) The festival sacrifice of dedication (8:62-66)
    g. The second divine appearance—a promise and a threat (9:1-9)

2. **Solomon the eminent king** (1 Kings 3:16—4:34; 9:10—10:29)
    a. Solomon's reign, official staff, and court. The size of the kingdom (4:1-28)
    b. The wisdom of Solomon (Proverbs) (4:29-34)
    c. The Solomonic judgment (3:16-28)
    d. Solomon's administration, trade, and commerce (9:10-28)

  e. The queen of Sheba (10:1-13)
  f. Solomon's wealth (10:14-29)

3. God allows adversaries to arise against Solomon (1 Kings 11)

  a. The foreign wives of Solomon and their worship (11:1-13)
  b. Hadad of Edom and Rezin of Damascus (11:14-25)
  c. Jeroboam (11:26-40)
  d. The length of Solomon's reign and his death (11:41-43)

Chs. 6-8, dealing with the building of the temple, constitute the core and dominant part of the section pertaining to Solomon (1 Kings 3-11). How important it was to the author can surely be seen in the way he deals but briefly and succinctly with all the other palace buildings (7:1-12). This, however, had nothing to do with their proportionate size, for the temple was but a small part of the palace complex, something like a court chapel. It is due to the significance it came to have in later times that the temple receives such a strong emphasis.

The temple building, together with its planning, erection, furnishing, and dedication, is really the only important continuous section in chs. 3-11. The way in which God revealed himself to Solomon at the beginning and at the end of the account gives to it a further special emphasis. On the night of a sacrificial feast, God, in a dream, granted Solomon a wish (3:4-15). The king did not request wealth and power but an "understanding mind." With this the emphasis on Solomon's wisdom begins. In response to his prayer (8) Solomon received an answer that was combined with a warning and a promise (9:1-9). God promised to cause his name to dwell in this house.

A series of individual reports, all dealing with Solomon's greatness and wisdom, have been lumped together before and after the account concerning the temple building:

1. In ch. 4 is an enumeration of his officials. Ch. 5:1-8 has to do with the extent of his kingdom and his royal household; 9:10-28, with his building program and the forced labor of the Canaanites who still remained. This passage deals also with trade and navigation, administration, and commerce; 10:14-29 pertains to his wealth.

2. Solomon's wisdom is extolled as in the case of no other king. He asked God for an obedient and understanding heart (3:4-15). In a difficult case he made a wise decision (3:16-28). "God gave Solomon wisdom and understanding beyond measure" (4:29). He was wiser than the renowned sages of the East (4:30-31). At his court wisdom literature was fostered. He composed proverbs about plants and animals (4:32-33). Thus people came from a great distance to become acquainted with his wisdom (4:34). In 10:1-13 there is a detailed account of such a visit from the queen of Sheba.

The section concerning Solomon nevertheless ends with a premonition of coming disaster. God permitted enemies to arise against him (11): foes from within (Jeroboam) and foes from without (Hadad of Edom and Rezin of Damascus). The reason given was the presence of heathen sanctuaries, built for Solomon's wives on the high places around Jerusalem. But this is probably intended only as a symptom of the way in which the kingdom had been transformed under Solomon.

With all manner of power and splendor it was now overrun with foreigners and had come to resemble in a dangerous way the governments of the surrounding kingdoms. Peace was indeed maintained as long as Solomon lived (5:4 f.), but dark clouds were already appearing.

D. THE HISTORY OF THE DIVIDED KINGDOM*

(1 Kings 12—2 Kings 17)

This section begins with the withdrawal of the northern tribes from the Southern Kingdom and the establishment of a separate kingdom in northern Israel (1 Kings 12). It ends with the destruction of North Israel and the message with which the historian concludes this epoch (2 Kings 17).

One can emphasize here only the most significant matters, that is, according to the two lines, presented by the Book of Kings, viz., those pertaining to the kings and the prophets (see above, pp. 104, 106).

1. The Kings

Jeroboam, one of Solomon's taskmasters (1 Kings 11:26-40), issued a summons, calling for separation from Judah, because Rehoboam, in following the advice of the young men of his court, did not agree to the justifiable demands of the northern tribes. Instead Rehoboam proposed to intensify the burden upon them (12:14). Jeroboam became ruler of the Northern Kingdom, established his residence at Shechem, and had calves of gold set up in Bethel and Dan. These were probably not intended as idols but rather as beasts of burden, carrying the *invisible* Yahweh. Jeroboam thus wanted to adhere to Yahweh, the God of Israel. A later age, however, looked upon this as the idol-worship that Israel had been forbidden to practice. To the one who wrote the history it was already an established fact that this way would ultimately lead to destruction, as he declares at the conclusion in 2 Kings 17:7-23.

The list of kings that ruled in Israel and Judah now follows. They are synchronized with one another in a way that the accession to the throne of the one king is dated according to the year of the other king's reign. This dating actually causes considerable difficulties. (The periods of rule on either side, when totaled up, do not agree.) The royal succession in the North as well as in the South, however, has on the whole been preserved. The respective kings at the same time have been evaluated merely on the basis of their attitude toward public worship. Only a few Judean kings receive a positive evaluation.

The most significant difference between the kingship in Israel and Judah consisted in the rapid interchange of the royal families in the Northern Kingdom. As a result, Israel did not establish a continuous dynastic organization. In Judah, however, the Davidic dynasty remained intact up to the end of the state despite various revolutionary disturbances.

In the North after Jeroboam there was an important king by the name of Omri, who established Samaria as the capital (1 Kings 16:15-28). He was succeeded by his son Ahab, who is portrayed quite negatively, inasmuch as our information concerning him is drawn almost entirely from the Elijah stories. It would follow, however, from the historical sequence that Ahab was an important king. He was not an idol-worshiper but one who wanted to be a worshiper of Yahweh. Jezebel, a Tyrian princess, was his queen. The great adversary of Israel at this time was Aram (i.e., Syria), with whom there were serious conflicts again and again (1 Kings 20, 22).

The next significant event was the coup d'état of Jehu (2 Kings 9-10), a bloody revolution in the name of Yahweh, in which the entire family of Ahab was annihilated. Another period of prosperity finally intervened for Israel under Jeroboam II (2 Kings 14:23 ff.). He was able to restore the old boundaries. This prosperity nevertheless was only superficial, for it was followed by a rapid decline. Assyrian attacks led to weakening and ultimately to the destruction of the Northern Kingdom under the final king, Hoshea (2 Kings 17).

Exceedingly little information has been provided in regard to the Southern Kingdom of Judah and its kings during this period. At first the Judean kings sought to regain their old power by warring against Israel. These attempts failed. King Jehoshaphat of Judah then appeared as an ally of Ahab, king of Israel (1 Kings 22); next Jehoram of Israel, as an ally of Ahaziah of Judah. The latter two were assassinated in the revolution of Jehu (2 Kings 9).

Thereupon the mother of Ahaziah usurped the throne and eliminated the royal family. Only one son of Ahaziah, Jehoash, was rescued. When he was seven years old he was elevated to the throne by Jehoiada the priest (2 Kings 11). There is information concerning his reforms and program of temple restoration (2 Kings 12). He had to pay tribute to the Arameans. When the Assyrians* threatened Palestine, a campaign was waged by Syria and Israel against Judah in order to force her to participate in an anti-Assyrian alliance (2 Kings 16, 17). This was the Aramean-Israelite war in 735-34 B.C. At that time Isaiah came before Ahaz, the Judean king (Isa. 7), and informed him that Jerusalem would be spared.

2. The Prophets

a. *The man of God at Bethel, Ahijah, and Jehu* (1 Kings 13:1–14:18)

Already in 12:21-24 there is the account of a man of God who forbade Rehoboam to fight with Israel. Ch. 13 tells in detail about a man of God from Judah who was given a message to proclaim against the altar in Bethel in regard to its impending fate; 14:1-18 tells about a message of doom that Ahijah of Shiloh pronounced against Jeroboam; 16:1-4 has to do with the prophet Jehu's message of judgment against the Israelite king Baasha.

b. *Elijah and Elisha* (1 Kings 17—2 Kings 9)

This great complex of prophetic narratives would hardly fit within the framework of the Book of Kings were it not for the fact that all the stories about these prophets are intimately connected with the political and royal history of these times. As one reads and makes a careful biblical analysis of this group of prophetic stories, it should be clear from the outset that one cannot place Elijah and Elisha on a par with the later literary prophets.

It is impossible for us to visualize what these prophets were like from a historical standpoint. Much that is reported about them will always remain strange and obscure. The two narrative groups, 1 Kings 17-19 (together with ch. 21) and 2 Kings 1-9, correspond to one another in the sense that the first group ends with the commission to anoint Jehu and Hazael (1 Kings 19:9-18) and the second, with the fulfillment of this commission (2 Kings 8:7-15; 9:1-15). The call of Elisha constitutes the connecting link between the two (1 Kings 19:19-21; 2 Kings 2).

(1) **The Elijah stories** (1 Kings 17-19, 21)

    a. Elijah pronounces judgment on Ahab and flees (17:1-6)
    b. The widow of Zarephath (17:7-24)
       ("the jar of meal and the cruse of oil"—v. 14)
    c. Elijah encounters Ahab (18:1-20)
    d. The divine judgment on Carmel (18:21-40)
    e. The rain comes (18:41-46)
    f. The flight from Jezebel (19:1-8)
    g. The divine appearance at Horeb (19:9-14)
    h. The new commission—the anointing of Hazael and Jehu (19:15-18)
       ("the seven thousand"—v. 18)
    i. The call of Elisha (19:19-21)
    j. Naboth's vineyard (21:1-29)

Ch. 17 begins by referring to a drought. At the end of ch. 18 is the statement: "And there was a great rain" (18:45). Vegetative life, on the whole, plays a much greater role in the Elijah-Elisha stories than in the later literary prophets.

The activity of Elijah, in helping the widow of Zarephath, saving her from death by starvation (17:7-16), restoring her son to life (17:17-24), demonstrates how a man of God affected the simple ordinary life of common people. It also calls to mind the narratives about Jesus, as do so many of the Elisha stories even more distinctly.

The other group of narratives exhibits Elijah involved in important political affairs. They tell of the divine judgment on Carmel in which a decision on behalf of the entire country was at stake (18:20-40), of the flight from Jezebel (19:1-8), and of the commission that required an action that was directly political (19:9-18).

Elijah resembles the later prophets most closely in the narrative of Naboth's vineyard (21). Amos would have been able to utter the word of judgment that he here pronounces against Ahab (21:19) in exactly the same way.

Before the second set of Elijah-Elisha stories there is introduced an account of the Aramean campaign (1 Kings 20, 22), in which other prophets appear. They utter words of good omen in 20:13-14, 28. Ch. 22 in particular gives an impressive demonstration of how a single prophet of judgment (Micaiah, ben Imlah), charged with announcing disaster, was arrayed against prophets of good omen who came forth in large numbers. The revelation he received reminds one of Isaiah 6 (1 Kings 22:19).

(2) **The Elijah-Elisha stories** (2 Kings 1-9)

    a. Elijah's message of judgment against Ahaziah (1:1-17)

    b. Elijah's ascent to heaven (2:1-12)

    c. The spirit of Elijah rests on Elisha (2:13-18)

    d. The miraculous deeds of Elisha (2:19-25)

    e. Elisha's message of good omen and his signs in the Moabite campaign of Jehoram (3:1-27)

    f. The miracles of Elisha near Gilgal (4:1-44)

    g. The healing of Naaman, the army commander (5:1-27)

h. The miracles of Elisha. Assistance in the Aramean war
    (6:1-33)
i. Elisha announces the liberation of Samaria (7:1-20)
j. The widow receives assistance (8:1-6)
k. The anointing of Hazael (8:7-15)
l. A disciple of Elisha anoints Jehu (9:1-15)

Elijah's last recorded message was one of judgment (2 Kings
1:1-17), which he had to announce to Ahaziah, because this king
had inquired of a foreign deity. In the case of Elisha, however, the
language of judgment disappears almost entirely. He was a man of
God that performed astonishing signs and wonders. In the narratives they are often bizarre and heightened into phantasy. One gets
a view here of Israel's early religion, which in many respects reminds one of the Middle Ages of the Western world. These miracle
tales have derived their characteristic features from popular tradition, the criteria and motifs of which must be kept in mind.

The narrative about Naaman, the Syrian commander-in-chief,
whom Elisha delivered from his malady, is an especially fine story.
His request for a burden of earth, in order to have something in his
own country that would unite him with the God who had healed
him, is an eloquent symbol of the beliefs pertaining to the deity
in that age.

Elisha often appears in the company of a prophetic group in
these stories. On one occasion a prophetic school is even described
distinctly (6:1). Elisha thus belongs to the line of prophecy that
is also found banded together at shrines and at court. They were
the cult prophets and the prophets of good news.

E. THE HISTORY OF JUDAH UP TO THE FALL
(2 Kings 18-25)

In the final section of the Books of Kings it is still possible to
give an account of two rulers who receive the historian's complete
approval. They were Hezekiah (chs. 18-20) and Josiah (chs. 22-23).
Between them ruled two wicked kings, Manasseh and Amon (ch.
21). After the death of Josiah the rapid downfall under Jehoiakim,
Jehoiachin, and Zedekiah (chs. 24-25) set in, leading up to the first
and second conquest of Jerusalem.

1. The eulogy of Hezekiah, the godly king, who purifies the worship and removes the high places. The victory over the Philistines (18:1-8)
2. Shalmanezer conquers Samaria (18:9-12)
3. Sennacherib threatens Jerusalem. Isaiah (18:13—19:37)
4. Hezekiah's sickness (20:1-11)
5. The embassy from Babylon (20:12-19)
6. Manasseh and Amon (21:1-26)
7. Josiah (22:1—23:37)
   a. The discovery of the "Book of the Law" (22:3-11)
   b. Its endorsement by the prophetess Huldah (22:12-20)
   c. The reform of public worship (23:1-27)
   d. Josiah is slain at Megiddo (23:28-30)
8. Jehoahaz (23:31-35)
9. Jehoiakim (23:36—24:7)
10. Jehoiachin. The siege and first captivity (24:8-17)
11. The siege and conquest of Jerusalem (24:18—25:21)
12. Gedaliah (25:22-26)
13. Jehoiachin is pardoned (25:27-30)

Two more times the Judean state, now the sole representative of Israel, reached a high point—under kings Hezekiah and Josiah. Hezekiah purged his land of the high places, gained another victory over the Philistines, and experienced a wonderful deliverance at the time Jerusalem was besieged by Sennacherib. Josiah carried out a reformation of the worship on the basis of "The Book of the Law"* found in the temple. He regained vast areas beyond the border of tiny Judah and ushered in what appeared to be a new and prosperous era.

But then came the collapse. Josiah opposed Pharaoh Neco, who wanted to lend support to Assyria against her new foes, the Babylonians and the Medes. Josiah was vanquished and fell on the battlefield. His son Jehoahaz was carried captive to Egypt by the Pharaoh and died there.

Under the last three kings of Judah, Jehoiakim, Jehoiachin, and Zedekiah (the period of Jeremiah's activity) there was a rapid series of changes, leading up to the complete collapse.** Jerusalem

---

*This book was the nucleus of Deuteronomy.
**This account is found also in Jer. 37-43.

was conquered and destroyed. Some of the people were carried away into exile.

Judah's history as an independent state was now at an end like that of Israel. A weak glimmer of hope may be evident in the final words of 2 Kings. They tell of how Jehoiachin was released from prison and accepted with great honor at the Babylonian court.

Those who survived were now faced with the question: "Is God's history with his people at an end? Is there still mercy for us in God's presence?" It is at this point that the message of Deutero-Isaiah begins.

Part Three

THE PROPHETS

X

History, Types and Forms of Prophecy

The history of prophecy extends from the beginning of the monarchy to the period beyond the exile. 1 Samuel—2 Kings give us information concerning the early history of prophecy preceding the literary prophets. The principal lines of development may be set forth approximately as follows:

	PROPHECY OF JUDGMENT	PROPHECY OF SALVATION (Cult prophecy)
EARLY HISTORY	Prophets in 1 and 2 Sam. 1 and 2 Kings	Prophets in 1 and 2 Sam. 1 and 2 Kings
PERIOD I (c. 750-700 B.C.)	Amos Hosea Micah Isaiah	
PERIOD II (c. 650-587 B.C.)	Zephaniah Jeremiah Ezekiel	Nahum Habakkuk
PERIOD III (The Exile)	→	Ezekiel Deutero-Isaiah
PERIOD IV (c. 520-470 B.C.)	Malachi	Haggai Zechariah
Dogmatic Disputation	←	→ Apocalyptic (Daniel)

In the above diagram two main types of prophecy are differentiated: the prophecy concerning welfare and the prophecy concern-

133

ing disaster. In addition, there is a distinction as to the address, governing all prophecy. The message of the prophet may be directed to Israel or to the nations. Whereas national oracles were words of judgment spoken almost exclusively against foreign nations, they contained good news for Israel.

Along with this fundamental distinction relating to the prophetic address, there is another which concerns its literary form. The books of prophecy contain not only (1) prophetic discourses but also (2) information (e.g., parts of Isaiah, Jeremiah, and the entire Book of Jonah), and (3) utterances directed to God, as in the Psalms (e.g., the laments of Jeremiah and the doxologies of Amos).

When reading the prophetic books it should be observed that the twelve Minor Prophets once formed a single book, somewhat equivalent in size to Isaiah. Like the Minor Prophets, Isaiah is also a body of diverse material, formed out of smaller books and collections. One should bear in mind this gradual growth out of smaller units in the case of each of the larger books of prophecy.

XI

Isaiah 1-39

Only chs. 1-39 belong to the prophet Isaiah of the eighth century B.C. Chs. 40-55 (Deutero-Isaiah), which is now generally recognized as prophecy coming from the exilic period, and chs. 56-66, usually termed Trito-Isaiah, must be dealt with separately.

First a survey of the main content of Is. 1-39:

A MESSAGE TO ISRAEL	MESSAGE TO THE NATIONS AND GOOD NEWS TO ISRAEL	INFORMATION	
Chs. 1-11 (12)*	Chs. 13-23	(Chs. 6-8)**	Chs. 24-27 (An apocalypse)
Chs. 28-32	Chs. 33, 34-35	Chs. 36-39	

A. THE MESSAGE OF ISAIAH (Isa. 1-12)

This is a collection of the utterances of Isaiah that once existed separately. At the heart is an account of Isaiah's call, exhibiting in a unique manner what a prophet is. It is clearly evident at this point that three things occur when God encounters an individual:

1. God appears as the Holy One (6:1-4)
2. Man discovers himself confronted by God, as a sinner in need of transformation (6:5-7).

°Translator's Note: Ch. 12 has been enclosed in parentheses according to the author because it is a psalm, concluding the collection.

°°Translator's Note: Chs. 6-8 contain prophetic messages in addition to information and have therefore been enclosed by parentheses according to the author.

    3. The man who has been transformed is sent forth by God as his messenger (6:8-11).

The story of Isaiah's call is followed by an account of his meeting with king Ahaz during the Aramean-Israelite war (7-8) and the consequences of this encounter. In connection with it is the statement: "If you will not believe, surely you will not be established" (7:9),* and a sign: "A young woman shall conceive and bear a son, and shall call his name Immanuel" (7:14).

Because of the king's unbelief the prophet became one who must wait. He had to "seal the teaching among (his) disciples" (8:16-18).

The conclusion to this section (chs. 6-8) is the good news in 9:1-7: "The people who walked in darkness have seen a great light. . . . For to us a child is born. . . . "

The story of the call (6) is preceded by a group of Isaiah's utterances in chs. 1-5 that are quite dissimilar in type. In the presence of a heavenly and earthly forum God draws up his indictment against his people who do not know their Lord:

> The ox knows its owner,
> and the ass its master's crib;
> but Israel does not know,
> my people does not understand (1:2-3).

Especially characteristic of Isaiah's prophecy is 1:10-17, a denunciatory cry against the insensitive, false sacrificial worship that was carried on, while gross injustice was being committed. "Your hands are full of blood!" he declares in v. 15.

A more extended message of judgment typical of Isaiah, which has a distinctly poetic power, is the "Song of the Vineyard" in 5:1-7. The prophetic declaration of judgment is set forth in a parable. God announces the destruction of a vineyard upon which he had expended so much labor in vain. "He looked to find right reason there, and all was treason; to find plain dealing, and he heard only

---

*Translator's Note: There is a play on words in this expression in the Hebrew: *'im lô' ta'amînû kî lô' tē'amā'nû*, which Moffatt reproduces in his rendering: "If your faith does not hold, you will not hold out."

the plaint of the oppressed" (v. 7).* Following the song is a series
of laments that deal primarily with social indictments.

The group of chapters (Is. 1-5) includes also redemptive promises,
viz., 2:2-5, which speaks of God's mountain at the end of days
(cf. Mic. 4:1-4) and 4:2-6, which refers to the wonderful presence
of God on Mt. Zion in the end time. Whether these promises are from
Isaiah or were added later to his utterances is a disputed question.
Ch. 9:7-20 (together with 5:25-29) contains a series of declarations
concerning judgment including the refrain: "For all this his anger
is not turned away and his hand is stretched out still" (vv. 12, 17,
21). Ch. 10 pronounces a woe upon Assyria, but the conclusion
(11:1-9) is once more a promise of welfare, telling of the shoot from
the stump of Jesse and his peaceful reign.

Ch. 12 concludes the entire section (chs. 1-11). It includes the
words of a psalm rather than those of prophecy. This twelfth chapter
presents the antiphonal response of the congregation in which
Isaiah's utterances were read and preserved. The book portion
(1-12) thus resembles the entire book (1-39) in its arrangement:

Words of Judgment Concerning Israel	Words of Judgment Concerning the Nations	Good News Concerning Israel	Information	Divine Praise
Chs. 1, 3, 5		Chs. 2, 4	Chs. 6-8	
Chs. 9, 10	Ch. 10	Chs. 9, 11		Ch. 12

B. ORACLES OF JUDGMENT AGAINST THE NATIONS**
(Isa. 13-23)

This collection of national oracles is to be interpreted as a group
of Isaiah's utterances, addressed to the surrounding nations. To them
were added additional oracles by unknown prophets, which are to

---

*Translator's Note: The above rendering is the version of Ronald Knox, who
in his free paraphrase has been able to reproduce the play on words in the original Hebrew as does the German rendering used by the author: "*Er hoffte auf
Guttat und sieh da, Bluttat! auf Rechtsspruch und sieh da Rechtsbruch.*" The
RSV renders the Hebrew literally: "He looked for justice (Heb. *mishpaṭ*) but
behold bloodshed (*mishpaḥ*), for righteousness (*tsᵉdāqāh*) but behold a cry
(*tsᵉʻāqāh*)."

be interpreted in the light of historical situations that were very much later.

The words of Isaiah in this collection are directed against Damascus (Aram) and Israel (17:1-7, a passage relating to the period of the Aramean-Israelite war), Assyria (14:24-27; 17:12-14; 18:1-7), Philistia (14:28-32), Egypt and Ethiopia (20:1-6), but also Judah and Jerusalem (22:1-14) and one of her officials (22:15-25).

All of these oracles against the foreign nations deal indirectly with Judah. Either Isaiah wanted his people to fear these powers or else he wanted to warn them against depending upon them. In ch. 20 Isaiah is commanded to walk naked and barefoot as a sign against Egypt and Ethiopia, who were the backbone of an anti-Assyrian coalition. His remarks to an Ethiopian legation (18) have the same meaning. They contain an illustration about God's watchful care, characteristic of the message of Isaiah: "I will quietly look from my dwelling like clear heat in sunshine, like a cloud of dew in the heat of harvest" (v. 4). It is matched perfectly by the passage that directs one away from feverish military preparations to the One who guides history: "But you did not look to him who did it, or have regard for him who planned it long ago" (22:11).

Later national oracles added to the words of Isaiah

1. Prophecies against Babylon (13, 14, 21)

a. The fall of Babylon (13:1-22)

b. A hymn of triumph over the downfall of the king of Babylon (14:1-23)

c. The watchman waits for the fall of Babylon (21:1-16)

These are all sayings of an unknown prophet from the time of the Babylonian exile, proclaiming the fall of Babylon. The hymn of scorn over the death of the king of Babylon is a magnificent poetical work that reproduces in a remarkable way the experience of the people at that time. "The whole earth is at rest and quiet; they break forth into singing" (14:7). "How you are fallen from heaven, O Day Star, son of Dawn!" (v. 12). This poem expresses in a deeply moving manner the way in which human power terminates in death.

There is in addition a series of utterances concerning judgment against other nations:

2. Moab (15:1—16:14)

3. Egypt (19:1-25)

4. Tyre (23:1-18)

Following the prophecies of judgment against Egypt (19:1-17) is a very remarkable promise of salvation (vv. 18-25). Here in a manner that is actually unique and unprecedented in the Old Testament is a foreglimpse of peace among nations: "In that day there will be a highway from Egypt to Assyria, and the Assyrian will come into Egypt, and the Egyptian into Assyria, and the Egyptians will worship with the Assyrians" (v. 23). In this time of peace Israel will not have a preferred place among the other nations: "In that day Israel will be the third with Egypt and Assyria, a blessing in the midst of the earth" (v. 24). At that time Egypt and Assyria will be blessed even as Israel.

C. THE ISAIAH APOCALYPSE (Isa. 24-27)

These four chapters could be viewed as a separate book of the Bible. They are an apocalypse, portraying the end of the world, and they belong to the latest portions of the Old Testament along with the Daniel apocalypse. The Isaiah apocalypse corresponds in many respects to the Revelation to John in the New Testament, in which there are also many individual expressions taken over from Is. 24-27. Similar also is the way in which descriptions of the end time are interspersed with hymns of praise.

The way in which the end of the world is portrayed is powerful: "The earth mourns and withers, the world languishes and withers; the heavens languish together with the earth" (24:4). "The earth is utterly broken, the earth is rent asunder, the earth is violently shaken. The earth staggers like a drunken man" (vv. 19 f.). Nowhere else in the entire Old Testament is the cessation of our world's moribund character depicted as here. "He will swallow up death for ever, and the Lord God will wipe away tears from all faces" (25:8). "Thy dead shall live, their bodies shall rise" (26:19).

D. THE "ASSYRIAN CYCLE" (Isa. 28-32)

In subject matter this section belongs together with chs. 1-11. Like the former section it includes primarily utterances of judgment against Israel and Judah. Again, as in that section, prophetic sayings have been arranged consecutively without any relationship to one another.

1. *"Woe* to the proud crown of the drunkards of Ephraim" (28:1-4)
   A *promise concerning salvation:* "A crown of glory" (28:4-6)
2. "The priest and the prophet reel with strong drink" (28:7-13)
3. The scoffers and the cornerstone (28:14-22)
4. "Does he who plows for sowing plow continually?" (28:23-29)
5. *"Ho* Ariel!" (29:1-8)
6. "A spirit of deep sleep" (29:9-12)
7. Lip service and hypocrisy before God (29:13-16)
   A *promise concerning salvation:* "A very little while" (29:17-24)
8. *"Woe* to the rebellious children" (30:1-5)
9. In the wilderness of the Negeb (Egypt's help) (30:6-7)
10. "Write it before them . . . sons who will not hear" (30:8-14)
11. "In quietness and in trust shall be your strength" (30:15-17)
    A *promise concerning salvation:* "The Lord waits to be gracious to you" (30:18-26)
    A scourge upon Assyria (30:27-33)
12. *"Woe* to those who go down to Egypt for help . . . The Egyptians are men, and not God" (31:1-3)
13. "The Lord of hosts will protect Jerusalem" (31:4-9)
    A *promise concerning salvation:* King and people of the future (32:1-8)
14. "You women who are at ease" (32:9-14)
    A *promise concerning salvation:* "Until the Spirit is poured upon us" (32:15-20)
15. *"Woe* to you, destroyer" (33:1)

As the above summary indicates, every chapter (with the exception of ch. 32) begins with a word of woe,* and at the end of a chapter or section there is usually a promise concerning salvation.

---

*Translator's Note: The R.S.V. has "Ho!" in ch. 29. The original Hebrew, however, has *hoi* = "Woe!" here as well as in 28:1; 30:1; 31:1.

This is clearly an arrangement of the one who collected the writings. He wanted thereby to give expression to the truth that the woe which the prophet was commanded to proclaim in his time was not the final word of God, even though Isaiah's preaching was indeed dominated by the same distinctive monotonous woe that is expressed here at the beginning of each chapter.

Special attention should be called to some of the sayings in this section:

Is. 28:14-22—To the rulers in Jerusalem who were basing their security on their covenants Isaiah announces: "God will do a strange deed." The statement implies that this security will be completely undermined. In the debacle, however, God is laying in Zion a new and different foundation that alone will guarantee security to those who believe.

> "Behold, I am laying in Zion for a foundation
> a stone, a tested stone,
> a precious cornerstone, of sure foundation:.
> 'He who believes will not be in haste' "(v. 16).

Is. 28:23-29—Following the comment concerning the cornerstone is another saying, unique to the entire Book of Isaiah. Here the prophet does not speak as a messenger of God but rather on his own behalf, as a man among men. The comment is in the nature of a dispute and presupposes that Isaiah was being attacked, because things had turned out in seeming contradiction to what he was announcing. The disaster he had proclaimed did not occur. To this he responds with a parable, based on the work of farmers, which necessarily must be different at different times. This, however, they have learned from the Lord, who does what is necessary at the proper time. "He is wonderful in counsel and excellent in wisdom."

Is. 30:15-17 is also a summons to faith. To those who were relying on their preparation for war and their weapons he announced the destruction of everything on which they were depending. At the same time, however, he referred to another possibility:

> For thus said the Lord God, the Holy One of Israel,
> "In returning and rest you shall be saved;
> in quietness and in trust shall be your strength."
> And you would not (v. 15)

The word from *Is. 31:1-3* is precisely in the same context:

> But [they] do not look to the Holy One of Israel. . . .
> The Egyptians are men, and not God;
> and their horses are flesh, and not spirit.

The utterances concerning judgment in chs. 28-32 state Isaiah's understanding of faith. He has given the concept its characteristic meaning.

E. A PROPHETIC LITURGY AND SUPPLEMENT (Isa. 33-35)

Ch. 33, which Gunkel* has termed a "prophetic liturgy," concludes this collection (28:1–33:1). Out of the national lament (vv. 2, 7-9) rises a redemptive promise looking forward to the final age.

Chs. 34 and 35 are a supplement. Ch. 34 depicts in bold colors the fall of Edom and all the pagan nations. Ch. 35 in contrast describes the future salvation, the untroubled joy of the final age. It concludes with an announcement of the return home:

> And the ransomed of the Lord shall return,
> and come to Zion with singing,
> with everlasting joy upon their heads;
> they shall obtain joy and gladness,
> and sorrow and sighing shall flee away (v. 10).

F. A CHRONICLE: THE THREATENING OF JERUSALEM AND ITS DELIVERANCE (Isa. 36-39)

1. The campaign of Sennacherib against Jerusalem
   Rabshakeh demands a surrender (36:1-22)
2. Isaiah announces the deliverance of the city (37:1-7)
3. New demands for surrender (37:8-13)
4. The prayer of Hezekiah (37:14-20)
5. Isaiah's promise to Hezekiah concerning welfare (37:21-35)
6. The departure of Sennacherib (37:36-38)
7. Hezekiah's sickness, healing, and prayer of thanksgiving (38:1-22)
8. The embassy from Babylon and the oracle of Isaiah (39:1-8)

---

*Translator's Note: Cf. H. Gunkel, *Einleitung in die Psalmen* (Göttingen: 1933), pp. 137, 408.

These four chapters to a large extent correspond with 2 Kings 18-20. If the Book of Isaiah is to be concluded with this chapter from the history of Israel, this then implies that the prophets of Israel were an essential element of that history. (The same is true of the Book of Jeremiah.) But it should be pointed out at the same time that the prophet Isaiah, who was sent to announce God's judgment, was at one with his people and their history in the most profound sense. Even though he had to announce the judgment of God against his king again and again, yet the moment the king in the temple lay bare before God the letter containing the Assyrian general's demand to capitulate, and then appealed to God for the threatened city of Jerusalem, king and prophet stood together before the Lord, from whom the one as well as the other expected everything.

XII

Isaiah 40-55 (Deutero-Isaiah)

The period of the prophecy of judgment concluded with the exile; for now the divine judgment that the prophets of the eighth and seventh centuries had proclaimed had been fulfilled. The prophets of the exile (Deutero-Isaiah, Ezekiel, and others whose identity is not known) now had the task of proclaiming to the defeated and scattered remnant of the people that God, despite everything, had not forsaken them. They still could expect redemption from him.

A. PROLOGUE (Isa. 40:1-11)

This is precisely the message of the prologue to Deutero-Isaiah (40:1-11), in which all the significant themes of his preaching are concentrated: God's command that his people be comforted, the ending of the time of service,* the preparation for the return home (vv. 1-5). Over against the lament of the people, who have no more hope, is set God's commission to the messenger that he proclaim to them his word that had survived the destruction. Verses 6-8 allude to the call of Deutero-Isaiah. God remains the Lord of history and the Victor. His booty is his people whom he will lead home (vv. 9-11).

B. THE FOURFOLD MESSAGE OF DEUTERO-ISAIAH

The message of Deutero-Isaiah, as indicated in the prologue, moves in two directions. It was supposed to call the defeated and

---

*Translator's Note: Cf. R.S.V. marginal reading. The German term is even stronger: *Frondienst,* i.e., forced labor. The Hebrew term *tsābā'* is a military term, usually rendered "war" or "host" in the R.S.V. It may have reference to service during wartime or even in worship (Cf. Num. 8:25; 1 Chr. 7:11).

despondent people of Israel out of their mood of complaint to a new hope. But at the same time it was meant to demonstrate that the God of the defeated nation of Israel was still continuing to carry on his activity in history.

(1)

The words addressed immediately to Israel proceed in the initial direction. These are, in the first place, the polemical and denunciatory utterances, in which the prophet responds to the complaints, objections, and accusations of Israel (40:12-31; 43:22-28; 45:18-19; 49:14-23, 24-26; 50:1-3). Then there are the promises concerning salvation in which Israel was assured of God's favor and help. These were the redemptive oracles (41:8-13, 14-16; 43:1-4, 5-7; 44:1-5, 12-13; 49:7-12; 54:1-6) and the announcements concerning salvation (41:17-20; 42:14-17, 18-25; 43:16-21; 45:14-16; 48:1-11, 17-19; 54:7-10). The utterances pertaining to salvation give a distinctive character to the entire message of the prophet.

(2)

Along the second directional line are a group of utterances that portray a courtroom scene between Yahweh, the God of Israel, and the gods of other nations. The legal action revolves around the claim as to who controls history (41:1-5, 21-29; 43:8-15; 44:6-8, 21-22; 45:9-13, 20-25; 46:9-11; 48:12-16). Here belongs also the word concerning Cyrus of Persia (44:24—45:7).

(3)

There is in addition a third set of sayings in which the cry of consolation in the prologue (40:1-2, 9-11) is picked up in a hymn of praise that echoes throughout the entire message of Deutero-Isaiah. This hymn already anticipates the coming deliverance. It praises the Redeemer and rejoices in the deliverance (42:10-13; 44: 23; 45:8; 48:20-21; 49:13; 52:7-12). The longer sections generally end with an "eschatological hymn of praise" of this type.

(4)

Finally a fourth principal group of passages should be mentioned. They are the "Songs of the Servant of the Lord" (42:1-4, 5-9; 49:1-6; 50:4-9, 10-11; 52:13—53:12).

All the sayings of Deutero-Isaiah cannot, of course, be distributed within the above four groups. They may, however, serve as guidelines.

C. AN ANALYSIS OF DEUTERO-ISAIAH'S MESSAGE

1. Words of encouragement

Deutero-Isaiah's discourse in 40:12-31 is directed to the one he addresses in v. 27: "Why do you say, O Jacob, and speak O Israel, 'My way is hid from the Lord, and my right is disregarded by my God'? Have you not known . . . ?" In four opposing statements the prophet rouses his people from this sense of resignation, by referring them to the One who is incomprehensible (vv. 12-17) and incomparable (vv. 18-24, 24-26). He points to their God, who is the Creator and Lord of history in relation to the nations (vv. 12-17), the mighty (vv. 23-27), the seemingly triumphant astral deities (vv. 25-26). He directs their attention, however, to the One who has stooped down from his lofty position in order to concern himself with the dire need of his people. He is the One who will give to the weary new strength for the return home (vv. 27-31). The proximity of Deutero-Isaiah to the language of the Psalms is evident in this chapter. In 40:12-31 the structure of the descriptive psalms of praise may be clearly recognized.

The polemical speeches (49:14-23, 24-26; 50:1-3) are of the same sort. They are directed against the grievances of the exiles who were complaining that God had abandoned (49:14), rejected (50:1), or could no longer help Israel (49:24-26). Ch. 43:22-28 is issued against another objection of the people, viz., that Israel had really served her God for a long time. She had brought him her sacrifices without fail. To this claim Deutero-Isaiah replies in the tradition of the earlier prophets. It was not God that Israel had served with her sacrifices. She had rather wearied him with her sins; yet now because of his abundant grace he is willing to forgive her sins. Ch. 45:9-13 is directed against the objection as to how Yahweh, the God of Israel, could effect a change in her destiny by means of a foreign king—through Cyrus. Deutero-Isaiah replies by alluding to the broad horizon of the One who has called this world into being.

2. Passages in defense of Yahweh as over against the heathen deities

With ch. 41 a series of legal proceedings begins between Yahweh and the gods of the nations. In these proceedings the God who had been vanquished and who thereby was thought to have been eliminated from history according to ancient conception lays claim nevertheless to the lordship of history in relation to the victorious national deities. He can advance two arguments against them:

a. He is the One who will bring about the coming turning point in history by rousing Cyrus to action.

b. He is the One who is announcing in advance the outcome of history.

Both his action and the proclamation of it are proof that the Lord abides over heights and depths as well as over all catastrophes. He is the "first and the last" (41:4), the One who provides for the former things and the things to come (41:22).

The gods of the nations cannot point to such a continuity that spans history. Their claims accordingly are weak (41:24-29). Israel, however, has been a witness to this faithfulness of God. Even though she is "blind and deaf" she nevertheless has eyes and ears (43:8) and can certify that he alone is God despite her little faith. Apart from him there is no savior (43:8-15; 44:6-8). When that which the Lord now proclaims is fulfilled, however, when even the mighty Babylonian empire is destroyed, then the summons to salvation will be issued to the "survivers of the nations." "Turn to me and be saved, all the ends of the earth! For I am God, and there is no other" (45:20-25). Some day every knee shall bow before him.

The Cyrus oracle (44:24—45:7) also belongs to this line of thought. After a solemn introduction in which God presents himself as Creator and Lord of history (44:24-27), the word is issued to the Persian king: "Thus says the Lord to his anointed, to Cyrus, whose right hand I have grasped . . . I will go before you . . ." (45:1 f.). This is a bold expression—"God's anointed"—addressed to a foreign king who is in the service of other deities. The comment that follows in 45:9-13 indicates how it immediately aroused offense and anger. God's activity, however, could be spoken of in this way, because it also took place "for the sake of my servant Jacob, and Israel my chosen" (45:4).

3. Oracles concerning salvation

The comfort that Deutero-Isaiah had to bring the people in their despair, the prophet expresses in the special form of the "oracles of welfare." The first oracle follows immediately after 41:1-5 in 41:8-13. In this form the suppliant who is pouring out his heart before God receives an answer from him.* At the heart of this promise is the call: "Fear not!" confirmed by a nominal sentence, "Fear not, for I am with you" (41:10), and a sentence containing a perfect verb, "Fear not, for I have redeemed you!" (43:1).

Each of the exiles who heard this oracle in Deutero-Isaiah's preaching recognized it as coming from the divine service. When it was now addressed to this remnant of God's people in their hopeless plight, the hearers must have noted that with this word had come to them the security of God's saving action in a foreign country.

These assurances of salvation are very much alike. This is due to their liturgical character. They have been expanded, however, in more outspoken declarations concerning salvation referring to the future. These tell about the coming deliverance.

Then comes a description of the road leading home (41:17-20), for which the desert will be transformed into a garden and upon which God will lead his people in wondrous fashion (42:14-17; 49:9-11; 43:2). From every distant place they will return (43:5-7; 49:12). This new exodus will be such a tremendous event that the exodus out of Egypt will pale in significance before it (43:16-21; 48:1-11). Out of the ruins will spring forth wondrous new things (49:17-23).

In 51:9—52:6 Deutero-Isaiah's message concerning salvation is expressed once more in an effective poem, beginning with a lament of the people who cry to God in their need: "Awake, O Arm of the Lord!" God responds by calling the people from their grief and weariness: "Rouse yourself, rouse yourself, stand up, O Jerusalem . . ." (51:17-23). "Awake, awake, put on your strength, O Zion . . ." (52:1-6), and concluding with a song of joy (52:7-12): "How beautiful upon the mountains are the feet of him who brings good tid-

---

*This relation of Deutero-Isaiah's promises concerning welfare to the priestly oracle was first perceived by Begrich.

ings, who publishes salvation, who says to Zion, 'Your God reigns.' "
In 54:8 this call to salvation, addressed to lonely Zion, reaches its
climax. "In overflowing wrath for a moment I hid my face from you,
but with everlasting love I will have compassion on you, says the
Lord, your Redeemer."

The 55th chapter returns again to the beginning—back to the
prologue. There the word of God stood opposite the lament of the
people as the one thing that had survived the catastrophe. It had
provided the reason for a message of comfort. Now at the end in
a simile it is once more stated that the word of God would accomplish the thing for which God had sent it. "It shall not return to
me empty, but it shall accomplish that which I purpose" (v. 11).
Then in the last verses of the book comes again the announcement
of the way leading home (55:12-13), as in the prologue (40:9-11).

4. The Songs of the Suffering Servant

The songs of the Servant of the Lord are inserted loosely throughout the book. They have, however, a close connection with one another. Ch. 42:1-4 is a divine word to the Servant. In 49:1-6 and in
50:4-9 the Servant himself speaks. Chs. 52:13—53:12 contain a
divine promise relating to the Servant together with a reflection of
the congregation on his suffering. Ch. 52:13-19 and ch. 53:11-12 are
the divine word at the beginning and the end that enclose, as within
a parenthesis, the reflecton of the congregation (53:1-10).

a. *Isa. 42:1-4* imitates the way a king is designated. God singles out
the Servant as his chosen one, equips him, and gives him his mission. "He shall bring forth justice to the nations." Verses 2 and 3
describe the mode of his activity: "A bruised reed he will not
break," also the goal of his activity: "till he has established justice
in the earth."

b. *Isa. 49:1-6.* Here the Servant himself speaks. In vv. 1-3 he refers
to his having been chosen by God (resembling 42:1-4). Then he reviews his prior work on behalf of Israel, which he would have had
to regard as a failure, were he not able to reply on God (v. 4).
Now, however, he has received a far greater commission from
God: "I will give you as a light to the nations!" (vv. 5-6).

c. *Isa. 50:4-9.* The servant speaks of his office that has a verbal character. Through it he is supposed to help the weary (v. 4). This office, however, is exposing him to suffering that he does not try to evade (vv. 5-6), for he trusts patiently in the sure help of God, who will intercede on his behalf (vv. 7-9).

d. *Isa. 52:13—53:12* begins like 42:1-4. God endorses the Servant whom he has chosen and with an allusion to his humiliation assures him of success and exaltation. A group of people now speak out in 53:1-10, a company who themselves were transformed through the Servant's work. They had seen his deep humiliation and had considered him a rejected man (53:1-3). But then the ones who had been transformed confess: "All this occurred for us!" They recognize the vicarious suffering of the Servant of the Lord (53:4-6). Deeply moved, they reflect on his way that had led even to death, a death in disgrace (vv. 7-9). Nevertheless they know that God will exalt his Servant through suffering, shame, and death (53:10). The conclusion is once again a divine word concerning the Servant—God will exalt and reward him for his vicarious suffering and death.

It is not possible here to enter into the extensive discussion that has taken place concerning the songs of the Servant of the Lord. The question as to whether the subject here concerns an individual or the people of Israel may perhaps be answered by stating that the Servant was indeed an individual who in his destiny and office represents the "Servant of the Lord" as he proceeds throughout the entire history of Israel.

The office of servant in the ministry of Moses and the prophet Jeremiah comes closest to the songs of the Suffering Servant. It has always been recognized that these songs point forward to the New Testament more clearly than any other text of the Old Testament.

XIII

Isaiah 56-66 (Trito-Isaiah)

Chs. 56-66 are appendices to the message of Deutero-Isaiah or the message of a third unknown prophet. These have been added later to the book. Their contrast to chs. 40-55 is so evident that they cannot be attributed to the same Deutero-Isaiah as prophet.

The following difference is most significant. Deutero-Isaiah was *only* a messenger of salvation. The message of Isa. 56-66, however, is intermingled with both salvation and judgment. This is due to a new situation. These chapters belong *after* the exile and were spoken once more in the land of Judah. The prophecies clearly reflect deep disappointment that the time of salvation had not been ushered in by the return from exile. Instead it had brought the difficult, barren, and hazardous task of establishing oneself in the old homeland.

A. A RENEWED MESSAGE OF SALVATION (Isa. 60-62)

Chs. 60-62 (together with 57:14-21) constitute the nucleus of the book. In them is renewed Deutero-Isaiah's message of salvation on behalf of those who had returned in disillusionment. The one speaking at this point understood himself to be divinely commissioned to renew the glad tidings (61:1-3). He issued the call to Zion: "Arise, shine; for your light has come, and the glory of the Lord has risen upon you" (60:1).

He sketches a picture of the period of salvation, reflecting the troubles of the immediate present. Those who were still dispersed would return (60:4), accompanied by abundance and wealth (vv. 6 ff.). The nations who had previously subjugated Israel would have

to minister to her salvation (vv. 10-16). Again the ruins would be
built up (61:4) and joy would return (61:3). Awaiting Zion would
be exaltation: "You shall be a crown of beauty in the hand of the
Lord" (62:3).

In a manner reminiscent of Deutero-Isaiah he also proclaims the
advent of salvation (62:10-12; 57:14-20). Closely connected with
these promises concerning salvation is ch. 66:6-14.

B. PROPHECIES CONCERNING JUDGMENT
(Isa. 56-58, 65-66)

A completely different emphasis is to be perceived at the beginning of the collection. Introducing it is a harsh, abrupt word of
judgment pronounced upon the watchmen and shepherds of the
people (56:9-12) who were concerned only about themselves. An
equally sharp word of judgment is pronounced upon the idolaters
(57:1-13).

The messenger receives the commission: "Lift up your voice like
a trumpet; declare to my people their transgression, to the house of
Jacob their sins" (58:1). This had to be proclaimed with power,
because the Israelites were making reference to their fasting and
basing thereon their claims before God, declaring: "Why have we
fasted, and thou seest it not?" (58:3).

The prophet exposes false worship with the severity and clarity
of the pre-exilic prophets, demanding in its stead justice and mercy.
"Is such the fast that I choose, a day for a man to humble himself?
Is it to bow down his head like a rush, and to spread sackcloth and
ashes under him? . . . Is not this the fast that I choose: to loose the
bonds of wickedness, to undo the thongs of the yoke, to let the
oppressed go free, and to break every yoke? Is it not to share your
bread with the hungry?" (58:5-7).

Ch. 59:1 f. in similar fashion is directed against the reproach that
God was not able to help. " . . . but your iniquities have made a
separation between you and your God." Then in 59:4-8 follows a
gloomy picture of the sins of the people. This changes into a national lament in vv. 9-20, as the people cry: "We look for light, and
behold, darkness." This is followed by a confession of sin in vv.

12-15a. On the strength of this confession God announces his beneficial intervention (vv. 15b-21).

There is still a reference to the people's guilt in 65:1-7 and 66:1-4, in particular idolatry. This is again an utterance relating to public worship that has become spurious. With such worship a life of simple righteousness is contrasted.

Typical of Trito-Isaiah are the words in which a definite distinction is set up between the righteous and the wicked (65:8-16; 66:5, 17; 66:22-24). Salvation is proclaimed to the one; judgment, to the other.

C. A LAMENT OF THE PEOPLE
(Isa. 59:9-20; 63:7—64:12)

Prior to the message concerning salvation that is at the heart of the book in chs. 60-62, there is an intimation of national lament (59:9-20). Directly following chs. 60-62 is an extensive lament of the people in 63:7—64:12, introduced by a historical psalm.* The lament begins with a petition in 63:15 and concludes with an anxious question in 64:12: "Wilt thou restrain thyself at these things, O Lord? Wilt thou keep silent, and afflict us sorely?" (Lam. 5 ends in similar fashion.)

D. MISCELLANEOUS MATTERS
(Isa. 56:1-8; 58:13-14; 65:16-25; 66:15-24; 63:1-6; 66:18-21)

Chs. 56-58 and 65-66 at the beginning and the end include other completely different sayings, in addition to the warnings concerning judgment already mentioned. These are:

1. Chs. 56:1-8 and 58:13-14, which deal with the observance of the Sabbath. During the exile the Sabbath had gained an increased significance and had become a symbolic token. Even foreigners and eunochs (contrary to Deut. 28) now receive a place among God's people by observing the Sabbath.

2. The promises in 65:16b-25 regarding a new heaven and a new earth (cf. Rev. 21:1) are definitely apocalyptic, as is also 66:15-24.

---

*This lament takes the place of the retrospective glance at God's previous saving activity, which is a characteristic feature in the historical psalms.

3. 63:1-6 produces an effect that is strangely weird in the message of Trito-Isaiah. It is a kind of triumphal song that uses the figure of treading grapes and speaks in glaring colors of God's coming destruction of the nations.

In contrast to this, Isa. 66:18-21 announces that even the nations (listed according to the names in the "Table of Nations" in Gen. 10) will ultimately see the glory of God and bring offerings to the Lord.

The following outline illustrates in general the arrangement of the material in Trito-Isaiah:

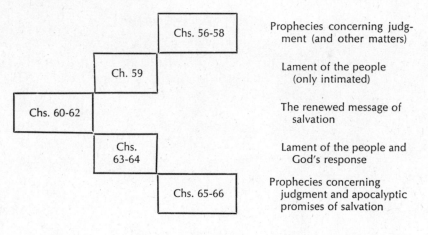

Chs. 56-58	Prophecies concerning judgment (and other matters)
Ch. 59	Lament of the people (only intimated)
Chs. 60-62	The renewed message of salvation
Chs. 63-64	Lament of the people and God's response
Chs. 65-66	Prophecies concerning judgment and apocalyptic promises of salvation

XIV

Jeremiah

All fifty-one chapters of Jeremiah (in contrast to the Book of Isaiah) have to do with one prophet—Jeremiah. There is no other prophet about whom there is so much to be learned. In connection with him the three principal forms of address present in the prophetic books appear with unusual clarity, viz., the prophetic message, informative material, and words directed to God.

Along with this is combined another three-fold division of material, resulting from the way the book of Jeremiah originated, three easily-to-be perceived literary strata, out of which it has grown.

The first consists only of *prophetic sayings*, gathered and arranged one after the other. The second is *an account of incidents* which occurred in connection with the suffering the prophet endured because of his preaching. It may be actually designated as Jeremiah's passion story, and probably originated with Baruch, the friend and amanuensis of Jeremiah (ch. 45). The third stratum is a *revision of Jeremiah's words*, written in a ponderous, sermonic style, the style of the Deuteronomic history. It like Deuteronomy contains an abundance of identical words and phrases.

The first literary stratum embraces essentially chs. 1-25. The Baruch narrative (stratum 2) begins in ch. 19, continued in chs. 28-29, and then extends uninterruptedly from ch. 36 to ch. 45. Stratum 3 has been interwoven with the other two strata to such an extent that it does not constitute an independent segment.

In its present form the Book of Jeremiah is arranged simply and clearly, as follows:

Utterances to Judah-Israel concerning judgment (Jer. 1:1—
    25:14)
Utterances to the nations concerning judgment (Jer. 25, 46-51)
Promises to Judah concerning salvation (Jer. 30-35)
The passion story of Jeremiah (Jer. 26-29, 36-45)
Historical appendix (Jer. 52 = II Kings 24:18—25:30)

The chart below illustrates how the various sections fit together:

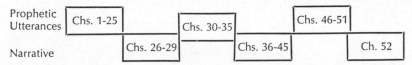

A. WORDS OF JEREMIAH TO HIS OWN PEOPLE
(Jer. 1-25)

1. His call and prophecies concerning judgment (1:1—10:25)

a. The call of Jeremiah (1:1-19. Cf. Isa. 6; Ezek. 1-3):

The call of Jeremiah differs from that of Isaiah primarily in the
sense that Jeremiah resisted the commission, saying: " . . . I am
only a youth!" (v. 6). It is evident here that the human side of his
office already stands out boldly in his prophecy, as in the case of no
other prophet.

The call is combined with a twofold vision (1:11-16), that has
been inserted between his induction (vv. 1-10) and his commissioning (vv. 17-19). The first vision tells him that God has been watch-
ing over his word; the second, that a catastrophe will be coming
upon the land. The two elements of a proclamation concerning
judgment are thereby indicated, viz., the intervention of God and
its result. The reason for this intervention is only hinted at in vv.
16-17.

As Jeremiah was now being sent forth (vv. 17-19) the gravity of
his mission was not concealed from him. He was informed: "I make
you this day a fortified city, an iron pillar and bronze walls" (v. 18).

b. Prophecies concerning judgment (2-10)

At the heart of chs. 2-10 is Jeremiah's temple address (7), which
should be read along with ch. 26, containing an account of the events
that followed. He here announces something that sounded shocking

to his audience. The temple in Jerusalem would become like Shiloh, i.e., like the sanctuary of the ark, destroyed by the Philistines in the time of the judges (Cf. 1 Sam. 1-6). For this announcement Jeremiah gives as a basis: "You have made the temple like a den of robbers!" In other words, they wanted to protect their wicked lives through their worship in the temple just as a robber protects his loot in his den. Ch. 26 reports how this warning concerning judgment almost cost Jeremiah his life.

Following the temple address (7:1-15) are sayings that deal also with public worship (7:16-20; 21-28; 7:30—8:3).

In chs. 2-6 is a passage that is characteristic of Jeremiah's preaching, viz., 2:1-13. In it Jeremiah hurls an accusation against the faithless nation, setting the indictment against the background of all the blessings God had bestowed upon his people (vv. 3-7). He points to other nations and asks: "Has a nation changed its gods?" (v. 11). Then he summons heaven and earth as witnesses to this unheard-of breach of faith, crying:

> "Be appalled, O heavens, at this,
>   be shocked, be utterly desolate, says the Lord,
> for my people have committed two evils:
>   they have forsaken me,
> the fountain of living waters,
>   and hewed out cisterns for themselves,
> broken cisterns,
>   that can hold no water" (vv. 12-13).

In 4:5-29 the approach of an enemy from the north (cf. 1:14b) is described in a poem that has the style almost of a ballad. He depicts the departure of the enemy: "A lion has gone up from his thicket, a destroyer of nations" (v. 7), then the panic he arouses, the headlong flight into the fortified cities, the enemy advance up to Jerusalem, the capital city. Chs. 5:5-17; 6:1-8, 22-26 deal also with the adversary from the north.

It was the task of the prophet not only to announce judgment. He was commissioned to do everything that might lead to a change of heart. Were there not still individuals or groups within the nation that had remained obedient? God had therefore appointed the prophet to be an examiner. As an assayer of metal uses fire, so Jeremiah had to dissolve the stubborn mass of the people to see if a good nucleus would still appear (6:27-30).

He received the commission to glean in the vineyard of his people (6:9-15). Thus he went from the simple folk to the educated people and the leaders to see if there might be one among them who would do good (5:1-6).

The note of lamentation, with which 8:4-7 begins, recurs again and again. This is the complaint concerning the incomprehensibility of Israel's backsliding. This apostasy is unbelievable (vv. 4-5) and unnatural (vv. 6-7). "Even the stork in the heavens knows her times," he says, "but my people know not the ordinances of the Lord" (cf. Isa. 1:3). God, wanting to reap a harvest among his people, had found an unfruitful fig tree (8:13). Ch. 8:18-22 is a national lament. The people who were so desperately sick cry out for help: "Is there no balm in Gilead?" (v. 22).

Ch. 9:17-22 is a summons to utter a dirge, a form utilized here by the prophet. Such an anticipatory dirge was a sinister announcement (cf. Amos 5:1-2). Death in this ballad is a person as in the songs and macabre dances of the Middle Ages. "Death has come up into our windows," Jeremiah cries, "it has entered our palaces." Verse 10 is also a lamentation over the land that had been laid waste. The conclusion of this section (10:19-20, 23-25) consists once again of plaintive words. Verses 23-25 are an excerpt from a prayer of lament.

2. Lamentations and prophecies concerning judgment (11:1—20:18)

a. Personal laments and confessions of Jeremiah

It is only within this section (chs. 11, 15, 17, 18, 20) that the laments and confessions of Jeremiah are found. There is nothing comparable to them in any other prophet. Only the lament of Moses and that of the Servant of the Lord in Deutero-Isaiah are similar. It is not the messenger of God speaking in these utterances but a human being, agonizing in his office. They constitute, therefore, a deeply moving witness, pointing to the future, indicating the importance that suffering was now to have in the life of the one whom God would commission.

(1) *The people of Anathoth* (11:18—12:6). The prophet sud-

denly became aware of the fact that his neighbors had planned to assassinate him without his having had any suspicion of the plot. How could God permit one, who had taken him so seriously, to be handed over to them without any defense? Jeremiah received an answer, informing him of still greater difficulties, yet making it clear that God was on his side.

(2) *Seized by the hand* (15:10-20). With an introductory cry of woe, Jeremiah complains to God of his loneliness: "I sat alone, because thy hand was upon me, for thou hadst filled me with indignation" (v. 17). He would gladly have been in the company of merrymakers. He longed for warm affection, for his loneliness had become unbearable. "Why is my pain unceasing, my wound incurable?" he cried. In his suffering he gave way to a dreadful accusation: "Thou hast been like a deceitful brook to me!" In reply God reprimanded him for his utterance and recalled him, yet renewing at that very moment the promise he had given him at the time of his appointment: "I am with you to save you and deliver you" (v. 20. Cf. 1:19).

(3) *Utterances directed against his enemies* (17:14-18; 18:18-23). Here Jeremiah speaks just as do the Psalms in the imprecatory laments. In the face of his enemies he clings fast to God and his promise.

(4) *Fire in my bones* (20:7-11). Jeremiah could stand it no longer. "For the word of the Lord has become for me a reproach and derision all the day long" (v. 8), he cries. Now he would like to cast off the burden. "If I say, 'I will not mention him, or speak any more in his name,' there is in my heart as it were a burning fire . . . and I am weary with holding it in, and I cannot" (v. 9). Here one hears the human side of Jeremiah, as he is torn between the word of his Lord that had brought him insult and the word of his Lord that had brought him joy and delight.

(5) *"Why was I born?"* (20:14-18). This final lament of Jeremiah is like a groan uttered in deepest despair (cf. Job 3). He curses the day in which he was born. To this complaint he also receives an answer. God does not permit him to be swallowed up in this despair.

Before each of these laments and matching them specifically is a divine commission, addressed to the prophet.

b. Other laments and prophecies of judgment

Ch. 11:1-14 introduces the section (11:1—20:18) and at the close Jeremiah is forbidden to make intercession (also in 14:11).

(1) *A national lament in a time of severe drought* (14:1—15:4).

Jeremiah sympathized with the suffering of his people and would like to have brought them good news but he was bluntly refused, as God told him: "Though Moses and Samuel stood before me, yet my heart would not turn toward this people" (15:1). Thus Jeremiah stood alone between the distress of his people and the wrath of his God. Out of this sense of loneliness his lament ascends.

(2) *A sign on behalf of the approaching judgment* (16:1-13).

Jeremiah's own life must become a sign of the approaching judgment. He was not permitted to have a wife or children (vv. 1-4). He could not participate in the mourning (vv. 5-7) or joys (vv. 8-9) of his neighbors. "I sat alone," he says, "because thy hand was upon me" (15:17).

(3) *Jeremiah at the house of the potter* (18:1-12).

The prophet was ordered to go to the shop of a potter. There the word of God came to him, "O house of Israel, can I not do with you as this potter has done?" (v. 5).

(4) *The prophet in prison* (19:1—20:6).*

Jeremiah was ordered to smash a clay flask in front of the Potsherd Gate. As he repeated the warning of judgment that this action signified, he was beaten by Pashhur, the priest, and put in the stocks. When he was released the next morning, he notified Pashhur of God's judgment. In the lament that follows this account, we hear: "The word of the Lord has become for me a reproach and a derision" (20:8).

In chs. 11-20 there are furthermore a whole series of denuncia-

---

*For an appreciation of this story (19:1-2a, 10-11, 14-15; 20:1-6) it is important to realize that it has been combined with another account (19:2b-9, 11b-13), which is a warning concerning judgment, uttered in the valley of Hinoam.

tory utterances. To the series belong also the acted parable concerning the burial of the waistcloth (13:1-11) and the parabolic saying about the jars of wine (13:12-14). In the midst of the section is a little collection of sayings (17:5-11), among which is the utterance: "The heart is deceitful above all things, and desperately corrupt; who can understand it?" (v. 9).

3. **Words to those exercising leadership** (21:1—24:10)
  a. Words directed against kings (21:1—22:30)
    (1) Answer to Zedekiah (21:1-10)
    (2) To the royal house (21:11—22:9)
    (3) To individual kings (22:10-30)
      (a) Shallum (Jehoahaz: "He shall not return" (22:10-12)
      (b) Jehoiakim: "The burial of an ass!" (22:13-19)
      (c) Jehoiachin: "The signet ring, torn off" (22:20-30)
  b. "Woe to the shepherds!" (23:1-8)
  c. Words directed against the prophets (23:9-40)
    (1) "Prophet and priest are ungodly" (23:9-12)
    (2) "The prophets of Samaria—the prophets of Jerusalem" (23:13-15)
    (3) "Visions of their own minds" (23:16-24)
    (4) "What has straw in common with wheat?" (23:25-32)
    (5) "You are the burden!" (23:33-40)
  d. The parable of the two fig baskets (24:1-10)

In these chapters the words of Jeremiah have been assembled and arranged from the point of view of their subject matter. Utterances concerning kings and prophets have been lumped together, interspersed with an observation about the shepherds, a comprehensive term used here for leaders.

In the oracles concerning the kings, the last stage of the royal history is reflected quite accurately. Jerusalem was still filled with lamentation over the death of king Josiah. Jeremiah then announces that Jehoahaz (Shallum), Josiah's son and successor who has been led captive to Egypt by Pharaoh, will never return.

Jeremiah directs a harsh word of judgment against Jehoiakim, informing him that he will die a violent death and that his dead body will be violated. The grounds for this is an accusation that the king has utilized his authority to exploit his subjects. At the same time Jeremiah makes reference to Jehoiakim's father Josiah, during whose reign justice and righteousness had prevailed.

Several sayings concerning Jehoiachin (22:20-30) have more the character of a lament. Jerusalem had been shocked by his fate. He had been carried off to Babylon after only three months' reign, tossed away as a worthless vessel.

Ch. 23:9-40 sheds a bright light upon the antagonism between Jeremiah, the prophet of judgment, and the prophets of welfare, who cry, " 'Peace, Peace,' when there is no peace" (8:11). They were appealing to their dreams and proclaiming a "God who is at hand," easygoing in relation to his hearers. God, however, had not sent them, Jeremiah declares. "Am I a God at hand, says the Lord, and not a God afar off . . . ?" (v. 23). "Is not my word like fire, and like a hammer which breaks the rock in pieces?" (v. 29).

The parable of the two fig trees concludes the words addressed to the leaders. It intends to say that the portion of the people left for destruction was definitely not the group that had been carried away captive but rather the contingent that had remained in Jerusalem under Zedekiah.

4. Conclusion to the collection of Jeremiah's prophecies concerning judgment (25:1-14)

This portion belongs to the third stratum and is an ideal example of the way in which Jeremiah's words were revised during the exile. Typical is the way in which his activity is here summarized in a retrospective manner. "For twenty-three years, from the thirteenth year of Josiah . . . to this day" (v. 3), also the way his activity is included with that of the earlier prophets: "Although the Lord persistently sent to you all his servants and prophets . . . yet you have not listened to me" (vv. 4, 7).

A passage that sums up everything in quite similar fashion is 11:1-8, introducing chs. 11-20. It too belongs to the exilic revision.

B. PROPHECIES OF JUDGMENT CONCERNING THE NATIONS (Jer. 25:15-38; 46:1–51:64)

In ch. 25:15-38 the figure of the intoxicating cup introduces the "Oracles against the Nations." "Take from my hand this cup of

foaming* wine," God says to Jeremiah, "and make all the nations
to whom I send you drink it. They shall drink and stagger and be
crazed because of the sword which I am sending among them"
(25:15 f.).

In an earlier form of the Book of Jeremiah the oracles against the
foreign nations were added at this point, as indicated still in the
Septuagint. That which has been stated already concerning Isa.
13-23 is relevant here also for Jer. 46-51. They do not all stem
from Jeremiah. As to origin, the national oracles are anonymous. In
all the collections for that matter there are sayings of various unknown prophets that have been taken over. The national oracles**
with the introductory section are as follows:

1. The cup of intoxication for
   the nations (with additions) (25:15-38)
2. Egypt (46:1-28)
3. Philistines (47:1-7)
4. Moab (48:1-47)

5. Ammon (49:1-6)
6. Edom (49:7-22)
7. Damascus (49:23-27)
8. Arab tribes (49:28-33)
9. Elam (49:34-39)
10. Babylon (50:1—51:64)

In the two declarations concerning Egypt (46:3-12 and 46:13-26),
the defeat of Pharaoh Neco at the Euphrates is presumed. The
one who had been victorious over king Josiah (d. 609 B.C.) was thus
defeated. This defeat was succeeded by Nebuchadnezzar's campaigns of conquest that extended down to Egypt. Philistia, which
was once such a powerful enemy of Israel, was also overrun by
the assault (47). One nation after the other of Israel's neighbors
fell, the drama of their collapse being portrayed magnificently.

That God is Lord over history finds emphatic expression to an
unusual extent in these oracles of Jeremiah to the foreign nations.
God's activity in the history of nations, however, is to be seen not
simply in the catastrophes which befall them. This is indicated by
the sentence at the end of the oracle to Edom: "But in the latter days
I will restore the fortunes of Elam, says the Lord" (49:39). This

---

*Translator's Note: R.S.V. has "wine of wrath" based on the Hebrew *ḥēmāh*.
The above rendering follows the German, which has adopted the reading
ḥemer "foaming wine." This is supported by the Septuagint rendering. Cf. Ps.
75:8, which also favors this emendation.

promise recurs in similar language in 46:26; 48:47; 49:6. These are all later additions, indicating that Israel could not remain content with only a partial view of God's activity in history.

The oracles concerning Babylon* (excluding 51:59-64) were added in chs. 50-51 to the collection of national oracles during the exile.

C. PROMISES CONCERNING SALVATION (Jer. 30-33)

These four chapters are a separate small collection, containing many dissimilar promises concerning salvation from various periods, extending from the time of Jeremiah into the post-exilic period.

(1)

It is quite certain that Jeremiah himself offers the good news in ch. 32 in connection with the purchase of a field. During the siege of Jerusalem, while Jeremiah was a prisoner at the court of the guard in the palace, he received an order to purchase a field from his cousin. As a kinsman he had the right of purchase. The field was near Anathoth in territory occupied by the enemy. The purchase is described in detail. Then follows the comment to which this parabolic act refers: "Houses and fields and vineyards shall again be bought in this land" (v. 15). This quiet and unpretentious word of Jeremiah concerning future welfare derives its significance and importance primarily from the situation to which it was addressed. The tired and bewildered people in the last stage of the siege were told, "All is not lost. There will again be an independent and peaceful existence in this place."

(2)

The good news in chs. 30 and 31 was probably addressed at first only on behalf of northern Israel in the early period of Jeremiah's ministry. In 31:5 f., for example, northern Israel is clearly addressed: "Again you shall plant vineyards upon the mountains of Samaria." This matches the summons to return addressed to North Israel in 3:12-13. Later these promises concerning welfare were extended to all Israel, that is, Israel and Judah.

---

*There are about 15 in all.

(3)

Whereas chs. 30-31 deal essentially with the announcement concerning the return home and the new happy life in the homeland, 31:31-34 contains a different kind of promise. At the outset it was probably a promise directed to Israel as a whole—the announcement of a new covenant. The newness here is viewed only in the sense that God's relationship to his people would be fundamentally altered. The epoch of the covenant that had been established at Sinai would be terminated. The new covenant would have as its distinctive feature the inscribing of God's will once for all in the hearts of his people. With this promise the institution of the Lord's Supper has been associated (Luke 22:20; 1 Cor. 11:25).

D. THE STORY OF JEREMIAH'S SUFFERING
(Jer. 26-29, 36-45)

1. The consequences of the temple sermon. The death of the prophet Uriah (26:1-24)
2. Hananiah and the yoke of the king of Babylon (27:1—28:17)
3. Jeremiah's letter to the exiles (29:1-32)
4. The fate of the scroll (36:1-32)
5. Jeremiah during the siege and conquest of Jerusalem (37:1—40:6)
   a. No one heeds Jeremiah (37:1-2)
   b. The inquiry of Zedekiah in the presence of Jeremiah (37:3-10)
   c. Jeremiah's imprisonment and release (37:11-21)
   d. Jeremiah cast into the cistern. His rescue by Ebedmelech (38:1-13)
   e. Final warning given to Zedekiah (38:14-28)
   f. The fall of Jerusalem (39:1-10)
   g. The liberation of Jeremiah (39:11-14)
   h. A promise concerning Ebedmelech's welfare (39:15-18)
   i. Jeremiah, liberated once again, goes to Gedaliah (40:1-6)
6 Gedaliah's governorship in Mizpah (40:7—41:18)
   a. Gedaliah becomes governor in Mizpah (40:7-12)
   b. The assassination of Gedaliah by Ishmael (40:13—41:10)
   c. Ishmael is driven out (41:11-18)
7. The flight to Egypt (42:1—43:13)

      a. An inquiry addressed to Jeremiah and his reply (42:1-21)
      b. The flight to Egypt against the advice of Jeremiah (43:1-7)
      c. Jeremiah announces Nebuchadnezzar's expedition against Egypt (48:8-13)
    8. Utterances of judgment against the idolatry in Egypt (44:1-30)
    9. Jeremiah's advice to Baruch (45:1-5)

It is the concluding chapter in Israel's history as a state that forms the background to the passion story of Jeremiah, beginning with the indignation aroused by his temple sermon (26). The mob wants to kill him, but he is rescued as if by a miracle. Contributing toward this rescue is a prophecy uttered by the prophet Micah a hundred years earlier (Micah 3:12). Another prophet, Uriah, however, is murdered by the king.

Through the reading of the scroll in which Jeremiah at God's behest dictates all his words, the preaching of the prophet is presented once more to the people, princes, and king (36). The king tears up the scroll and burns it. Something decisive thereby occurs. Jeremiah and Baruch at the same time narrowly escape death. The king during whose reign both events occur is Jehoiakim. Then the first blow falls. Jerusalem is conquered, and the first exiles are carried away in 597 B.C.

Under Zedekiah Jeremiah has his worst controversy with the prophets of good news (37:1-2). In ch. 28 his encounter with Hananiah is impressively described. Jeremiah has to tolerate Hananiah's seizing and breaking of the yoke he was carrying on his shoulders as a symbol. God did not intervene or grant him a word at the moment. While the prophets of good news triumph, he has to remain silent. Only later is he able to respond with the word that had been given to him.

His letter to the exiles in Babylon is also directed against the prophets of good news (29). He tells the exiles to begin to work and pray on behalf of the people among whom they are now living. Thus for the first time in the Bible intercession on behalf of those not belonging to the people of God is commanded.

Now comes the last act, the seige and conquest of Jerusalem (37-40). Jeremiah remains faithful to his commission to the last moment. He guarantees that God's judgment upon his people will now be executed by a foreign conqueror. He does not himself, however, evade the fate of his people, which he had proclaimed throughout his life, but he sympathizes with their suffering up to the last moment, as one who was hated, imprisoned, and distrusted.

Since he is given a choice after the collapse, he throws in his lot with the remnant that remains in the land, only to encounter disobedience, stubbornness, and apostasy here too. In the end he has nothing but the saving word of God, of which he declares: "Thy words became to me a joy and the delight of my heart" (15:16).

The advice that Jeremiah gives his companion Baruch apply also to himself:

> Behold, what I have built I am breaking down,
> and what I have planted I am plucking up. . . .
> And do you seek great things for yourself? (45:4 f.)

Baruch concludes his narrative with these words.

XV

Ezekiel

The Book of Ezekiel on the whole resembles Jeremiah, as the following outline* indicates:

1-24	A. PROPHECIES OF JUDGMENT CONCERNING JUDAH AND JERUSALEM (1-24)
25-32	B. PROPHECIES OF JUDGMENT CONCERNING NEIGHBORING NATIONS (25-32)
33	C. THE WATCHMAN (33) (Cf. chs. 3, 18)
34-39	D. PROMISES CONCERNING SALVATION (34-39)
40-48	E. THE NEW TEMPLE (40-48)

It is easy to summarize Ezekiel's prophecy, because of the way in which the main sections have been arranged, subdivided, and linked with one another. A striking connection is to be observed, for example in the way Ezekiel was commissioned to his office as a watchman. He received this commission at the close of his call to become a prophet (3:16-21), prior to the warning concerning

---

*Translator's Note: The author indicates that he has placed sections 34-39 under sections 1-24, because these chapters have the same addressee. Chs. 25-32 on the other hand, are addressed to a different group. Sections 40-48 have been set apart from the sections above, because it is a unit by itself. To conform with the author's comments above and on p. 175 the outline has been slightly modified.

judgment. At the beginning of the promises concerning salvation (33:1-9) he receives the commission again. Thus a link which binds together the two parts of the book is clearly indicated.

A similar relationship becomes evident when there is a direct allusion to the promises concerning salvation in the final utterance of chs. 1-24, viz., 24:15-27. This concludes: "On that day a fugitive will come to you to report to you the news" (v. 26). Ezekiel had already been informed of the death of his wife whom he was not to mourn until news had come of the fall of Jerusalem (24:15-27). Precisely this is reported in 33:21 f., and then Ezekiel's message concerning salvation begins.

The words of Ezekiel are in part dated. From 593-571 B.C. he worked by the river Chebar in Babylon (1:1, 3; 3:15). There he had come with the exiles in the year 597 B.C. Whether he worked in Jerusalem as well is a controversial question. (Cf. the account of his removal there in 8:1-4.)

A. PROPHECIES OF JUDGMENT AGAINST JUDAH AND JERUSALEM (Ezek. 1-24)

1. The call of Ezekiel (1-3)

The call of Ezekiel is unusually detailed. The vision of the throne chariot (1:4—2:7) is followed by the commissioning of the prophet, couched in the form of a symbolic act. Ezekiel was supposed to devour a scroll upon which indictments had been written. Then he was equipped for his task. God said: "Like adamant harder than flint have I made your forehead" (3:9).

In these chapters one encounters a series of features that are found in the calls of Isaiah (Isa. 6) and Jeremiah (Jer. 1). On the other hand, they are already suggestive of apocalyptic in the detailed way they describe the chariot of God.° At the conclusion Ezekiel was appointed as a watchman. Here something novel in relation to earlier prophecy becomes evident—man as an individual comes within the purview of the message of the prophet who is required to bring this message before each individual. But now a separation takes place between the righteous and the wicked, as

---

°The four beasts (1:5-14) became symbols of the evangelists.

over against the word, and the prophet can no longer be held responsible for the wicked who reject his message.

2. Symbolic acts (4:1—5:17)

A series of strange and partially bizarre symbolic acts ensue in this section, all alluding to the destruction of Jerusalem. With a brick and iron plate Ezekiel, for example, has to portray the siege of Jerusalem (4:1-3). Another sign represents the scant and unclean rations that were available during the siege (4:9-17). At the conclusion of this cluster of parabolic acts there is a detailed warning of judgment directed to Jerusalem (5:5-17). God declares: "I will execute judgments in the midst of you in the sight of the nations."

3. Prophecies of judgment concerning Judah and Jerusalem (6:1—7:27)

These utterances belong in the strictest sense together with chs. 4-5, for they resume the warning concerning judgment (5:5-17). The disastrous word uttered against the mountains (6:1-10) is significant. "Son of man,* set your face toward the mountains of Israel, and prophesy against them" (6:2).

The theme of ch. 7 is: "The end has come!" Amos** had already said this in similar fashion (8:1-3). A comparison between these utterances will demonstrate the constant as well as changing factor in prophecy—from Amos to Ezekiel.

4. The abominations in Jerusalem (8:1—11:25)

The prophet was transported in a vision toward Jerusalem (8:1-4). At the end of the revelation in Jerusalem he was transferred back to the river Chebar in Babylon. At this time it was again expressly stated that this occurred in a vision. "Then the vision that I had seen went up from me. And I told the exiles all the things that the Lord showed me"(11:24-25).

The prophet saw idolatrous abominations in the temple of Jeru-

---

*This is the typical mode of address for the prophet throughout the entire Book of Ezekiel.

**Translator's Note: Amos was a prophet of the eighth century (cf. below p. 185; Ezekiel, of the sixth century B.C.

salem. Nowhere is this idolatry described so concretely as here in Ezek. 8. All kinds of idol worship, the Tammuz cult, and solar worship are dealt with (8:5-18). This was followed by an overwhelming vision, in which Ezekiel saw the destruction of the city and its inhabitants (chs. 9, 10). His intercession on their behalf was rejected (9:8-10). It is characteristic of Ezekiel that he draws a distinction between the righteous and the wicked in connection with the judgment of the city's inhabitants. The city itself would be completely destroyed and desecrated. The glory of God is represented as leaving the city (10:18 f.; 11:22 f.). In 43:1, where the new temple is described, it again enters the temple.

5. Prophecies of judgment against Judah and Jerusalem (12:1—24:27)

This large conglomerate series of warnings concerning judgment is again introduced by symbolic acts, in which Ezekiel has to portray, in advance, the coming destruction of Jerusalem. During the night he digs through the wall of his house as commanded, picks up his baggage that has been laid out, and hurries off into the darkness. In answer to the questions of his associates, he gives the explanation of these actions (12:1-16). A melancholy symbolic act follows, in which Ezekiel is supposed to eat his bread with fear and drink water with trembling in order to show how the coming destruction of Jerusalem will threaten the peace of every individual. A long series of warnings concerning judgment is then introduced:

    a. The irrevocability of the judgment (12:1—15:8)
       (1) Symbolic act: flight out of Jerusalem (12:1 16)
       (2) Symbolic act: meal eaten in fear and trembling (12:17-20)
       (3) It will not be delayed any longer (12:21-28)
       (4) Against the false prophets who "have not built up a wall" (13:1-16)
       (5) Against the false daughters of prophecy, who "encourage the wicked" (13:17-23)
       (6) God will not reply to idolaters (14:1-11)
       (7) Only Noah, Daniel, and Job could be delivered (14:12-23)
       (8) The worthless wood of the vine (15:1-8)

Only one group of people is singled out by Ezekiel in this accusation. They are the prophets, i.e., the prophets of welfare, "who daub the walls with whitewash" (13:11). Because they cry, "Peace!" when there is no peace (13:10),* they are frustrating Ezekiel's crucial mission. "You have not gone up into the breaches," he says, "or built up a wall for the house of Israel" (13:5).

The elders wanted to receive instruction from God through the prophet. Ezekiel refused them by alluding to the idolatry of the nation (14:1-11). Divine judgment could now no longer be averted. Even Noah, Daniel, and Job could no longer rescue Judah. The nation was worthless as the wood of a vine, which can only be burned. The entire first section (chs. 12-15) has as its distinctive feature an emphasis upon the irrevocability of judgment.

    b. A historical résumé (16:1—24:17)
         (1) Jerusalem, the harlot (a history of Israel) (16:1-63)
         (2) The great eagle (a historical allegory).
             The perjury of Zedekiah (17:1-24)
         (3) "I will judge you . . . every one according to his ways" (18:1-36)
         (4) Lament concerning the royal family (19:1-14)
         (5) The history of Israel, a history of backsliding (20:1-49)
         (6) A sword over Ammon and Judah (21:1-32)
         (7) "Israel has become dross" (22:1-31)
         (8) Oholah and Oholibah, the adulterous sisters (23:1-49)
         (9) The rusted pot (24:1-14)
      (10) The unlamented death of Jerusalem (24:15-27)

At the very moment when judgment was past recall, the prophet saw the entire preceding history of Israel crowding in upon him. In three chapters (16:1-63; 20:1-44; 23:1-49) he projects a historical review that embraces centuries of time. In this résumé of a history that consisted only of sin and unfaithfulness, one is prone to see only the superficialities: the bizarre forms and figures that from our point of view are a one-sided caricature and an exaggeration. Something significant, however, in theology as well as the history of ideas, has been concealed under this manner of expression, viz., the disclosing of significant historical relationships that

---

*This accusation is taken over literally from Jeremiah 6:14.

only can be seen in such a one-sided manner, as over against the actions of God. These embrace history on a broad scale. When Ezekiel, moreover, handles historical data with the utmost freedom there is even in this a demonstration of the way he adjusts contexts that overlap. This is what makes historical reflection in the modern sense first possible.

In the remaining passages of chs. 16-24 this grasp of historical facts and relationships is also evident. Ch. 17 is a historical allegory concerning two great eagles, in which Ezekiel describes historical movements affecting that period of time. The second conquest of Jerusalem was launched during the reign of Zedekiah because of his breach of oath as a vassal. Ezekiel viewed this last period of Judah's history, therefore, in exactly the same way as did the prophet Jeremiah. Even his lament over the fate of the last kings (ch. 19) corresponds to the respective oracles of Jeremiah concerning them (Jer. 21-22).

Ezekiel reveals in ch. 21 his remarkably broad and profound historical outlook. He suggests that the fall of Jerusalem from the standpoint of the Babylonian conqueror was only one act among others.

Ch. 22 summarizes again, in broad outline, the accusation against the people of God and comes to the conclusion: "The house of Israel has become dross to me" (v. 17). The figure of the rusted kettle (24:1-14) says the same thing.

*   *   *   *   *

At the heart of the warning concerning judgment (chs. 12-24) is the remarkable *eighteenth chapter,* which is especially significant in respect to Ezekiel's theological point of view. It begins with a proverb that was circulating among the remnant of the people: "The fathers have eaten sour grapes and the children's teeth are set on edge" (cf. Jer. 31:29). Against the background of the broad historical outlook in chs. 16, 20, 23, this proverb and its significance is quite understandable. Ch. 18 was placed at the heart of this section precisely for this reason. Ezekiel, however, declares: "This proverb is now no longer valid!" With the fall of Jerusalem an epoch had been concluded. Those who remained were no longer to be affected by the sentence of judgment upon all Israel. To them would be given the opportunity of individual decision. "The son shall not suffer for the iniquity of the father," he says, "nor the father suffer for the iniquity of the son; the righteousness of the righteous shall be upon himself, and the wickedness of the wicked shall be upon himself" (v. 20).

Just as the section (chs. 12-24) began with acts of symbolic import, it concludes with one of this kind (24:15-27). Informed about the death of his wife, the prophet was forbidden to mourn over her as a sign pointing to the unlamented death of Jerusalem.

B. ORACLES AGAINST THE FOREIGN NATIONS*
(Ezek. 25:1—32:32)

Whereas the national oracles in the older prophets are lumped together without any obvious order (Amos is an exception), they give evidence of a well-defined order in Ezekiel. This again fits in with his broadly developed understanding of history. The oracles have been arranged from a geographical standpoint: first, the small adjoining nations in the east and west—Ammon, Moab, Edom, and Philistia (25); then in the north Tyre, which at that time had gained new significance, also Sidon, (26-28); finally Egypt in the south (29-32).

Special attention should be called to the magnificent poetic allegory concerning Tyre, the ship of splendor. "Thus says the Lord God: O Tyre, you have said, 'I am perfect in beauty' . . . so you were filled and heavily laden in the heart of the seas. Your rowers have brought you out into the high seas. The east wind has wrecked you in the heart of the seas . . . all the inhabitants of the coastlands are appalled at you; and their kings are horribly afraid" (27:3, 25 f.).

The announcement of the downfall of the fortified city of Tyre was not fulfilled—at any rate not immediately. Nebuchadnezzar laid siege to Tyre for a long time, yet did not subdue it. At this point Ezekiel himself corrects his earlier announcement (29:17-21). Nebuchadnezzar was supposed to get Egypt (so he says here) in

compensation for his arduous but unsuccessful siege against Tyre.*
This prophecy is an important illustration of the fact that a prophetic
announcement does not preclude its being later corrected.

C. THE WATCHMAN (Ezek. 33)

Chs. 3, 18, 33 occupy a key position in the entire Book of Ezekiel. In chs. 3 and 33 the office of prophet is newly defined as that
of a watchman having supervision specifically over the message of
judgment (introduced in ch. 3) as well as the message of salvation
(introduced in ch. 33).

The responsibility of a watchman as over against that of a messenger is increased in this respect that he, like a watchman in a
tower (33:1-9), must see to it that everybody actually hears the
cry of alarm. His responsibility, however, then ceases; for once an
individual hears the warning his own responsibility begins.

The cry of a watchman thus brings about a separation between
those who listen to the call and those who reject it. This is what
ch. 18, which is at the heart of the prophecy of judgment, is saying.
Therefore the announcement concerning the office of watchman in
ch. 33:1-9 is followed by a call for conversion and a promise to those
who were converted (cf. vv. 10-20; 18:23). The oracles relating to
salvation (chs. 34-39; 40-48) are then introduced.

Now the fugitive from Jerusalem, who had already been announced at the end of the prophecy concerning judgment (24:
26 f.), comes and reports that the city has fallen. This is the moment
that Ezekiel's preaching concerning judgment, which now has
fallen, changes to preaching concerning salvation.

D. THE COMING REDEMPTION (Ezek. 34:1–39:29)

1. The bad shepherds and the good shepherd (34:1-31)
2. A word of judgment concerning Edom (35:1-15)
3. Good news concerning the mountains of Israel (36:1-15;
   cf. ch. 6)
4. The cleansing of Israel (36:16-38)

---

*This prophecy has been included with the oracles against Egypt in chs.
29-32.

    5. The resurrection of the dry bones (37:1-14)

    6. The reunion of those who were separated (37:15-28)

    7. Gog and Magog; the assault and downfall of secular power
       (38:1—39:29)

At the heart of this section is Ezekiel's vision about the raising of the dry bones from the dead (37:1-14). The prophet, while gripped by the hand of God, sees a valley full of dry bones. At God's bidding he utters the commanding word that causes human forms again to rise, then the word calling forth the quickening spirit. "And they lived, and stood upon their feet, an exceedingly great host" (v. 10). In the explanation offered the prophet concerning this vision, he receives the commission to announce that the nation is bound to rise to new life. This is to counter the lament of the people: "Our bones are dried up, and our hope is lost" (v. 11).

Closely related to ch. 37:1-14 are the words that precede and follow—a promise of healing for the two deepest injuries of the past:

    a. Israel, defiled by her manifold guilt, shall again become clean (36:16-38). "I will sprinkle clean water upon you," God promises, "and you shall be clean. . . . A new heart I will give you, and a new spirit I will put within you" (v. 25 f.). (Cf. Jer. 31:31-34).

    b. Israel, rent asunder, shall be reunited (37:15-28). " . . . And I will make them one nation in the land . . . and they shall all have one shepherd" (vv. 22, 24). Ch. 34 speaks in detail about this one shepherd, beginning with the proclamation of woe upon the evil shepherds (cf. Jer. 23) and the announcement of the new and good shepherd. "I will set up over them one shepherd, my servant David," God promises, "and he shall feed them. . . . And I, the Lord, will be their God, and my servant David shall be prince among them" (vv. 23 f.).

There still remain but two sections, which link the promise concerning salvation with the oracles against the foreign nations, viz., chs. 35-36 and chs. 38-39. In chs. 35-36 Ezekiel is ordered to proclaim disaster over the mountains of Edom, salvation over the mountains of Israel. The prophecy of judgment relating to Edom (35) is in this passage, because the prophet was leveling an indictment against her for her scandalous behavior during and after the fall of Jerusalem. On the other hand, the doom he once had had to pronounce over the mountains of Israel (6:1-10) is now changed to welfare (36).

Chs. 38-39, a section that is textually very difficult, depict the assault of a northern power against the new state of Israel, only to suffer a complete collapse on the mountains of Israel. This passage clearly points already over to the apocalyptic literature.

E. THE NEW TEMPLE AND THE NEW WORSHIP
(Ezek. 40:1—48:35)

1. The temple in which the glory of God re-enters (40:1—43:27)
2. The attendants in the new temple (44:1-31)
3. The partition of the land. Duties of the prince (45:1-25)
4. The place of public worship for prince and people (46:1-24)
5. The wonderful fountain of the temple (47:1-12)
6. The boundaries and partition of the land (47:13—48:35)

This amazing conclusion to a prophetical book with its view of the future temple and the worship therein gives prominence to the priestly side of Ezekiel's discourses. At the same time, however, it points beyond to Haggai and Zechariah, the post-exilic prophets who were closely associated with the temple and its worship. What is said in ch. 47 concerning the wonderful temple fountain demonstrates that Ezekiel was speaking of the final age.

XVI

The Twelve Minor Prophets

The twelve minor prophets were once combined in one biblical book. Of these prophets, Amos and Hosea of the Northern Kingdom and Micah of the Southern Kingdom belong to the period of Isaiah (cf. table above p. 133); Nahum, Habakkuk, and Zephaniah, to the period of Jeremiah; Haggai and Zechariah, to the early post-exilic period. Malachi is about fifty years later. Joel, Obadiah, Jonah are post-exilic but cannot be dated exactly.

HOSEA

The Book of Hosea consists almost entirely of prophetic oracles, strung together as a rule in unsystematic fashion. It is unusually difficult to provide biblical helps to get at its content.

A. PERSONAL ACCOUNTS RELATING TO HOSEA
(Hosea 1-3)

The first section (1:1—3:5) contains two accounts, one in the third person (1:2-9) and the other in the first person (3:1-5), in which the prophet is commanded to perform a symbolic act--the marrying of an adulterous woman. Ch. 1 mentions that she bore him three children, to whom he gave names: Jezreel, Not-pitied, Not-my-people, all referring to the coming judgment. Later the names were changed to titles having a redemptive significance (1:10—2:1), although probably not by Hosea himself.

Between the two personal accounts is a warning concerning judgment (2:2-13), interpreting the symbolic act. This is a charge

178

leveled against the way public worship had been contaminated by the Canaanites. It states that Israel had been serving Canaanite deities in the land, because she thought they were essential for her necessities of life. But in doing this she had been disloyal to the one who actually had provided these gifts and so must now receive the punishment of an unfaithful wife.

In ch. 2:14-23 God announces a great transformation: Israel must once more go into the wilderness and then everything would become new. "I will betroth you to me in righteousness and justice, in steadfast love, and in mercy," God says (2:19). Along with this transformation the names of the children would also be changed.

B. PROPHECIES OF JUDGMENT AGAINST ISRAEL, (Hosea 4:1–14:9)

There now follows but one other large block of individual sayings (4:1–14:9), arranged one after the other. With few exceptions they are prophecies of judgment, directed against Israel.

1. Legal proceedings (4:1–5:7)

This section consists mostly of sayings in the form of legal proceedings (e.g., 4:1–"Hear . . . the Lord has a controversy with the inhabitants of the land." They are for the most part accusations of infidelity.

- a. "No faithfulness or kindness, and no knowledge of God in the land" (4:1-3)
- b. The priests: "They feed on the sin of my people" (4:4-11)
- c. "My people inquire of a thing of wood" (4:12-14)
- d. "Enter not into Gilgal" (4:15-19)
- e. Accusation against the leaders (5:1-2)
- f. "The spirit of harlotry is within them" (5:3-7)

2. A warning concerning judgment, the lament of the people, and God's reply (5:8–6:6)

Ch. 5:8-14 is a comprehensive and especially harsh announcement concerning judgment. It begins with a cry of alarm: "Blow the horn in Gibeah" (5:8), and fashions God's case against his own people in alarming imagery. "I am like a moth to Ephraim," he says, "and like dry rot to the house of Judah. I will be like a lion to Ephraim, and like a young lion to the house of Judah" (5:12, 14).

Here begins the lament of the people (6:1-3), hinted at in a few sentences. The people, moved by God's wrath, want to return to him. Ready for repentance, they expect God now to show favor toward them. But God's reply (6:4-6), foreshadowing indeed his mercy, views the people as they are: "What shall I do with you ... ? Your love is like a morning cloud, like the dew that goes early away" (v. 4). The prophetic message of judgment (v. 5) was therefore necessary. "For I desire steadfast love and not sacrifice, the knowledge of God rather than burnt offerings" (v. 6).

3. Prophecies concerning judgment (6:7—9:9)

Following this comment at the heart of chs. 4-9 is once more a list of utterances concerning judgment:

    a. The cities of Israel—places of outrage (6:7-11)
    b. "By their wickedness they make kings glad" (7:1-7)
    c. "Woe to them, because they have strayed from me!" (7:8-16)
    d. "They have broken my covenant" (8:1-3)
    e. Kingship and idolatry (8:4-10)
    f. The piling up of sacrificial worship (8:11-14)
    g. Exile as recompense for the unfaithful (9:1-6)
    h. Mockery and persecution of the prophets (9:7-9)

There is no prophet who has judged kingship as such so sternly as Hosea. "In their wickedness they anoint* kings," he says (7:1-7). "They set up princes, but without my knowledge" (8:4-10). Kingship and idolatry are linked most intimately in this statement.

One learns almost nothing about the prophet Hosea himself in his book except for the symbolic act (chs. 1, 3) and the comment (9:7-9), which in a few sharp sentences intimates how he had been mocked and persecuted as a spokesman for God. This word of

---

*Translator's Note: This is based on the German rendering of v. 3, which follows a different reading of the Hebrew (*yimshehû* in place of *yesammehû*). The rendering of the R.S.V.: "By their wickedness they make kings glad" is based on the latter.

Hosea points over to Jeremiah (chs. 11-20) and the Suffering Scrvant of the Lord.

4. A historical review (9:10–13:16)

Most of the sayings in this section are linked up with a historical review. It was from this point of view that they were perhaps also grouped together.

    a. "Like grapes in the wilderness I found Israel" (9:10-17)
    b. "Israel is like a luxuriant vine" (10:1-2)
    c. "They tremble for the calf of Beth-aven (= Bethel)" (10:3-8)
    d. "From the days of Gibeah you have sinned" (10:9-10)
    e. "Ephraim was a trained heifer" (10:11-13a)
    f. "You have trusted in your chariots" (10:13b-15)
    g. "When Israel was a child I loved him" (11:1-9)
    h. The return home of Israel (11:10-11)
    i. Israel, a liar from the beginning (11:12—12:10)
    j. "There is iniquity in Gilead" (12:11-15)
    k. "Men kiss calves" (13:1-4)
    l. "It was I who knew you in the wilderness" (13:5-8)
    m. "Where now is your king to save you?" (13:9-11)
    n. "O death, where are your plagues?" (13:12-16)

Ch. 11:1-9, as the heart of this section, is especially significant. It sets the announcement of judgment against the background of the history that had led up to this result. The history had started with Israel's election at the time of her deliverance from Egypt. Apostasy, however, had set in immediately. "The more I called them, the more they went from me" (v. 2). And now in the period that had followed, God's loving concern for Israel was standing in radical opposition to the Baal apostasy that had flung his loving concern to the winds. God's concern was expressed in the words: "I led them with cords of compassion" (v. 4). The judgment upon Israel therefore was now unavoidable (vv. 5-6). The love of God for Israel, however, did not grow cold. "How can I give you up, O Ephraim," he says. "My heart recoils within me, my compassion grows tender. . . . For I am God and not man; the Holy One in your midst!" (v. 8 f.).

In these utterances there is frequent reference to the happy period of Israel's beginning. But then with the settlement in Canaan the covenant with God had been frequently put in jeopardy. The wealth of the country, the adoption of the Canaanite forms of worship (13:1-4), kingship (13:9-11), the reliance on personal strength or on coalitions with the great northern or southern powers—all had been contributing factors. Worthy of note is the completely negative estimate of Jacob in 12:4-7, 13.

The conclusion of this section is 13:12-16. At this point the text causes peculiar difficulties. The saying (v. 14), which Paul cites in 1 Cor. 15:54 f. does not have the meaning perhaps of a promise but should be translated: "Shall I redeem them from the power of Sheol? Come with your plagues, O death! Come with your pestilence, O Sheol!"*

5. A promise concerning salvation (14:1-8)

A call to repentance is followed by a confession, to which God responds by a promise concerning salvation: "I will heal their faithlessness; I will love them freely, for my anger has turned from them" (v. 4). It is not certain whether this promise originated with Hosea himself or was affixed later to the collection of his prophecies.

6. A wisdom saying (14:9)

The wisdom saying with which the Book of Hosea concludes is noteworthy. It is a witness from the period, when a devotional type of wisdom occupied itself with the Scriptures.

✳   ✳   ✳   ✳   ✳

JOEL

In the brief Book of Joel one finds prophecy that is decidedly cultic in character. It is for the most part a prophecy concerning

---

*Translator's Note: The German, followed here, uses exclamations to render the obscure phrases of the Hebrew and thereby emphasizes the lack of anxiety with which the prophet awaited whatever death or Sheol might hold in store for him. Cf. Moffatt's translation: "Nay, come, Death, with your plagues! Come, Death-land, with your pestilence!"

welfare. For an appreciation of the book, it is important here to take 1:1—2:27 as a unit and 2:28—3:21 as supplementary.

A. A PROPHETIC LITURGY: A NATIONAL LAMENT
(Joel 1:1—2:27)

A national lament extends throughout chs. 1 and 2, providing a kind of framework to the book, as follows:

A lament: the awful drought (1:15-20)
A call to repentance (2:12b-14)
A petition (2:17b)
    God's response (2:18-20)
    Objective: the praise and acknowledgment of God (2:26-27)

1. A summons to lamentation or fasting

Both the lament in 1:15-20 and the petition in 2:17b are introduced by an extensive call to lamentation or fasting. Ch. 1:5-14 is a grand summons to lamentation, arranged according to the social ranks to which it is addressed: drunkards (vv. 5-7), farmers or vinedressers (vv. 11-12), priests (vv. 13-14). Both times the announcement of a locust plague introduces the call to lament or to fast. In 1:2-4 there are four different words describing locusts; and in 2:1-11 there is a detailed description of their invasion. In 2:12b-14 is inserted a call to repentance.

2. The divine response

After the petition, "Spare thy people, O Lord!" (v. 17b), the divine response follows in vv. 18-20, introduced by the words: "Then the Lord became jealous for his land and had pity on his people. The Lord answered and said to his people . . . . "

The divine response, introduced in this way[*] explains why the little Book of Joel was included in the collection of prophetic books. The cult prophets had the ministry of intercessory prayer, and a part of this ministry was also the duty of communicating God's response to the people at the time of a national lament.

---

[*]2:19b-20 is the oracle concerning salvation. This is followed by a promise of salvation (vv. 21-23) in the style of Deutero-Isaiah and by an account of the results of God's intervention (vv. 24-25).

3. Praise and acknowledgment of God

Linked with the promise concerning welfare is 2:26-27, which has as its object the praise and acknowledgment of God.

Up to this point the plan of Joel may be understood on the basis of the national lament, as follows:

1. Announcement of the plague	(1:2-4)		(2:1-11)
2. Call to lamentation	(1:5-14)	to repentance	(2:12b-14) (2:15-17a)
3. Lament and petition	(1:15-20)		(2:17b)
4. God's response a. Assurance of welfare b. Consequences		(2:18-20, 25) (2:19b, 21-23) (2:24-25)	

5. Objective: praise and acknowledgment of God (2:26-27)

B. A SERIES OF PROCLAMATIONS (Joel 2:28—3:21)

To the prophetic liturgy has been attached a series of proclamations, as follows:

1. The outpouring of the Spirit (2:28-29. Cf. Acts 2)
2. The great and fearful day of the Lord (2:30-32)
3. The destruction of the nations in the valley of Jehoshaphat (3:1-3, 9-17, 4-8)
4. Salvation for Judah; disaster for other nations (3:18-21)

These utterances are all prophecies of good news too, expressed partially in the form of warnings of disaster against foreign nations. They border, however, on the apocalyptic style of writing.

The end time is announced, bringing God's final judgment upon all nations in the valley of Jehoshaphat (= "Yahweh judges"),* together with the time of salvation for Israel. This will be an age of undisturbed happiness and spiritual endowment for all of God's people.

---

*This corresponds to the day of judgment in the New Testament.

AMOS

The structure of Amos is simple and easy to perceive. The blocks
of material may be arranged, as follows:

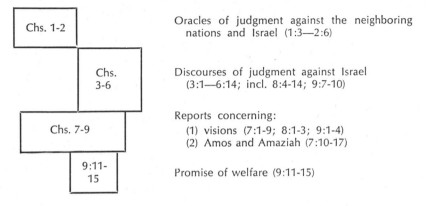

Chs. 1-2	Oracles of judgment against the neighboring nations and Israel (1:3—2:6)
Chs. 3-6	Discourses of judgment against Israel (3:1—6:14; incl. 8:4-14; 9:7-10)
Chs. 7-9	Reports concerning: (1) visions (7:1-9; 8:1-3; 9:1-4) (2) Amos and Amaziah (7:10-17)
9:11-15	Promise of welfare (9:11-15)

The superscription (1:1) mentions the period of Amos' activity
in the time of Uzziah, king of Judah, and Jeroboam II, king of
Israel. The more precise dating, "two years before the earthquake,"
indicates that the period of his activity was quite brief.

Amos was a Judean, working in northern Israel. After a short
period of time, however, he was banished from the country (7:10-
17). It is expressly stated that he was not a professional prophet
(i.e., a cult prophet) but a shepherd (7:10-17).

A. ORACLES OF JUDGMENT AGAINST THE NEIGHBORING NATIONS (Amos 1-2)

1. Damascus (1:3-5)
2. Gaza (1:6-8)
3. Tyre (1:9-10)
4. Edom (1:11-12)
5. Ammon (1:13-15)
6. Moab (2:1-3)
7. Judah (2:4-5)

These all have the same construction and exhibit well the structure of a prophetic word of judgment, as follows:

a. basis—the accusation and its elaboration

b. declaration—God's intervention and its effect. It should be
noted moreover that the basis for the judgment might include in-

fractions of international law. The oracle of judgment against Moab (2:1-3), for example, has to do with a transgression against Edom. It was thus what we would call a violation of international law. Yahweh, the God of Israel, is here assumed to be the Lord of history and accordingly a preserver of justice also outside of Israel.

The oracle concerning Judah (2:4-5) was appended, later, when Amos' words were transmitted in Judah's tradition, after Amos was expelled from Israel. This is an example of how prophetic utterances became a direct address to people of later times. The oracles concerning Tyre and Edom (1:9-12) were also probably appended later.

To these national oracles that were probably once intended as good news for Israel, Amos attached a pronouncement of judgment against Israel and thereby gave these words a new turn, viz., that Israel would by no means have the guarantee of salvation simply because God punished other nations for their wickedness. On the contrary, to be chosen does not mean security but rather increases one's responsibility. "You only have I known of all the families of the earth: therefore I will punish you for all your iniquities" (3:2).

In the oracle against Israel (2:6-16) with which the series in chs. 1-2 concludes, a social indictment, typical of Amos, is drawn up:

> They sell the righteous for silver,
>   and the needy for a pair of shoes—
> they that trample the head of the poor into the
>   dust of the earth,
>   and turn aside the way of the afflicted;
> a man and his father go in to the same maiden,
>   so that my holy name is profaned;
> they lay themselves down beside every altar
>   upon garments taken in pledge;
> and in the house of their God they drink
>   the wine of those who have been fined. (vv. 6-8).

Amos then contrasts this indictment with all the good that God had done for Israel (vv. 9-12) in order to indicate the reason for the special responsibility of the chosen people, the reason for the severity of the announcement (vv. 13-16).

B. DISCOURSES OF JUDGMENT AGAINST ISRAEL
(Amos 3:1—6:14; 8:4-14; 9:7-10)

The opening and closing words in the primary section of the Book
of Amos repudiate a confidence in election which is leading to a
sense of security. For the statement in 3:1 f., which harks back to
1:3—2:16, belongs together with the closing words in 9:7-10. There
Israel is advised in all seriousness that she has no advantage whatsoever over other nations either as a sinful or a chosen nation. "Did
I not bring up Israel from the land of Egypt," God says, "and the
Philistines from Caphtor and the Syrians from Kir?" (9:7).

Inasmuch as 3:1 f. still reflects chs. 1-2, Amos 3:3-8 is the real
introduction to the main part of the book. This passage replaces the
story of the call in other prophets. It alludes but vaguely to the call
of Amos, however, because it leads to the inescapable call of God
that summons a man into his service in the series of results that are
inevitable. "The lion has roared; who will not fear? The Lord God
has spoken; who can but prophesy?" (v. 8). The series of announcements concerning judgment follows at this point:

1. "They store up violence and robbery" (3:9-11)
2. "I will smite the winter house with the summer house"
   (3:12-15)
3. "You cows of Bashan!" (4:1-3)
4. "Come to Bethel and transgress!" (4:4-12)
5. "Fallen is the virgin Israel (5:1-3)
6. "Seek me—do not seek Bethel!" (5:4-6)
7. "Seek good and not evil!" (5:14-15)
8. "Woe to you who turn justice to wormwood!" (5:7, 10-13)
9. "Woe to you who desire the day of the Lord!" (5:18-20)
10. "I hate your feasts" (5:21-25)
11. "Woe to those who are at ease!" (6:1-7)
12. "I abhor the pride of Jacob" (6:8-11)
13. "Are they better than these?" (6:2, 13-14)
14. "You who trample upon the needy" (8:4-7)
15. "On that day . . . " (8:9-10)
16. Hunger for the word (8:11-13)

It should become evident to anyone trying to read these chapters
(3-6) in consecutive order that each of the sayings exists by itself

and ought to be noted and expounded individually. One ought actually write them down and impress them on the mind in such a way that each of them individually would have an effect. There should be a wide interval between each utterance, even as when they were once spoken.

In the accusations that Amos here hurls, there are three groups that stand out at first glance:

a. The social indictments, especially typical of Amos (2:6-8; 3:9-11; 3:12-15; 4:1-3; 5:7-11; 8:4-7)
b. The charges against false worship (2:8; 3:14; 4:4-12; 5:4-6; 5:21-25)
c. The accusations against a false sense of security (5:18-20; 6:1-7; 6:8-11; 6:13-14)

C. INFORMATIVE ACCOUNTS (Amos 7:1–8:3; 9:1-4)

1. The visions (7:1-3, 4-6, 7-9; 8:1-3; 9:1-4)

These five visions all begin: "Thus the Lord showed me; behold. . . . " In them Amos sees a swarm of locusts (7:1-3), a consuming flame (7:4-6), a plumb line in God's hand (7:7-9), a basket of summer fruit (8:1-3), the Lord as he smites the capitals of the altar (9:1-4). The first two deal with plagues that are often the occasion for a national lament, viz., drought and locusts. Actually a national lament is also intimated, in which the prophet as intercessor for his people begs that there may be a gracious response to their lament (7:2, 5). Both times the wrath of God was averted, implying that the plague had been turned aside through intercession. Here is a hint of the earlier concern of the prophet.

Now, however, comes the turning point. What the prophet witnessed in the next two visions was interpreted to him, as follows: "I will never again pass by (i.e., forgive) them" (v. 8). Following this comment, the prophet became a messenger of judgment.

The third and fourth visions refer clearly to the two elements in a proclamation of judgment: the divine intervention, referred to in the plumb line that was let down by God, and the result of his intervention, indicated by the basket of summer fruit, which was interpreted as, "The end has come!"*

---

*The Hebrew word for "summer fruit" (*qayts*) resembles the word for "end" (*qets*).

The final vision demonstrates the inescapability of the judgment that had been announced in the two previous visions.

In a magnificently concentrated form the five visions embrace the task of the prophetic messenger of judgment, set within the background of the prophet's intercessory office.

2. Amos and Amaziah (7:10-17)

In a single scene Amos' activity is presented here in such a way as to bring out all the important elements. His warning of judgment (7:9a) evoked a ban against speaking in the royal sanctuary at Bethel. This ban was announced by Amaziah, the priest, who was carrying out the king's order. Amos guaranteed the truth of his own message but refused to be classed with the professional prophets. His credentials were simply his Lord's command, as he says: "The Lord took me from following the flock, and the Lord said to me, 'Go, prophesy to my people Israel!' " (v. 15). To the prophet Amaziah, Amos had the following to say—he together with his entire family would also be involved in the coming judgment. This was probably Amos' final word in Israel.

D. A PROMISE CONCERNING WELFARE (Amos 9:11-15)

"In that day I will raise up the booth of David that is fallen . . . . " Thus begins this promise concerning welfare; then it refers to the time of salvation at the end of days. It is questionable whether or not these words originated with Amos himself. It was customary for communities who transmitted prophetic warnings of judgment to append promises of welfare to many of these collections.

Even if these words did not originate with Amos, however, his message did contain here and there faint hints that judgment was not God's final word concerning his people Israel. Such an example is in 5:14-15: "Perhaps the Lord will be gracious to the remnant of Joseph."

E. DOXOLOGIES (Amos 4:3; 5:8-9; 9:5-6)

In conclusion, a special group of sayings in the Book of Amos should be mentioned. These are the doxologies in 4:13; 5:8-9;

9:5-6. They are utterances in praise of God, more specifically praise of the Creator, appearing quite unexpectedly in these three passages. Read together they amount to a psalm of creation or part of one.

Here is an impressive testimony to the continuing vitality of Amos' words within the community of later generations. The deep emotion of those who read Amos' words of judgment and who were aware of their fulfillment is expressed in the way these words of divine praise have been added. In them God is glorified for his government of the universe.

*   *   *   *   *

OBADIAH

This is a tiny collection of originally anonymous oracles, dealing with Edom and coming from various periods. They could belong to a larger collection of oracles against the foreign nations, e.g., Jer. 46-51. Several verses from Obad. 1-14 are found in Jer. 49. The oracles against Edom became a separate little book, because they were ascribed to a prophet Obadiah, about whom one can learn nothing—neither in this collection nor anywhere else.

As in several other passages, Edom was accused because of her conduct at the time of the conquest of Jerusalem (note esp. vv. 9-10). There is an announcement that she would be destroyed and expelled from her land. As also in many passages, the Edom oracles have been combined with the proclamation of the day of the Lord, which would bring ultimate judgment upon the nations and final redemption for the people of God.

1. **Announcement of the conquest of Edom** (1-9)
    a. Tidings from the Lord (1)
    b. Edom's insignificance (2)
    c. In spite of your secure clefts of rock (3-4)
    d. The completeness of your destruction (5-7, 9)
    e. Edom's wisdom belongs to the past (8)

2. **Then Edom's violence against Israel will be avenged** (10-15a)

3. **The day of the Lord—destruction on the foreign nations, deliverance for Zion** (15b-21)

JONAH

The Book of Jonah is the tale of a prophet. It contains no prophetic oracles. The narrative is directed against an exclusivism that was becoming obdurate; but it also lauds the mercy of God, which embraces all creatures and breaks through the barriers imposed by men. This it does in opposition to a vexation that wonders how God can give Gentiles happiness and success.

1. Jonah flees from the duty of preaching against Nineveh (1:1-3)
2. The storm and Jonah's surrender to the judgment of God (1:4-12)
3. Jonah is thrown into the sea. The storm subsides (1:13-16)
4. The amazing rescue of Jonah and his prayer of thanksgiving (2:1-10)
5. The new commission, the sermon on repentance, the conversion, and the averting of the judgment (3:1-10)
6. Jonah rebels and is reproved. God's compassion on all creatures (4:1-11)

The Book of Jonah arose in the late post-exilic age, when particularism became a great danger for the faith in late Judaism. This exclusivistic spirit expected that Israel alone would be saved, that the Gentiles only would suffer disaster.

Nineveh had not been in existence now for a long time. It is depicted as a great legendary city of past ages. The way Jonah was swallowed up by a great fish was intended as a symbol, viz., that God initiates his work of deliverance on behalf of a person, when he is engulfed by a hopeless abyss. A psalm of praise was therefore put into Jonah's mouth, while he was down in the body of the fish. (This is a psalm of thanksgiving exactly as it might have stood in the Psalter.)

The overarching mercy of God, which extends from the eulogy of one redeemed individual, crying, " . . . yet thou didst bring up my life from the Pit, O Lord my God" (2:6), even to the many children and animals in a great city of the world, is wonderfully evident in this book.

MICAH

Micah, a contemporary of Isaiah, prophesied in Judah during the time of Jothan, Ahaz, and Jezekiah (1:1). One can learn nothing about him personally in his book. It contains no informative accounts, no national oracles, but only warnings of judgment against Israel and Judah (chs. 1-3; 6:1—7:6) promises concerning salvation (chs. 4-5), and part of a national lament (7:7-20). Ch. 3 includes warnings of judgment, addressed to those exercising leadership.

A. WARNINGS CONCERNING JUDGMENT
(Micah 1-3; 6:1—7:6)

1. **Utterances against Israel and Judah** (1:1—2:13)
   a. "The Lord is coming forth" (1:2-7)
   b. Up to the gates of Jerusalem (1:8-16)
   c. "Those who devise wickedness and work evil upon their beds" (2:1-5)
   d. A preacher for this people (2:6-11)
      Supplement: "I will gather Jacob" (2:12-13)

2. **Words to those exercising leadership** (3:1-12)
   a. "Who eat the flesh of my people" (3:1-4)
   b. "Concerning the prophets who lead my people astray" (3:5-8)
      ("But as for me . . . " v. 8)
   c. "You heads and rulers who build Zion with blood" (3:9-11)
   d. "Zion shall be plowed as a field" (3:12)

3. **Utterances against Judah** (6:1—7:6)
   a. "The Lord has a controversy with his people" (6:1-5)
   b. "He has showed you, O man, what is good" (6:6-8)
   c. "The treasures of wickedness in the house of the wicked" (6:9-16)
   d. "Put no trust in a neighbor!" (7:1-6)

The collection begins with a comment that embraces the entire message of Micah (1:2-7). The nations of the earth are called as witnesses. God appears to conduct a trial against his people because of the sins that emanate from Jerusalem and Samaria. In this initial utterance of the collection (chs. 1-3) the collapse of Samaria is announced (1:6-7); in the concluding utterance, the collapse of Jerusalem (3:9-12). But even in the comment that immediately follows the initial utterance, there is an announcement that the blow will reach "to the gates of Jerusalem" (1:8-16).

The indictment of Micah was primarily a social one. Thus ch. 2:1-5 condemns the inordinate greed of the rich, who "covet fields, and seize them; and houses, and take them away" (v. 2); ch. 2:8-10 criticizes the enslavement of debtors; ch. 6:9-16, commercial fraud and the piling up of wealth. The vehemence of this accusation is expressed in the contrast—"Can I forget the treasures of wickedness in the house of the wicked, and the scant measure that is accursed?" (6:10). In ch. 7:1-6 Micah directs his remarks against the collapse of community life, in which nobody could trust another person any longer. The indictment against the "heads and rulers" is also a social one. He indicates that they were exploiting the people (3:1-4) and impoverishing the nation (3:9-12), even they "who build Zion with blood and Jerusalem with wrong" (v. 10).

It is clear that Micah's preaching was disagreeable to them and that they wanted to silence him (2:6, 11). Micah, however, was confident of his mission; for he declares: "But as for me, I am filled with power, with the Spirit of the Lord, and with justice and might, to declare to Jacob his transgression and to Israel his sin" (3:8). So he had to speak also against the prophets, "who cry 'Peace' when they have something to eat" (3:5).

B. PROMISES CONCERNING SALVATION
(Micah 4:1–5:15)

Micah 4:1-4 is like Isa. 2:1-4. Only 4:4a, which is in accord with the social note in Micah's prophecy, has been added. The exile is announced in 4:6-13:

> Writhe and groan, O daughter of Zion, like a woman in travail;
> for now you shall go forth from the city and dwell in the open
> country; you shall go to Babylon (vv. 9-10a).

But simultaneously the deliverance from exile and the gathering of the dispersed is mentioned:

There you shall be rescued, there the Lord will redeem you from
the hand of your enemies (v. 10b).

In ch. 5:1-5 is a prophecy directed to Bethlehem, proclaiming the
coming of the Messiah. It is followed by further promises concerning salvation in vv. 6-8 and vv. 9-14.

C. A NATIONAL LAMENT (Micah 7:7-20)

The conclusion to Micah is part of a national lament that begins
with a confession of trust (7:7. Cf. Hab. 2:1):

> But as for me, I will look to the Lord,
>   I will wait for the God of my salvation;
>   my God will hear me.

The "I" who speaks here is Zion (v. 11), who is enduring the time
of suffering with great assuredness, knowing that God will once
more help her. "He will again have compassion on us," she says,
"he will tread our iniquities under foot. Thou wilt cast all our sins
into the depths of the sea" (v. 19).

*   *   *   *   *

NAHUM

This book deals with the fall of Nineveh in the year 612 B.C.
Nahum was a contemporary of Jeremiah. His book is to be understood as an announcement of the conquest of Nineveh or a kind of
festive liturgy to celebrate emancipation from the Assyrian yoke.
It probably contains announcements that had been previously
issued concerning the fall of Nineveh. After the city fell, these were
then gathered for the liturgical tradition, just as they had been
handed down.

In any case, Nahum belongs to the prophecy of good news, presented in the form of national oracles. These were produced in a
form for public worship in such a way that the oracles against
Assyria (1:11, 14; 2:1; 2:3—3:19) have become associated with a
promise concerning welfare directed to Israel (1:15; 2:2; 1:12-13).
The order of the verses has thus been upset. The book as a whole
is introduced by a fragmentary hymn of praise.

A. AN ACROSTIC PSALM OF PRAISE (1:2-10)

The psalm of praise (1:2-10) is alphabetic* and includes a divine epiphany in 1:3b-6 (as in Judges 5; Ps. 18; Hab. 3 and frequently elsewhere). The earth-shaking advance of God corresponds to the assault of the enemy against Nineveh (2:1-13).

B. GOOD NEWS FOR ISRAEL (1:15–2:2; 1:12-13)

The good news for Israel (1:15–2:2; 1:12-13) is reminiscent of Isa. 52:7 ff. It is a pledge concerning welfare, introduced by an invitation. This is followed by an announcement of good news. It concludes with the words: "And now I will break this yoke from off you and will burst your bonds asunder." With this the principal section is introduced, viz.,

C. ANNOUNCEMENT OF NINEVEH'S DOWNFALL

1. The destruction of the city (1:11, 14)

It was from Nineveh that the plan for Israel's annihilation had emanated. Now Yahweh had decided on the destruction of that city itself.

2. The Assault Against Nineveh (2:1-13)

The coming conquest of Nineveh is portrayed impressively with poetic power.** At the conclusion is the word of the Lord of history: "I will cut off your prey from the earth, and the voice of your messengers shall no more be heard" (v. 13).

3. Woe Concerning the Bloody City (3:1-17)

She "betrays nations with her harlotries" and now sinks in shame and ruin. Nineveh was no better than the Egyptian Thebes, which had been destroyed in all its splendor. The countless officials, scribes, and tradesmen who had engulfed the subjugated lands would now be no more (3:8-17). The oracles concerning Nineveh conclude with a lament: "Your wound is grievous!"

---

*Only to the Hebrew letters *lamed* ("l") or *samek* ("s").

**Ch. 3:2-3 is also a part of this description.

HABAKKUK

The Book of Habakkuk belongs to approximately the same period as Nahum. Here too the subject revolves around the annihilation of a powerful tyrant, under whom Israel was suffering oppression. The oppressor may have been Assyria here also, although this is not stated explicitly. Whereas Nahum, however, already anticipates liberation from the tyrant, Habakkuk speaks out of the misery of the oppression. Nahum opens with a psalm of praise. But Habakkuk has as its distinguishing feature a psalm of lament—an individual lament, in which the need of the people is nevertheless implied. The parts of the psalm may be traced throughout the whole book:

Accusatory lament (1:2-4)	The coming of the conqueror (1:5-11, 14-17)
Lament and confession of trust (1:12-13)	
The divine response (2:1-4)	The five-fold woe concerning the enemy (2:5-19)
Advent of God (3:3-15)	The prophet's response (3:16)
	Laudatory vow and eulogy (3:17, 18, 19)

A. A LAMENT (Hab. 1:2-4, 12-13)
AND AN ANNOUNCEMENT (1:5-11, 14-17)

The lament is first interrupted by an announcement in 1:5-11 that God is raising up a powerful conqueror* whose description is continued in vv. 14-17. This is a bold and amazing portrayal. "Their own might is their God," he says. "Therefore he sacrifices to his net and burns incense to his seine" (vv. 11, 16). Habakkuk's confession, "Thou hast ordained them as a judgment; and thou, O Rock, hast

---

*"Chaldeans" in v. 6 is uncertain. The Septuagint adds here "powerful."

established them for chastisement" (v. 12), links together both lament and proclamation.

B. THE DIVINE RESPONSE (Hab. 2:1-4)

In 2:1-4 God again returns answer. The prophet* is to act as a mediator, delivering God's answer to the people who have been lamenting and imploring God from the depths of their despair. He becomes a watchman (2:1) in the very sense indeed that he cannot yet proclaim good news as a present reality but can encourage them to wait patiently. For the promised deliverance "will surely come, it will not delay" (v. 3b). Its arrival, however, will bring about a separation. *Only* the righteous will live by his faithfulness (or by his faith). Cf. Rom. 1:17.

C. THE FIVEFOLD WOE CONCERNING THE ENEMY (Hab. 2:5-19)

In 2:5-19 there follows a fivefold woe against the powerful, malicious conqueror. This provides the reason for his destruction. The woes include blistering indictments against the politics of a great nation that has swallowed up little nations (v. 5) and heaped up power and wealth, thereby incurring guilt that will someday be avenged (vv. 6-8). This is a nation that has recklessly utilized men, animals, and material for its power (vv. 9-18). "For the stone will cry out from the wall, and the beam from the woodwork respond" (v. 11).

D. THE ADVENT OF GOD (Hab. 3:1-15)

The promised intervention of God (2:1-4) is anticipated in (3:3-15) by a powerful portrayal of the divine epiphany. God comes, and this advent convulses the whole creation. Its aim, however, is salutary. "Thou wentest forth for the salvation of thy people, for the salvation of thy anointed" (v. 13).

---

*In the Book of Habakkuk the office of cult prophet is again evident.

E. THE PROPHET'S RESPONSE (Hab. 3:16-19)

The prophet was deeply moved by this vision (3:16), but he is able to conclude his lament with a laudatory vow and a divine eulogy (3:18-19), while waiting for the coming of God.

*　*　*　*　*

ZEPHANIAH

Zephaniah was a contemporary of Jeremiah, active probably around 630 B.C.,* specifically as a prophet of judgment, to which order he also belongs.

The collection of his sayings has been arranged in the same way as in Jeremiah, Ezekiel, and other prophets:

Utterances of judgment concerning Judah (1:2—2:3; 3:1-8)
Oracles against the foreign nations (2:4-15)
Promises of welfare for Judah (3:9-20)

A. UTTERANCES OF JUDGMENT CONCERNING JUDAH (Zeph. 1:2–2:3, 3:1-8)

A withering judgment is pronounced upon the wicked nation that has bowed down in idolatry to other gods rather than to its own. The aftereffects of the wicked period under Manasseh and Amon may perhaps be detected in these words. This is expressed in 1:10-13 by the graphic accusation concerning "the men who are thickening upon their lees." They were the men who no longer took God seriously but said: "The Lord will not do good, nor will he do ill" (v. 12). To this generation that had become entirely corrupt "the day of the Lord" was announced. It would be "a day of darkness and gloom" (vv. 14-18). The hymn *Dies irae dies ille* (Day of wrath, that day of mourning!) is a paraphrase of these words.

In 2:1-3 a warning and a call to conversion is once more issued, "before there comes upon you the day of the wrath of the Lord."

---

*He was probably the great-great-grandson of king Hezekiah. Cf. 1:1.

The same possibility *(vielleicht)* as in Amos 5:15* holds open the door—"Perhaps you may be hidden in the day of the wrath of the Lord."

Ch. 3:1-8 is a woe for the rebellious city. The ones especially indicted are those exercising leadership—the princes, judges, prophets, and priests. "Her priests profane what is sacred," he says, "they do violence to the law" (v. 4). God had warned the city by many a grievous fate (vv. 6-7), but she had not accepted correction. The judgment was now inevitable (v. 8).

B. ORACLES OF JUDGMENT AGAINST OTHER NATIONS
(Zeph. 2:4-15)

These include Philistia (vv. 4-7), Moab and Ammon (vv. 8-11), Egypt (fragmentary) (v. 12), Assyria (vv. 13-15).

C. PROMISES CONCERNING JUDAH'S WELFARE
(Zeph. 3:9-20)

Verses 9 and 10: "Yea, at that time I will change the speech of the peoples to a pure speech, that all of them may call on the name of the Lord and serve him with one accord . . . ," are an addition to the warning of judgment in v. 8. This is one of the sayings that anticipate a pure and united worship for all nations in the final age.

Ch. 3:11-15 includes a description of the purified remnant in Zion and a song of praise of those who have been saved. A promise concerning welfare, addressed to Zion, constitutes the conclusion: "Do not fear, O Zion . . . the Lord, your God, is in your midst" (v. 16).

*   *   *   *   *

(Note: The last three prophets belong to the post-exilic period.)

Haggai, Zechariah, and Malachi were active in Judah at the beginning of the post-exilic period: Haggai, in the year 520 B.C.; Zechariah, from 520 to 518 B.C.; Malachi, probably around 470 B.C. Haggai and Zechariah belong to the line of cultic prophets. The sayings of both deal essentially with the rebuilding of the temple and public worship.

---

*Translator's Note: "It may be that the Lord, the God of hosts, will be gracious to the remnant of Israel." In the German, *vielleicht* (perhaps) is used in both passages.

HAGGAI

A. APPEALS TO BUILD THE TEMPLE
(Hag. 1:1-14, 15; 2:15-19; 2:1-5)

Haggai issues here a warning for the people not to forget the temple in their concern for rebuilding their own houses. It is to the lack of a temple that he attributes the meager crops since the return. Once the temple has been rebuilt, everything would improve. Haggai was given a hearing, and the building was begun.

B. SPECIAL PROMISES CONCERNING THE TEMPLE
(Hag. 2:6-9) AND TO ZERUBBABEL (2:20-23)

Both promises have been combined with a warning of judgment upon the foreign nations. God would shake heaven and earth and destroy the heathen empires, but he says, "I will fill this house with splendor" (2:7). God would choose Zerubbabel as his servant. He declares: "I will . . . make you like a signet ring" (2:23).

C. A PRIESTLY TORAH (Hag. 2:10-14)

In accordance with a kind of priestly torah (i.e., law) Haggai pronounces "this people" (the Samaritan element of the nation?) unclean.

*   *   *   *   *

ZECHARIAH

Zechariah was a contemporary of Haggai. His dated oracles extend from 520 to 518 B.C. Only chs. 1-8, however, should be interpreted on the basis of this period. In chs. 9-14 the words of a later unknown prophet have been added, as in the case of the book of Isaiah. This unknown prophet has been called Deutero-Zechariah. Whether all the words in chs. 9-14 originated with one prophet must remain an open question. They belong to parts of the Bible that are difficult to understand. Much that we can no longer figure out has been hinted at here or deliberately obscured.

Zechariah 1-8
A. A SUMMONS TO REPENT (Zech. 1:2-6)

This passage introduces an appeal for conversion, reminiscent of the earlier (pre-exilic) prophecy and based upon it. The ponderous style (e.g., the frequently repeated, "Thus says the Lord") indicates its remoteness from earlier prophecy.

B. THE SEVEN NOCTURNAL VISIONS OF ZECHARIAH
(Zech. 1:7—6:8)

1. The visions:
   a. The horses (1:7-15)
   b. Four horns and four smiths (1:18-21)
   c. The man with the measuring line (2:1-5)
   d. The lampstand and the two olive trees (4:1-5, 11-14)
   e. The flying scroll (5:1-4)
   f. The woman in the ephah (5:5-11)
   g. The four chariots (6:1-8)

Certain features are common to all the visions. Thus the introduction is followed by a description of that which the seer observed. He then poses a question as to the significance of what he has seen, and an angel (the *angelus interpres*) gives him the explanation. All the visions end with an announcement of good news.

In the lament, "O Lord of hosts, how long wilt thou have no mercy on Jerusalem and the cities of Judah?" the *first vision* (1:7-15) indicates the situation for which the vision was given. The explanation holds out the prospect of a change, not so far away as yet. "We have patrolled the earth, and behold, all the earth remains at rest," declares the man, riding on a red horse, standing among the myrtle trees.

The *second vision* (1:18-21) in its reference to the four smiths alludes to the powers who will rise up against the oppressors of Israel (the four horns).

The man with the measuring line in the *third vision* (2:1-5) refers to the size of a Jerusalem that has been liberated.

The two olive trees in the *fourth vision* (4:1-5, 11-14) designate the anointed officials, Zerubbabel and the high priest Joshua, with whom the period of salvation for Jerusalem is to begin. The divine presence is implied by the lamps.

The *fifth and sixth visions* (5:1-4, 5-11) indicate the expulsion of evil from the new Jerusalem. (The flying scrolls contain curses that strike the wicked in their hiding places, and the woman in the ephah personifies the evil that was being removed from Jerusalem.)

The *last vision* of the four chariots with horses of different colors (6:1-8) suggests the approaching judgment of God upon the nations of the earth.

With these visions of the prophet Zechariah apocalyptic writing begins. Many of the most varied symbols, ideas, and esoteric events have been employed here to unveil a wonderful future for the people to whom the prophet spoke. They are intended to indicate the endless possibilities available to God in bringing about salvation. The line of apocalyptic proceeds from Zechariah to Daniel and then to the many apocalypses that arose in the next centuries but were no longer admitted into the canon.

2. Prophetic utterances:

The series of nocturnal visions is interrupted by isolated prophetic sayings:

    a. A promise of salvation for Jerusalem and the temple (1:16-17)

    b. The summons for departure from the "land of the north." Judgment befalls Israel's oppressors. God, however, will find a dwelling place in Zion (2:6-13)

    c. The installation of Joshua and Zerubbabel (3:1-10; 4:6-10)

    d. A crown for the "Branch" (6:9-15)

These words stand within a context. Thus what was revealed by intimation in the nocturnal visions and in the imagery with its semblance of reality [*in die Wirklichkeit überspielenden Bildern*] has been adapted to the actual situation of post-exilic Judah in the words of this prophet of good news. Zechariah proclaims that the time of salvation will begin for Judah, when the building of the temple is completed. Thus the Lord says: "I have returned to Jerusalem with compassion" (1:16, 17). This will be the turning point. Jeru-

salem will rise again together with the temple, and the cities of
Judah will overflow with prosperity. All the exiles will return. Judgment will be executed against their enemies, and God will once
more find a dwelling place in Zion (2:6-13).

The new order, however, would begin in Zion, with Joshua, the
high priest, being absolved of accusation. (As high priest he would
be a substitute for the guilt of the entire nation. Here Satan appears before God as an accuser—3:1-8). A turban was put on
Joshua's head as a symbol of the dignity that would grant him free
access before God. It was also a token of the time of salvation.
Ch. 4:6-10* is immediately connected with this passage. It is a
promise to Zerubbabel concerning his welfare. He will surmount all
obstacles (This is the meaning of "the great mountain" in 4:7) and
will bring the temple to completion. "He shall bring forward the
top stone amid shouts of 'Grace, grace to it!'" is the promise.

But then he was supposed to fashion a crown (so the prophet
Zechariah was commanded) and set it on the head of the "Branch."
For this "Branch" would be king, even the Messiah, in the time
of salvation. By "Branch"** only Zerubbabel can be meant. He,
moreover, was designated in this way. In our text, however, it is
Joshua who receives the crown and is called the Branch (6:11 f.).
Here the history of the text reflects the actual sequence of events. In
those days (still during the period of Zechariah's activity) Zerubbabel was recalled from his office as governor, never again to be
mentioned. The expectation that he would become the Messiah after
the completion of the temple was not realized.

C. THE QUESTION CONCERNING THE FASTS
(Zech. 7:1-14)

An inquiry was directed to Zechariah concerning the fasts that
had been established in the fifth month, commemorating the fall
of Jerusalem and the end of the Judean state. "Should they be
continued?" the people asked. The reply of the prophet was a twofold one: first, he contrasts the spurious feasts with those that

---

*In its present position it is interrupted by the fourth vision.

**According to Isaiah 11:1 this is a frequent description for the Messiah.

were pleasing to God. He does this by making a reference to the earlier prophets (7:4-14). His actual answer, however, is given in the promises concerning welfare in ch. 8: "The fast of the fourth month, and the fast of the fifth, and the fast of the seventh, and the fast of the tenth, shall be to the house of Judah seasons of joy and gladness . . . " (v. 18).

D. PROMISES CONCERNING WELFARE
(Zech. 8:1-23)

Ch. 8 contains a comparatively long series of assorted promises concerning welfare, all introduced with an expression that had already become formal: "Thus says the Lord." God will again dwell in Zion. It will be given a new redemptive name, and everyone, from little children to old people, will participate in the prosperity. Those who are still far off will re-return, and God "will sow well-being" (v. 12).* Jerusalem will become a center of attraction. "Many peoples and strong nations," he says, "shall come to seek the Lord of hosts in Jerusalem" (v. 22).

DEUTERO-ZECHARIAH
(9:1—14:21)

The collector has provided a supplement to the Book of Zechariah in chs. 9:1 and 12:1, in each case with the superscription: "An oracle. The word of the Lord."** No previous research concerning these supplements has as yet been able to shed any light on the meaning of these words. Only one principal feature that extends throughout both parts (i.e., chs. 9-12 and chs. 12-14) is evident. This is the announcement concerning a period of salvation for Zion, which is combined with utterances concerning judgment. This one characteristic also links these supplements with Zechariah's prophecy (1-8).

There are individual passages that apparently contain allusions

---

*Translator's Note: This is a reading based on the German version, which had adopted a slightly emended Hebrew text. The R.S.V. has "There will be a sowing of peace" which is a literal rendering of the Hebrew.

**Translator's Note: This is the German rendering. The original Hebrew could be understood in this way rather than as the R.S.V. has it: "An oracle. The word of the Lord. . . . "

to contemporary events, as, for example, the strange historical allegory about "the shepherd of the flock, doomed to slaughter" (11:4-17); but its meaning is as obscure to us as the other references.

The call for Zion to rejoice, because her king is coming (9:9) is reminiscent of Deutero-Isaiah. Matt. 21 adopted it for the account of Jesus' triumphal entry into Jerusalem. The reference to Judas' thirty pieces of silver is derived from 11:13.

The concept of the remnant has been phrased in such a way that it announces the extermination of two-thirds of the people. A third part is to be refined by fire. The original relationship to God will then be resumed. "I will say, 'They are my people,'" declares the Lord of hosts, "and they will say, 'The Lord is my God'" (13:9).

* 　 * 　 * 　 * 　 *

MALACHI

This collection originally had the same superscription as the two supplements to Zechariah: "An oracle. The word of the Lord." The name "Malachi" (= my messenger) was derived from 3:1. Later it became a part of the superscription. Nevertheless, the voice of a definite prophet with distinct ways of expressing himself is to be clearly discerned in these four chapters.

Just as Zechariah already tends toward apocalyptic writing, so does Malachi toward dogmatic disputation. All six utterances exhibit the same characteristics. Thus the prophet picks up an opinion that is opposed to his own, making it the basis for a dialectical comment.

1. "I have loved you," says the Lord.
   But you say, "How hast thou loved us?" (1:2-5)

2. "If then I am a father, where is my honor?"
   You say, "How have we despised thy name?" (1:6—2:9)

3. "Why are we faithless?"
   "You have been faithless to your wife, your companion" (2:10-16)

4. "You have wearied the Lord with your words."
   Yet you say, "How have we wearied him?" (2:17—3:5)

5. You say, "How shall we return?"
   "Will man rob God? Yet you are robbing me." (3:6-12)

6. You say, "How have we spoken against thee?"
   You have said, "It is vain to serve God" (3:13—4:3)

7. An admonition to keep the law (4:4)

8. Elijah's announcement before the day of the Lord (4:5-8)

Malachi no longer has the supreme authority that the ancient prophets had. Yet with the energy that has been given him he opposes a growing unbelief, an incipient alienation from God (cf. esp. 3:14 f.). After the exile it is only in Malachi that the earnestness and clarity of the pre-exilic prophets of judgment is found. He points forward in 3:1-5 to a day of judgment, as he cries, "Who can endure the day of his coming?" (3:2).

Part Four

THE WRITINGS

XVII

Essence and Purpose of the Writings

The third part of the Old Testament canon is not on a par with the first two parts: the law and the prophets. Thus the New Testament can designate the Old Testament simply as "the law and the prophets," (Matt. 7:12; 22:40; Luke 16:1; Acts 13:15; 24:14; Rom. 3:21).

In essence and purpose this third part is a response. It grew out of and was formed around the Psalter, which is also essentially a response to God's deeds and words.

Closely related to the Psalter are Lamentations and Job, in which lament and divine praise are a primary component. As a second primary constituent, Job includes wisdom discourses and is thus closely linked with the wisdom books—Proverbs and Ecclesiastes. Words of wisdom also occur in the Psalter (see below). Israel in later times understood the language of wisdom also as a response to God's word—pious reflection seemed close to plaintive and laudatory response. Understood in this way the Psalms and the wisdom literature constitute the heart of the Hagiographa.

The work of the Chronicler (1 and 2 Chron., Ezra, Neh.) was added as a supplement to the historical books. Daniel, an apocalypse, was included as a supplement to the prophetical books.

Finally there is the Megilloth, a collection of five festival scrolls, adopted into the canon as readings for a series of consecutive festivals in the late Jewish community. These are the Song of Songs, Ruth, Lamentations, Ecclesiastes, and Esther. The Song of Songs, Esther, and Ecclesiastes were held for a long time in dispute.

XVIII

The Psalms

It is extremely difficult to survey the Book of Psalms in its entirety. One possibility for getting this general view is furnished by the psalm types. Another means, however, is also provided by the way the Psalter grew out of smaller collections. In the very first stages, the various psalms were not arranged consecutively in a mechanical fashion but rather according to their subject matter. What is still to be perceived concerning this?

A. COLLECTIONS DISCERNIBLE WITHIN THE PSALTER

In the Book of Psalms, as we now have it, there is one small collection accepted into the Psalter, which may be clearly recognized, viz., the *ma 'ălôth** psalms (= pilgrim psalms?). These are psalms 120-134.

Preceding this collection is Ps. 119, which is a tribute to the law. It is unique in the Psalter. (The only other psalm that resembles it is Ps. 19b.) It seems quite likely that Ps. 119 once terminated a psalm collection. Now, however, it has a formal as well as an internal correspondence to Ps. 1, which is also an indirect tribute to the law, but in the way that a man who accepts God's law in his life and directs his life according to it is counted as blessed. Both psalms are representative examples of devotional wisdom or the piety connected with the law. Neither one is a psalm any longer in

---

*Translator's Note: *ma 'ălôth* is a Hebrew term, rendered "Degrees" in A.V. and "Ascents" in R.S.V. Its exact meaning has never been explained beyond doubt. It refers apparently to songs sung by pilgrims, *ascending* to Jerusalem.

the strict sense of the term but rather a religious meditation. Hence it may be assumed that there was once a Psalter, beginning with Ps. 1 and ending with Ps. 119. An external proof of this (still apparent today) is the absence of superscriptions for Ps. 1 and Ps. 119.

Collections discernible within the present fivefold collection of the Psalter are as follows:

1. Book 1 (Ps. 1-41)

a. *The Psalms of David* (3-41)

If we should seek for additional collections within Ps. 1-119, there is a collection of Davidic psalms (3-41), indicated by the superscriptions. Its concluding psalm coincides with the end of the *First Book of Psalms* (1-41), as indicated by the doxology at the end of Ps. 41. Apart from the question as to the meaning of the Hebrew term *l^e Dawid,* Ps. 3-41 (which are so designated) exhibit in common a very important feature. They are all songs of an individual type. (Ps. 19 and 24 alone are exceptions.)

2. Books 2 and 3 (Ps. 42-89)

a. *Elohistic psalms* (42-83)

With Ps. 42 the so-called "Elohistic" psalter begins, that is to say, the divine name *Elohim* replaces *Yahweh* in Ps. 42-83.

(1) Psalms of the Sons of Korah (42-49):

Starting with Ps. 42 is a group of Korah psalms (42-49), in which is included a number of songs of a congregational type (44-48). These were evidently at one time an independent collection. Ps. 42 f. and 49 now enclose them at the beginning and the end.

(2) Psalms of Asaph (73-83)

The same is true of the Asaph psalms (73-83), which have personal laments at the beginning and the end (73 and 83). Within this bracketed group are included congregational songs*, national laments, and hymns of Zion. Actually most of the national psalms of the Psalter are included within the above two collections, viz., 42-49 and 73-83.

---

*Only the latter part of Ps. 77 is congregational in type.

(3) Psalms of David (51-72)

Between them is the Elohistic psalter of David (51-72). It contains personal psalms almost exclusively, even as Ps. 3-41. The *Second Book of Psalms* (43-72) concludes likewise with a Davidic psalter—in this case an Elohistic one.

b. *Supplement* (84-89)

There is in addition a supplement. This is a small group of Korah psalms (84-88 exclusive of 86) plus the Royal psalm 89, which terminates the *Third Book of the Psalter* (73-89). The observations noted above apply also to this supplement: the psalms are again congregational in type and include national laments (85, 89) and hymns of Zion (84, 87).

The two large collections, i.e., the Psalms of David (3-41) and the Elohistic psalter (42-83) together with Ps. 84-88, have Royal psalms at the beginning and the end.

3. Books 4 and 5 (Ps. 90-150)

a. *The "Yahweh is king" Psalms* (93-99)

The next distinctive group is Ps. 93-99. These are psalms that begin with the expression "Yahweh is king."* (Ps. 90-92 have no apparent relationship to them.) To this group has been added as a doxology Ps. 100.

b. *Psalms of praise* (103-107, 111-118)

Two additional groups of psalms, expressing praise, follow, viz., Ps. 103-107 and 111-118. (To this group 135 and 136 probably belong, separated now by 119 and the Songs of Ascents)** Ps. 117 is probably the closing doxology to Ps. 111-118. Ps. 118, a liturgical psalm, was later appended.

---

*Translator's Note: RSV renders Hebrew *Yahweh* as "the LORD."

**Translator's Note: Between these two groups are the following isolated psalms:

(1) Ps. 108, which is a composition based on parts of two other psalms, viz., 57-7-11 and 60-6-12.

(2) Ps. 109, an Imprecatory psalm.

(3) Ps. 110, a Royal psalm. Cf. Westermann, C., "Zur Sammlung des Psalters," in *Forschung am A.T.*, München, 1964, p. 336.

c. *The Songs of Ascent* (120-134)

To the collection of psalms, beginning with Ps. 1 and ending with Ps. 119, the Little Psalm Book (120-134) has been added. It is likewise a complete unit, including only one certain pilgrimage song, viz., Ps. 122. The Hymns of Zion (125, 126, 132), however, are closely related to it. Ps. 134 is the closing doxology.

d. *Psalms of David* (140-143)

The next apparent collection is 140-143, consisting of four Davidic psalms. They are four personal laments, Ps. 138 and 139 at the beginning and Ps. 145 at the end have probably been appended to this collection.

e. *Miscellaneous psalms*

Ps. 135-136, as noted above, belong to the psalms of praise—the Hallelujah psalms (111-118). Ps. 137 and 144 stand alone. The former is actually not a psalm at all but a national hymn. Ps. 144 is a composite work, made up of various psalm fragments.

f. *Psalms of praise* (146-150)

A series of hymns (146-150), dominated by an urgent summons to praise, concludes the Psalter. Ps. 150 stands in place of a closing doxology for the *last book of Psalms* (107-150), i.e., Book 5. With this the collections that are to be distinguished in the Psalter have been singled out.

What conclusions are to be drawn from the above survey?

(1) It is apparent at once that personal lament, the most frequent type of psalm in the Psalter, is confined almost entirely to the first half of the Book of Psalms—specifically to the two large collections (Ps. 3-41 and 51-72). In addition, there is but one other little collection of such psalms, viz., Ps. 140-143. Outside these three blocks of material they occur only sporadically in other collections (e.g., 77, 94, 102, 109).

(2) The larger groupings of psalms, expressing praise, are found only in the second half of the Psalter. All collections after Ps. 90

include them except Ps. 140-143 (personal laments) and the songs of ascent (120-134). It is clear therefore that the first half of the Psalter contains predominantly psalms of lament; the second half, psalms of praise.

(3) The superscriptions give evidence of several categories. All the groupings of Davidic psalms contain predominantly personal psalms (primarily laments). The national or congregational psalms appear almost only in the Korah and Asaph groups, except for the Songs of Ascents, which are chiefly congregational.

(4) The psalms of praise serve frequently as a conclusion to the individual collections, as do the doxologies at the end of the present books within the Psalms (41:14, Book 1; 72:18 f., Book 2; 89:52, Book 3; 106:48, Book 4; 150, Book 5.) Ps. 134 is the conclusion to the collection (120-133); Ps. 117, to Ps. 111-118; Ps. 100 to Ps. 93-99; Ps. 145 possibly to Ps. 140-143.* All the psalms of praise, preceding Ps. 90, perform this function (Ps. 18 and 19, 33 and 34, 40, 65, and 66).

(5) The Royal psalms, which seem to be a separate collection, appear only as separate additions throughout the entire Psalter. Ps. 2 and 89 as noted above bracket the two large collections (Ps. 3-41 and 42-88). Ps. 20, 21, 72, 101, 110 perform a similar function.** It is evident that they have been added to the existing collections according to their messianic interpretation rather than on the basis of their original cultic significance as it pertained to the respective ruler.

(6) The Psalter does not include a clearly-to-be-discerned liturgical collection. Wherever there are liturgies they have been inserted in the existing collections.

---

*Translator's Note: Cf. Westermann, "Zur Sammlung des Psalters," *op. cit.*, p. 342.

**Translator's Note: In a special communication the author suggests that these psalms have been inserted into or attached to smaller collections.

(7) The criteria according to which collections in the Psalter may be recognized exhibit two basic distinctions: first personal psalms are distinguished from those that are congregational in type; then psalms of lament from psalms of praise. These two distinctive features are unmistakably evident. They must therefore have been important for the determination of a psalm to those who collected them and handed them down. These criteria coincide exactly with the fundamental distinctions that are followed in determining psalm types.

The arrangement of the various collections noted above may be portrayed as follows:

Ps. 1

Ps. 3-41   Psalms of David

Ps. 42-49   Korah psalms

Ps. 51-72   Psalms of David

Ps. 73-83   Asaph psalms

Ps. 84-88   Korah psalms

Ps. 42-83 are Elohistic psalms

Ps. 93-99   The Lord is king
Ps. 100   Psalm of praise

Ps. 103-107   Psalms of praise

Ps. 111-118   Psalms of praise

Ps. 119

Ps. 120-134	Pilgrim psalms

Ps. 135-136	Psalms of praise

Ps. 138-139	Personal psalms of praise
Ps. 140-143	Personal laments
Ps. 145	Psalm of praise

Ps. 146-150	Psalms of praise

B. PSALM TYPES DISCERNIBLE ON THE BASIS OF WORSHIP

To this initial survey a further classification of personal psalms must be added; for the psalms have developed out of Israel's public worship. Each one individually contains within itself a worship event. It is a part of the worship life. Even though the events lying behind the psalms can often no longer be perceived, nevertheless they are always to be assumed. When one listens to a psalm, one should not ask: "What ideas does it contain?" but rather: "What is being fulfilled in the words of this psalm?"

1. Personal laments

The Davidic psalms, as we have seen, contain predominantly personal laments. This is the most frequent type in the Psalter.

a. *Psalm 13 as an example of this type*

Psalm 13 gives one a clear indication of the significance and structure of this type. It begins with a fourfold question: "How long?" This is the deep, heartfelt sigh of one who has suffered pain for a long time and can no longer keep silent. The two first questions: "How long . . . wilt thou forget . . . wilt thou hide . . . ?" are a complaint directed against God, i.e., a divine indictment (using indictment here in the formal sense).

In the next two questions—"How long must I bear pain?" and "How long shall my enemy be exalted over me?" there follows a personal lament and a lament concerning a foe. Following the lament is a petition. At first the petitioner beseeches God to turn to him; as he cries, "Consider and answer me!" Then he asks for God's helpful intervention: "Lighten my eyes! (i.e., Cheer me up again!)" The petition is combined with reasons intended to influence God.

Now comes a "but." This "but" appears frequently in the midst of the psalms of lament, indicating always a turning point—a step forward out of the lament. Evident in this "but" is the violent agitation of these psalms. A confession of faith is introduced at this point: "But I have trusted in thy steadfast love." In conclusion, there is a promise, directing the attention away from lament to joy.

b. *The character of the laments*

(1) Their diversity in plan

This simple plan lies at the basis of all the personal laments. At the same time, however, there is not one that is identical with another. The constituent parts of a psalm vary to such an extent that each of the approximately seventy personal laments is an individual production. The order of sequence may vary. Thus for example the confession of confidence often comes between the lament and the petition. One or several of the elements may be missing; a petition may appear two or three times. The emphasis may fall entirely on one element—on the lament concerning an enemy perhaps or on the confession of confidence. Themes from other psalm types may also appear.

(2) Their generality in content

It is difficult for us to understand these psalms, because the specific trouble about which the psalmist is complaining can hardly ever be determined. This is part of the very essence of these psalms, however. They have all been uttered over a long period of time (often centuries in duration) before being recorded. During this long period of use they have been polished to such an extent that

that which is individual or unique has merged entirely into that
which is typical.

These psalms were actually supposed to express the varied suffering of many dissimilar people. We ought never therefore recognize only a single individual behind one of these psalms but always
a long succession of people who have prayed. That is why a specific circumstance is not even evident in such a vivid and directly
appealing lament as Ps. 13. This also explains why troubles which
are quite diverse are described in many psalms—sickness and persecution perhaps (e.g., Ps. 22).

The exact occasion for the suffering, therefore, is hardly a basis
for distinguishing between groups of personal laments. Though sickness (Ps. 22, 38, 102) and false accusation (Ps. 7, 35, 37, 69) are
frequently mentioned, it is oppression and persecution by enemies
that predominate (in about 36 psalms). Only that which is typical
is ever mentioned about these enemies too. Thus they threaten the
one who is praying; they conspire against him; they seek to bring
about his downfall. The imagery to express this usually comes from
three spheres:

a. They set nets and snares for the psalmist (140:5 f.)
b. They threaten him like wild animals (17:11 f.)
c. They attack him like soldiers (11:2),* ridiculing him and
   gloating over his misfortune.

The enemies are wicked and treacherous men, blasphemers, fools,
contemptuous of God (10:3; 28:5; 36:1). All these comments concerning the psalmist's enemies, however, are so general that it is impossible to identify specific persons or classes of people. We can
only say that a community, affected by profound contrasts, is here
depicted—a community in which a dominant class has been pitted
against a defenseless one. The ones who pray describe themselves
often as the poor and the needy, which accords with this situation.

When the psalms of lament are viewed from this standpoint,
they become a vivid witness on behalf of the importance of placing

---

*Translator's Note: The author suggests 7:13 as an example for (c): "Wieder
schärft er (d.h. der Feind) sein Schwert." The R.S.V. rendering of this
passage, however, refers this passage to God. Ps. 11:2, a more appropriate
reference, on the basis of the English, has therefore been substituted.

one's dependence on God and finding shelter in him from the adversities over which one is fretting. Not a single one of these psalms, however, continues on as a lament [except perhaps Ps. 88]. Everyone exhibits some kind of anticipation that reaches beyond the adversity.

c. *Types of laments*

(1) The confession of trust became incorporated within a psalm of its own in the case of the *psalms of confidence* (Ps. 23; 27:1-6; 63; 71; 131). In the case of others, like Ps. 22, lament has passed over immediately into a hymn of praise.

(2) In one group confession of sin is much more prominent. These so-called *penitential psalms* (Ps. 6, 32, 38, 51, 102, 130, 143) became unusually prominent in the Christian tradition. There is in these psalms, however, simply forgiveness of sins, i.e., it is not meant as a forgiveness that delivers from some specific need.

(3) There is another group, moreover, that contains a marked note of *personal integrity* (Ps. 5, 7, 17, 26). These psalms belong particularly to the prayers of the falsely accused.

(4) Certain psalms reflect the bitter vexations felt by those who prayed, while seeing the good fortune of the wicked (Ps. 37, 49, 73). Here contemplation is combined with prayer. Ps. 73 points clearly in the direction of the poem of Job.

2. Personal psalms of praise

Matching the personal laments are the personal psalms of praise (the informative psalms of praise or the psalms of thanksgiving). These are Ps. 9, 18, 30, 31b, 32, 34, 40:1-12; 66:13-20; 92 (107)* 116 (118)* 138. The one who had been rescued from his trouble would enter the sanctuary, bring an offering (66:13f.), and tell others what God had done for him (66:16). This account has a definite plan, beginning with a recollection of the distress which is often described as the state of having been bound or seized by death, the grave, or Sheol. The suppliant continues: "I cry to thee—thou hast heard me—thou hast delivered me." The psalm then frequently becomes

---

*Translator's Note: Ps: 107 and 118 also belong to the Psalm liturgies according to the author.

a tribute to God, at the heart of which is the overwhelming wonder of the deliverance. "His anger is but for a moment," cries the psalmist, "but his favor is for a lifetime" (30:5). The themes of informative or confessional praise are found in many other passages also outside the Psalter (in Luke 1 and 2 for example).

3. National laments

Besides the personal laments the Psalter includes also national laments—not many, however. These are Ps. 44 (60),* 74, 79, 80, 83, 89. There are themes and reminiscenses of laments also in Ps. 82, 85, 90, 106, 115. (The national laments that are complete are all in the Korah and Asaph collections.) Such laments are included also in the Book of Lamentations and the prophetical books (Jer. 14; Isa. 63 f.; Hab. 1; Joel 1 f.) and frequently alluded to in Deutero-Isaiah. The setting for a national lament appears often in the Old Testament. Whenever it says, "Then the children of Israel cried to the Lord," there is an implication of such a lament. Joel 1 f. describes in detail what happened in such a situation.

The plan of the national lament is similar to that of the personal lament. It also has a salutation, a complaint (in three parts), a petition with reasons attached, and a confession of confidence. In place of confession there is frequently a recollection of God's previous saving activity. There is also a difference in that the national lament expects a divine answer to follow upon the complaint and petition—a promise concerning welfare that could be proclaimed in place of this by a man of God.

This is expressed in an especially clear manner in Ps. 85. After the petition (vv. 4-7) a single voice begins: "Let me hear what God will speak; for he will speak peace . . ." (v. 8, cf. Jer. 14:11; 2 Chron. 20:3-17).

Ps. 80 is an unusually fine example of a national lament. Following the introductory petition (vv. 1-2) comes the lament (vv. 4-7), in contrast to which there is the recollection of God's previous saving activity (vv. 8-11) in the figure of a vinedresser. This figure is continued in the accusation against God, picked up once more in vv.

---

*Translator's Note: Ps. 60 was used by the compiler of Ps. 108; vv. 6-12 are the same as 108:7-13.

12 f., declaring that God himself is destroying what he has planted. In the complaint addressed to God, the two typical questions are: "Why?" (v. 12) and "How long?" (v. 4). The twofold petition (vv. 14 f.) is continued in a wish directed to both queries. The psalm concludes with a vow of fidelity (vv. 18 f.).

There are also national psalms of confidence to be found especially in Ps. 123 and 125, also Ps. 90 (by intimation).

4. National hymns of praise

There are national hymns of praise that correspond to the national laments. These celebrate God's help after the danger has been averted. Ps. 124 and 129, both belonging to the Songs of Ascents (120-134), are informative psalms of praise of this type. The sense of deliverance felt by the one who has been rescued is expressed here with remarkable directness:

> Blessed be the Lord
> who has not given us
> as prey to their teeth!
> We have escaped as a bird
> from the snare of the fowlers;
> The snare is broken,
> and we have escaped!
> (124:6, 7)

The oldest extant hymn of national praise is the song of Miriam (Ex. 15:1 = v. 21). It is this song to which the late historical psalm 106 refers when it states: "Then they believed his words; they sang his praise" (v. 12). But this eulogy which gives an account of God's acts on behalf of his people has developed along other traditional lines. It has acquired a special form in the hymn of victory (Judges 5) and in the hymn of the Lord's epiphany, who comes to his people's aid (Ps. 18:7-15; Hab. 3:3-15); and it has become a historical composition, proclaiming God's mighty acts on behalf of his people. For this as well as other reasons there are almost no specimens of it represented in the Psalter.

5. Hymns

Descriptive psalms of praise or hymns are found in the first part of the Psalter (Ps. 8, 19a, 29, 33, 57:7-11; 65; 66:1-7). Thereafter

they occur from Ps. 90 and on in the sections mentioned in the survey at the beginning. There are also many outside the Psalter, viz.,
Isa. 6:3; 12; Jer. 10:6-16; the doxologies in Amos but especially
Deutero-Isaiah and Job. In the New Testament they are found especially in Luke 1-2 and in Revelation.

The descriptive psalm of praise is Israel's true song of worship
in praising God. Ps. 113 provides a simple and clear example of its
construction. The introduction to most psalms of praise is the call
to worship, expressed imperatively (113:1-3). The call to extol God
extends throughout time (v. 2) and space (v. 3). The reason for
this call is given in the main section of the Psalm (vv. 4-9). At the
heart of it are the clauses:

> Who is like the Lord our God in the heavens and the earth,
> who is seated on high, who looks far down?*

This clause expresses what divine eulogy has to say about God in
a final, simple, and remarkably impressive statement:

He is the One who is majestic and sublime, towering above everything. Yet at the same time he stoops down from his exalted place
to help those who are in the depths. This assertion in Ps. 113 is
developed in such a way that v. 4 describes the grandeur of God,
vv. 7-9 his condescension. That God looks far down implies that
he detects dire need there in the depths and then meets it in wonderful fashion. "He raises the poor from the dust and lifts the needy
from the ash heap" (v. 7). The way he exalts is then portrayed by
two examples in v. 8 f.

This arrangement is found again in Ps. 33. The principal section,
however, has been expanded. Thus praise of the divine majesty is
worked out in greater detail in the way God is extolled as Creator
(vv. 6-9) and as Lord of history (vv. 10-12). This portion passes
over into praise of the divine Helper, the One who saves (vv. 13-19a)
and preserves (v. 19b). The same arrangement may be found in
Ps. 136 and in other psalms of this type.

There are numerous special groups in the case of the psalms of
praise:

---

*Translator's Note: This follows the author's rearrangement of the text, plac-
ing v. 6b after 5a.

a. Creation psalms, derived from praise of the Creator (Ps. 8, 19a, 104, 139, 148. Cf. also Amos 4:13; 5:8 f., 9:5 f.; parts of Deutero-Isaiah and especially Job 38 ff.).

b. Historical psalms, evolving out of praise of the Lord of history. One can notice, for example, the development from Ps. 33:10-12 to Ps. 136:10-22 to Ps. 78 and 105. Ex. 15 and Deut. 32 belong here also.

c. One group is distinguished by the way it emphasizes an urgent summons to praise (Ps. 95a, 100, 145, 148, 150). Here instrumental accompaniment is given special prominence.

d. Festal songs or liturgies, praising God. These were used at the time the ark of the covenant was carried in procession (Ps. 24, 132?), in the case of the festal hymn (Ps. 118), in the liturgy of thanksgiving (Ps. 107), in the psalms of the Lord's kingship (Ps. 47, 93, 96-99) and his manifestation in power (Ps. 29, 50).

6. Psalms of pilgrimage and Hymns of Zion

The Psalter contains only one pilgrim song (Ps. 122). There must surely have been a great number of them at one time; for there are many allusions to them (in Isa. 2 and Jer. 31:6, for example). The Psalter has instead a number of hymns of Zion (Ps. 46, 76, 84, 87). These are closely related to the pilgrim songs. A tradition concerning the choice of Zion as the mountain of the Lord lies behind them. Before the city gates the great battle of nations takes place, in which God remains victorious, entering triumphantly into his city. This divine victory is celebrated by a procession in connection with which there is an exquisite poetic expression concerning confidence in the city that has been protected and rescued by God.

7. Psalms of benediction

Pilgrims coming to the sanctuary received a blessing as they departed. This was considered essential for everyday life. The blessing is mentioned in the liturgy of Ps. 118 (v. 25 f.). An almost identical blessing is at the end of Ps. 129, also Ps. 134:3. When the ark was carried in procession (Ps. 24), a final blessing was pronounced (v. 5). In Ps. 67 the congregation receives a blessing in answer to their prayer—also in Ps. 115:9-15.

Ps. 91 and 122 demonstrate a special kind of blessing, received by an individual. In both instances a man expresses his confession of trust and then receives an assurance of blessing from the priest. Ps. 128:4 f. also mentions this.

8. Royal psalms

These are Ps. 2, 18, 20, 21, 45, 72 (89), 101, 110, 132. Ps. 2 and 110 are connected with royal enthronement, promising the king victory, success and divine assistance. Ps. 132 links a promise on behalf of Zion with one on behalf of the Davidic dynasty, both of whom were divinely chosen. It is probably a song for a festival in which this election was celebrated. Ps. 45 is a royal wedding song, a purely secular composition that has come into the Psalter through the later interpretation suggesting that "king" here refers to the Messiah. Ps. 72 is an intercession on behalf of a king. Ps. 20 and 21 contain a petition and a thanksgiving on his behalf as do also Ps. 61, 63, 132. Ps. 89 is a royal lament.

In the case of the Royal psalms, one must carefully distinguish between their original meaning, according to which they once referred to real kings of Israel and Judah, and the one which prompted their later adoption into the Psalter on the basis of their messianic interpretation.

9. Wisdom psalms

In later times prayerful piety and wisdom were in accord with one another in Israel. In the Songs of Ascents there are found several proverbs of wisdom (127:1-2, 3-5; 133). They could have appeared in the Book of Proverbs without any alteration. They have nothing to do actually with the Psalms but are maxims dealing with everyday life.

Ps. 37 is a wisdom poem in which a wise man warns against becoming envious of wrongdoers and urges instead trust in God. Ps. 49 and 73 are troubled by the question concerning the prosperity of the wicked. In them personal lament and wisdom have been combined.

In the psalms of thanksgiving (31:23; 32:6 f.; 40:4-8) there appear features characteristic of the language of wisdom. The genuine psalms of wisdom (1, 112, 128) distinguish between the righteous and the wicked. To this group belong also the psalms in praise of the law (119, 19b).

A concluding remark concerning a systematic study of the Psalms:

In order that you may really come to know the Psalms, you ought to copy down a number of typical examples from each of the categories that have been indicated here. This should be done in such a way that you would immediately recognize their literary structure. Thus as you would continue to read each new psalm, it would exhibit that which was already well known as well as its own distinctive character. It would be still better if you would memorize a psalm from each major group in order to compare each new psalm with this example.

XIX

The Book of Job

The Book of Job has a clearly planned structure that is easy to discern. It has been set within a framework of an older narrative concerning a devout, long-suffering individual named Job (1:1—2:10; 42:7-17).

The poem about Job grows out of the visit of his three friends who came to comfort him in his misery (2:11-13). The dialogue begins (ch. 3) and closes (chs. 29-31) with a lament of Job. Contained within this lament are three speech cycles (chs. 4-14; 15-21; 22-23), in which Job's answer follows intermittently the speech of a friend. The third cycle consists of only one of the friends' speeches and the response of Job (chs. 22-23). The original arrangement of the following chapters (24-27) can no longer be apprehended; for they contain only fragments. As the friends depart there is a concluding comment in an involved poem of wisdom (ch. 28). This comes before Job's final lament in chs. 29-31, which concludes with a demand that God appear. This is followed immediately by the appearance of God (38:1).

In the opinion of many expositors, the speeches of Elihu (chs. 32-37), which intervene at this point, are later insertions. Chs. 38:1—42:6 add to the initial dialogue between Job and his friends a second one between Job and God. God answers Job "out of the whirlwind" in two discourses, after which Job speaks twice (40:3-5; 42:2-6). With this the poem is joined once more with the narrative framework (42:7-17).

226

The plan of the book may be represented, as follows:

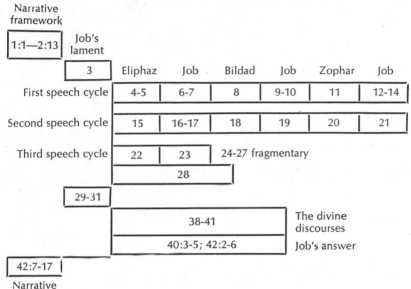

Narrative
framework

| 1:1—2:13 | Job's lament |

| | 3 | Eliphaz | Job | Bildad | Job | Zophar | Job |

First speech cycle: 4-5 | 6-7 | 8 | 9-10 | 11 | 12-14

Second speech cycle: 15 | 16-17 | 18 | 19 | 20 | 21

Third speech cycle: 22 | 23 | 24-27 fragmentary

28

29-31

38-41 — The divine discourses

40:3-5; 42:2-6 — Job's answer

42:7-17

Narrative
framework

A. THE NARRATIVE

The narrative is so simple and direct that it does not need any special biblical exposition.

B. THE DIALOGUE BETWEEN JOB AND HIS FRIENDS (Job 3-31)

1. The speeches of Job

a. The laments

The traditional forms of the personal lament, as known from the Psalms, furnish the structural elements of Job's laments in chs. 3, 29-31 and in the successive speeches. The lament begins in ch. 3 with Job's cursing the day of his birth. This is the harshest form of the lament, and his friends at once shrink back from it, reprimanding him now rather than consoling him. The lament continues under the three aspects known from the psalms: personal lament, lament concerning one's enemy,* and indictment against God.

(1) Lament concerning the enemy

Lament concerning one's enemy is much less evident in the discourses of Job. In its place is his controversy with his friends, appearing at times at the beginning of his speeches. In the first speech (6:13-27) there is a detailed statement that his friends have failed him. He uses the illustration of a deceitful brook (i.e., a dried-up river bed). In 19:13-19 this complaint is extended to include all his associates. They have all turned away from him. In the final lament (30:1-15) Job considers himself at last completely abandoned and despised. To him God's seeming hostility is even worse. At the height of his complaint in 16:9-14 and 19:7-12 Job draws up an indictment against God in the form and language of a hostile accusation.

(2) Personal lament

It is surprising that complaint concerning illness assumes such a minor role in Job's discourses. It is only in 7:3-5 and in the final lament (30:17-30) that it is expressly mentioned. (Perhaps 19:20, 27c should be added.) In the beginning of ch. 6 (vv. 1-12) Job describes rather the gravity of his suffering (vv. 2-3a), its reality (vv. 5-7), its intolerability (vv. 11-12). In 7:1-10 his suffering (vv. 3-5) is extended to include the hopelessness of human existence and especially the way it tends toward death. Already in ch. 3 too this extension is evident, and the theme is picked up in the subsequent discourses. Thus 9:25-31 is another complaint concerning life's brevity. With it Job's second discourse concludes (10:18-22). In the third discourse (14:1-15) this complaint is dominant. Verses 1-5 deal more with the external aspect, i.e., the transitory character of life; vv. 7-12 with the inner aspect, i.e., its hopelessness. This section (14:1 ff.) is especially impressive from a poetic standpoint.

(3) Accusation against God

Already at the time Job curses the day of birth, this charge is

---

*In the course of the dialogue the friends of Job become his enemies.

lodged. It is put into words at the close of ch. 3: "God has hedged me in" (v. 23). And in the first discourse Job justifies his words of despair with the comment: "The arrows of the Almighty are in me; my spirit drinks their poison . . . " (6:4). In 7:11-21 this theme is developed. Verses 12-16 are declarative statements essentially; vv. 17-21 questions. The two primary forms of complaint against God in the Psalms are also declarations and questions (Why? How long?).

In Job's second discourse (chs. 9-10) the accusation against God is dominant. It erupts in bitter sarcasm in 9:17-23, the way for it having been prepared by Job's concurrence with Bildad that a man can never be just before God (vv. 2-3, again alluded to in vv. 14-16). He declares that God is like a raging tempest that seizes a man and crushes him. Indeed God permits might to take the place of justice. In vain Job had maintained his innocence before him (v. 21 f.). The imagery of v. 17 is further exaggerated into the satire of a raging demon in v. 23. In ch. 10 the accusation terminates in a question as to why: "Why, O God, do you oppress me? Why do you despise the work of your hands?" The contradiction implicit in these questions is broadly developed in vv. 8-12. With it praise of the Creator borders closely on accusation. At the conclusion the accusation is intensified in the imagery that depicts God as hostile. In the questions concerning why (vv. 18-19) his complaint then reverts once more to its starting point—"Why was I born?" There is here a span, extending from ch. 3 to the end of ch. 10.

After the third discourse (chs. 12-14) the accusation reaches a climax in ch. 9 that is never again surpassed. It is replaced by a formal legal dispute with God. In 13:23-27 Job questions God concerning the legal basis of his action against him. The different points of the accusation, raised by Job in the preceding speeches, are here concentrated and summarized as in a bill of indictment. With this the charge against God is terminated (at the end of the first speech cycle).

The fourth and fifth discourses of Job contain in place of this the complaint lodged against God as an enemy (16:9-14; 19:7-12). Since God did not respond to Job's questions in 13:23-27, Job must now assume that he has become his enemy (19:6, 11, 21 f.). Here

at the close the same metaphor appears as at the beginning (3:23)
—God has blocked the way of the one who is complaining (19:8).

b. Wishes and petitions

Several other features in Job's discourses are included in his lament, viz., wishes and petitions. As every lament shows a tendency
toward petition, so the laments of Job lead on to prayers or long-
ings, which (in the order of their occurrence) manifest quite clearly the progression in Job's speeches. Three series of such petitions
and desires correspond to the three divisions of the discourse
section.

(1) The desire of Job to die (3:11-13, 21 f.; 6:8-10; 7:15 and
an echo in 10:18 f.) issues immediately out of the cry at the beginning. It is the desire of one who cannot hold out any longer. Apparent at the same time is a gradual decrease from the longing implied in the outcry of ch. 3 to that which is but an echo in 10:18 f.
After this it never appears again.

(2) The wish (or petition): "Let me alone!" (7:16b; 10:20 f.;
14:6; 13-15; 9:34 f.; 13:21 f.) extends through all three speeches
of the first cycle. This also is as yet a quite elementary petition,
arising out of the most extreme affliction. This wish often occurs together with a lament concerning the transitory character of life. In
9:34 f. and 13:21 f. this wish leads to a third desire, viz., to meet God.

(3) In the second cycle of speeches the desire of Job as expressed
in his third and fourth discourses is the same. Job thus pleads that
his case may be heard and an answer found in spite of his death
(16:18-22; 17:3; 19:23 f.). In both passages this desire is combined
with a confession of trust. In the seventh and last discourse of Job,
the one desire to meet God still remains (23:3-12). The speech
begins immediately with it: "O that I knew where I might find him!"
(v. 3). It is preceded by Eliphaz' wholesale denunciation (ch. 22).
Job no longer responds to it. He can now turn only to God in order
to place his cause before him. Only at the end is this desire again
picked up in the final words of the concluding lament (31:35-37).

Against the demand of his friends that he confess his sin Job
protests his innocence. To begin with he asserts his innocence in

the presence of his friends (6:28-30; cf. 19:6). But already in the second discourse Job turns to a higher court: "I am innocent!" (9:21; cf. 9:29-31; 10:6). Out of the despairing cry comes a resolve in the third discourse: "I will defend my ways to his face" (13:15 f., 18, 23). To this is added a similar comment in 23:7, 10, 12 in Job's final speech. Here it is linked with the desire to stand in God's presence. Both together constitute the conclusion of Job's lament in ch. 31. The grand oath concerning his innocence, together with his desire to appear before God, comes at the end.

c. Confession of trust

A confession of trust occurs only in two passages, in both instances, however, at a high point, when the accusation against God assumes the form of a complaint concerning the enemy. This is in the first two speeches of the second cycle (16:19-21 and 19:25-27). In 16:19 ff., it is combined with a cry of despair: "O earth, cover not my blood!" The only thing that still remains for him now is the court of justice beyond death. Thus he must appeal to God against God—"that he would maintain the right of a man [in a contest] with God" (16:21), and he knows "even now my witness is in heaven, and he that vouches for me is on high" (16:19).

In ch. 19 the confession of confidence occurs in the same context. Corresponding to 16:19 is 19:25-27: "But I know my attorney lives and an advocate will arise for me beyond the dust . . . I will see God and my eyes will behold one who is no longer unknown."* Job expects the benefit of justice *despite* the judgment of death, *contrary* to his own death. The concept of a life after death is not meant here. Job expresses rather the certainty that even though he must die he will still receive justice from God.

2. The arguments of the friends

Over against the laments of Job are the arguments of his friends, who over and over again advance one basic argument:

---

*Translator's Note: The meaning of these verses is obscure in the Hebrew. The above is based on the German rendering of these verses. Cf. R.S.V. "For I know that my Redeemer lives, and at last he will stand upon the earth . . . then without my flesh I shall see God, whom I shall see on my side, and my eyes shall behold and not another."

transgressors will perish. In the first two speech cycles this is found in all six discourses of the friends. Each of them emphasizes in this way the authority lying behind his address. Thus Eliphaz appeals to his own experience; Bildad to the tradition of the fathers. Zophar wants God himself to speak to Job.

In all three discourses of the second cycle the fate of the wicked is the only argument, now continued along two lines: the whole life of the transgressor is on display (e.g., 15:20), and a reason for the fate of the transgressor is provided. Thus Eliphaz maintains that Job has rebelled against God (15:25-28); Bildad declares that he has set snares for the righteous (18:7-8); Zophar makes a similar charge (20:19-21). In each of the three discourses of the second cycle one of the three gifts that survive death is singled out: the blessing of progeny (15:29-33), abode (18:5-6, 14 f., 21), and possessions (20:12-18).

Matching the theme concerning the fate of transgressors is one which concerns the prosperity of the godly. In the first cycle of speeches each of the three friends alludes to it. In the second cycle it is entirely lacking, although it occurs once more in the final discourse of Eliphaz. As a third argument the statement is added that no man is righteous before God (4:12-21; 15:14-16; 25:4-6). Job agrees definitely with this (9:2).

Otherwise Job does not argue like his friends. Only once in his final address (ch. 21) does he offer a counter-argument. Thus he picks up what his friends say concerning the fate of the wicked and carries it a little farther, calling in question the view that the end of the transgressor may necessarily be always a dreadful one. He finds support for this simply in experience and says to his friends: "Your theory does not agree with actual fact." Job realizes how dangerous his comments here are (vv. 5-6), and it is understandable that they are followed by a sweeping condemnation of Job by his friends (ch. 22).

3. Divine praise in the discourses of Job and his friends

All sections of the Book of Job include words in praise of God. It is by design that portions containing divine praise occur almost without exception in the first cycle of speeches—in the case of Job as well as his friends. In the second cycle it is entirely lacking on both sides.

In the first cycle of speeches Job and his friends still have something in common in that they both extol God. That they both can give assent to God in their praise is still a common basis on which they stand. The increasing bitterness of their dialogue is indicated by the way divine eulogy disappears in the second speech cycle.

The development of divine eulogy is the same as in the Psalms. Praise concerning God's majesty pours forth in adulation of the Creator (chs. 9-10) and the Lord of history (ch. 12). The same motifs are found also in the discourses of Job's friends. The artistry of the poet is revealed by the different ways in which the same motifs of divine praise appear in the speeches of Job and his friends.

C. THE DIVINE DISCOURSES (Job 38-41)

Job terminates his final lament by demanding a hearing (31:35-37). Behind this request is the desire that God may really answer him. Job gets this wish fulfilled. God answers him (38:1; 40:1, 6). The reply indeed does not contain either an indictment, imposing a penalty (31:35), or the exoneration that Job has eagerly anticipated (16:19-21; 19:25). But God does answer him, even though the meaning behind this answer remains hidden. The One who was challenged by Job speaks as the Challenger, asking Job himself: "Who are you? Are you the Creator?" These questions are amplified in an indirect praise of the Creator.

1. God created the world (38:4-15)

2. God alone knows and keeps an eye on his creation (38:16-24)

3. God guides and rules over his creation (38:25—41:34)

    (a) In the heavens—in the case of constellations and precipitation (38:25-38)

    (b) On earth—in relation to animals (38:39—41:34)
    Within this passage is included a description of God as the Lord of history:

        (1) The resumption of Job's challenge (40:6-7)

        (2) The Judge of the world (40:8-10)

        (3) He brings the mighty to ruin (40:11-14)

    (4) Behemoth (40:15-24)

    (5) Leviathan (41:1-34)*

God's activity in creation is here portrayed so comprehensively as in no other passage in the Bible. It has obviously two sides: his majestic reign (e.g. 38:8-11) and his loving care (especially in his conduct toward animals, 38:39—39:30). In this description the contrasting character of God's majesty and goodness are merged in praise of the Creator. When God is extolled these as a rule stand side by side. It is in this way also that the significance of God's reply to Job is indicated.

The original conclusion of God's address was probably 41:10-11, which refers at the outset to Job's question: "Who has hardened himself against him and succeeded?" (9:4). In response to this demand (31:35-37) God, as conceived by Job, has to demolish him. The divine discourses, however, leave Job unhurt. They put him again in his proper place—the place of creature who must bow before his Creator (42:6); and they thus tacitly indicate at the same time the benevolence of the Creator, who shows mercy to his creation. Job's answers (40:3-5 and 42:1-6) indicate that he understood God's speeches in this way.

D. THE SPEECHES OF ELIHU (Job 32-37)

These are a later expansion of the Book of Job, an insertion that clearly contains an opinion as to the solution of the Book of Job. Job does not express himself at all here. He is rather the subject of the discourse. This is evident in ch. 34, where his case is discussed before a group of wise men, and he is condemned as a transgressor

---

*Translator's Note: In his monograph on the literary structure of Job (Westermann, C., *Der Aufbau des Buches Hiob,* Tübingen, 1956) the author has the following comment concerning the present position of the detailed description of Behemoth and Leviathan, which follows rather loosely upon 40:6-14: "It is possible that the poet himself may have purposely inserted the description of Behemoth and Leviathan at this point as a cryptic amplification of the theme—"God, the Lord of history." This would then signify that both animals are here to personify the powers of history. They symbolize the great powers as the author of the Book of Job perceived and understood them to be" (p. 87). Job is thus implying in veiled language that God is also Lord over these powers.

(34:7-8, 34-37). The friends, however, were also reproved "because they had found no answer and had thus put God in the wrong" (32:3).* This is not correct, inasmuch as the final words of Job's friends contain a clear indictment of Job (ch. 22).

The speeches of Elihu perceive the solution in the disciplinary significance of suffering. Since Job did not accept this divine chastening he was condemned. Elihu's speeches disregard the real despair and anguish of Job with a judgmental indifference that is shocking. They were intended, however, in this very way to be a passionate apology for God.

---

*Translator's Note: R.S.V. has "although they had declared Job to be in the wrong." The Hebrew originally had "they had thus put God in the wrong," a reading which the author has adopted. Cf. *The OT, an American translation,* by J. P. Smith *et al.*: "And against his three friends his wrath blazed, because they found no answer, and so had put God in the wrong."

XX

The Proverbs

It is almost impossible to provide biblical helps that will lay bare the content of the Book of Proverbs. This is not even necessary, for we do not need to know or examine the enormous quantity and variety of individual proverbs. It is enough to glance here at the primary forms and principal themes of proverbial wisdom.

A. THE ARRANGEMENT OF PROVERBS

The way in which the Book of Proverbs is arranged indicates clearly the two basic forms of wisdom: poems (chs. 1-9) and epigrams (chs. 10-31).

1. The wisdom poems (Prov. 1-9)

Chs. 1-9 contain poems, generally advocating wisdom or else admonishing or inviting us to seek it.

    a. The significance of a book of wisdom (1:1-6)
    b. Wisdom which comes from fear of God (1:7)
    c. Warning against the temptations of the wicked (1:8-19)
    d. Wisdom's sermon on repentance (1:20-33)
    e. The admonition of a father to his son (2:1-22)
    f. The recommendation concerning wisdom and piety (3:1-35)
    g. Wisdom's farewell blessing (4:1-27)
    h. Wisdom's cry at the city gate (8:1-36)
    i. Dame Wisdom and Dame Folly issue their dinner invitations (9:1-18)
    j. Warning against a loose woman* and adultery (5:1—7:27)

---

*Translator's Note: The original Hebrew has *zārāh* "strange woman" (cf. A.V.), which R.S.V. has rendered "loose woman." The reference is apparently not to foreign prostitutes but to women of loose character who have left their husbands (Cf. Prov. 2:17 ff.).

2. The proverbs of wisdom (Prov. 10-31)

The real Book of Proverbs, which begins in ch. 10, contains two basic collections:

    a. The proverbs of Solomon (10:1—22:16)
    b. The proverbs of the men of Hezekiah (25:1—29:27)

There is in addition a series of appendices to these two primary collections, as follows:

    c. The words of the wise (22:17—24:22)   }   added to chs.
    d. Also these sayings of the wise (24:23-34)   10-22

    e. The words of Agur (30:1-14)
    f. Numerical proverbs (30:15-33)   added to chs.
    g. The words of Lemuel (31:1-9)   25-29
    h. Praise of a capable housewife (31:10-31)

B. THE FORM AND CHARACTER OF A PROVERB

The formal structure of a proverb is very simple. It usually consists of a distich of parallel lines, sometimes in a series of two or on rare occasions three distichs. From this point on it already has developed into a wisdom poem.

There are three principal forms:
    1. A simple assertion
    2. An antithetical statement
    3. A maxim expressed in the form of an imperative

Sometimes there is also a question together with an answer, indicating a riddle.

The wisdom proverb is really the oldest and simplest literary form. Knowledge or discernment, which for us today has illimitable ramifications, is presented here in its first stage. This is a wisdom developing as yet within the life of a community and presented in a simple proverbial form. It is a wisdom that is more practical than worldly, embracing all areas of being and accumulating experiences that have become mellowed therein.

C. THE PRINCIPAL THEMES OF PROVERBIAL WISDOM

The proverbs in the above-mentioned collections give no evidence of having been arranged according to subject matter (except possibly in only a few passages). They must therefore be classed according to areas treated by them, as follows:

1. Human existence

a. Observation and comparison

The simplest proverbial form is that of the declarative sentence. It may involve a simple observation in which is portrayed some discovery concerning man himself or his environment, animals, plants, fellow-men. Under observation come comparisons in which similarities and differences are portrayed and hidden associations discerned. Such observations, for example, are grouped together in the numerical proverbs of ch. 30. Verses 24-28 are the result of long attentive observation of animals. In vv. 18-19 the noting of various ways of behavior leads to a presentation of the concept of movement.

In the abundance of comparisons (especially in chs. 25-26) the prototype of the parable, which played such an important role in the teaching of Jesus, may be seen.

b. Observations concerning mankind

Reflection and wonder concerning human existence is reflected in these words:

> The spirit of man is the lamp of the Lord,
>   searching all his innermost parts (20:27).
> As one face alongside another face,
>   so differ the hearts of men (27:19).*
> A man without self-control is like a city broken
>   into and left without walls (25:28).

c. Words and deeds

The proverbs reflect on human utterances, their healing as well as their destructive effect. This is developed quite concretely. The prov-

---

*Translator's Note: This is a rendering of the German, which is based on the Septuagint rendering of the verse. The R.S.V., following the Hebrew quite literally, has: "As in water face answers face, so the mind of man reflects the man."

erbs are aware of wholesome and healing words as well as patho-
logical and injurious words. They wonder at the power of human
language for good and evil.

> A word fitly spoken
>> is like apples of gold in a setting of silver (25:11).
> There is one whose rash words are like sword thrusts (12:18).

The proverbs speak of good behavior, doing good, helping, pro-
moting peace. They concern themselves, however, more frequently
with the many possibilities of doing evil, as they expose, warn,
reprove:

> The way of the guilty is crooked,
>> but the conduct of the pure is right (21:8).*
> The beginning of strife is like letting out water (17:14).

2. Man in community

These proverbs have to do with friend and foe, with people according to their rank, with the young and the old, women, slaves,
even with table manners.

> A friend loves at all times,
>> and a brother is born for adversity (17:17).
> When your enemy hungers,
>> give him bread to eat (25:21).

Quarrelsome and dissolute women are denounced (27:15; 11:22).
At the same time there is praise of a capable housewife in ch. 31, a
poem with which no other in all antiquity can be compared.

Young people are frequently admonished to respect old people
(13:1; 19:26; 20:20). Children, however, also receive their just
claim in the comments about upbringing.

Section 22:17—23:11, which includes rules of table etiquette, corresponds closely to a section from the Egyptian book of wisdom,
entilted, "The Instruction of Amenemope." This book was discov-
ered in 1888.

---

*Translator's Note: The author has suggested this substitution for the passage
in the German text: "Behold, how good and pleasant it is when brothers dwell
in unity" (Ps. 133:1).

Israel learned a great deal from other people, especially in questions pertaining to cultural matters, as the superscription, "The words of Agur of Massa" (30:1) perhaps also indicates.

It is evident from the large number of proverbs dealing with slaves that there was a humane attitude manifested toward them.

3. Labor and property

A group of proverbs has something to say in regard to work and possessions—concerning the farmer, his cattle and land. They praise men who are industrious, ridicule those who are lazy, contrasting the poor and the rich. A life of simplicity is recommended as opposed to all striving after illicit gain. Spontaneous and sincere generosity, alleviation of want and need are a part of this simple and upright way of life.

> A worker's appetite works for him;
> his mouth urges him on (16:26).

> As a door turns on its hinges,
> so does a sluggard on his bed (26:14).

> Better is a little with the fear of the Lord
> than great treasure and trouble with it.
> Better is a dinner of herbs where love is
> than a fatted ox and hatred with it (15:16-17).

> Happy is he who is kind to the poor (14:21b).

4. People in public life

This is a more marginal sphere of proverbial wisdom. Legal conduct indeed was still so much a part of life in general that it too was frequently reflected upon in the proverbs. Injustice is sharply condemned along with partiality and any kind of bribery. There is a warning against unfounded and premature accusation (24:28; 25:7 f.); for false and deceitful testimony is the most serious threat to a community (12:17; 14:5; 19:28).

As far as the proverbs were concerned, the state was still embodied completely in the monarchy. Thus there is a group of proverbs pertaining to kings. A democratic element, however, is not lacking. The advice in general is directed toward the welfare of the public (11:14).

> He who justifies the wicked
>> and he who condemns the righteous
>> are both alike an abomination to the Lord (17:15).

> Like a roaring lion or a charging bear
>> is a wicked ruler over a poor people (28:15).

5. Wisdom and folly, education leading to wisdom

The praise of wisdom extends throughout the Book of Proverbs: "Happy is the man who finds wisdom . . . " (3:13-15). It comes from God (2:6) and is the first fruits of his creation (8:22-31). It makes men able to speak and listen (16:21; 18:15). It is "appreciation for existence." "The wisdom of a prudent man is to discern his way" (14:8). It is a source of life and good fortune (13:14; 19:8) and has an effect also on one's neighbor: "The lips of the wise feed many" (10:21).

Prudence is a part of wisdom. It is the wise man's demeanor. He exercises moderation and is able to control himself (14:17; 16:32).

Folly is not merely stupidity but an attitude toward life. Its principal characteristic is thoughtlessness (25:28). The fool is a windbag, unable to control himself. He flies into a blind rage (19:2) and does not know how to exercise moderation (17:24).

> Folly is the chastisement of fools (16:22).

> Everyone who is arrogant is an abomination to the Lord (16:5).

There is a warning sounded against the fool and an announcement that the proud will fall.

Especially frequent is the way in which wisdom and folly are contrasted. There are 52 proverbs containing such a contrast, 39 of which are in chs. 10-15. The nature of wisdom and folly is differentiated (15:14), with praise reserved for wisdom, reproach for folly (14:27). The consequences of both are portrayed (12:19).

A good deal of space is devoted to an exhortation to wisdom, especially in the poems of chs. 1-9. One can cultivate it. It is amazing how many proverbs deal with upbringing. Fostering of wisdom is shown to be of great significance for one's whole life. Fostering here implies chastisement and reproof (29:15), although there seems to be a tendency to put the word above the paddle:

A rebuke goes deeper into a man of understanding than a hundred blows into a fool (17:10).

There are even proverbs which manifest a careful study of the child, his nature and his needs (20:11; 22:6). The goal of education is a wise son, in whom parents may take delight (10:1; 13:1; 15:20).

6. The righteous and the wicked

The largest group of proverbs (about 85) deal with the righteous and the wicked. The contrast between them is concerned frequently with that of the wise and the foolish, but it refers more pointedly to the relationship with God (as in Ps. 1).

The godly man is mindful of that which is good (11:27). He shuns evil (13:5) and rejoices in the right (21:15). His words are choice silver (10:20). He walks in uprightness, fearing God (14:2). He is concerned about the rights of the poor (29:7). He gives sound advice (12:20) and has regard for animals (12:10). The wicked are depicted as the opposite of the godly in all this. This does not need any further amplification.

Matching this is a description of the fate of the godly man and the transgressor, a theme of many proverbs. The righteous flourish like a green leaf (11:28; 14:11). The light of the righteous rejoices; the lamp of the wicked will be put out (13:9). They will be overthrown and destroyed (10:9; 11:5).

7. Mankind and God

The first part of the Book of Proverbs begins (1:7) and ends (9:10) with an admonition to fear God. This recurs repeatedly (1:29; 2:5; 3:7; 8:13; 16:6). Quite similar is the summons to trust (3:5; 18:10; 16:20; 3:23-26). Fear of God and trust are here two aspects of the same attitude.

There is seldom any reference in the proverbs to worship, sacrifice, or prayer. God and his actions are certainly mentioned, however. Words in praise of God occur (15:3, 11; 17:3; 21:30). In all the delight over the capacity to understand there is not meanwhile a forgetfulness of the Creator in this.

> The hearing ear and the seeing eye,
> The Lord has made them both (20:12).

The boundary of all human planning and activity lies within the activity of God (19:21; 20:24; 10:22; 16:33).

The Book of Proverbs is full of contrasts. In an incomprehensible way God is beyond their sphere (22:2; 29:13), corresponding to the statement from the Sermon on the Mount:

> For he makes his sun rise on the evil and the good,
> and sends rain on the just and the unjust (Matt. 5:45).

At the end of Proverbs is a comment, hinting vaguely at the problem which even wisdom as a whole fails to solve:

> The man says, "I am wearied over God.
> I am wearied over God and am at an end" (30:1).*

And the final comment is: "What is his name, and what is his son's name?" (30:4).

---

*Translator's Note: This rendering is based on the German of the Zurich Bible, followed here by the author. Cf. Moffatt's similar version: "The cry of the man weary with the quest for God: 'I am weary, O God, weary and worn in vain.'" The R.S.V. has simply transliterated the obscure Hebrew terms: "The man says to Ithiel, to Ithiel and Ucal."

XXI

The Megilloth

The Megilloth are five rather brief writings, quite diverse in content. They have one thing in common, however, in that they were each read publicly at one of the great annual Jewish festivals: the book of Ruth at the Feast of Weeks (Pentecost), the Song of Solomon at the Passover festival, Ecclesiastes at Feast of Tabernacles, Lamentations at the commemoration of the destruction of Jerusalem in 587 B.C. (the ninth of Ab), the Book of Esther at the Purim festival. *Megilloth* is a Hebrew word meaning "scrolls."

THE BOOK OF RUTH

The Book of Ruth is a short story whose setting is in the period of the judges. It endeavors to explain how a Moabite woman came to be an ancestress of king David. The whole account is imbued with the conviction that God was the one who had prepared the way for Ruth, the Moabitess, so that she came to Judah from her homeland with the mother of her dead husband. God had ordained that she there become the wife of Boaz, David's ancestor.

Like Gen. 24 it is also a story of guidance, taking important strands from the history of God with his people and lovingly weaving them into an account of simple, everyday happenings. Thus in the common, ordinary events reported in the Book of Ruth, God had prepared that which he wanted to grant his people in the anointed one—king David. The plan of the book is as follows:

1. Introduction: famine and the journey abroad (1:1-5)
2. The return home with Ruth (1:6-22)
3. The gleaning and meeting in the field of Boaz (2:1-22)
4. On the threshing floor of Boaz (3:1-18)
5. The conclusion, the marriage, and the birth of the child (4:1-22)

THE SONG OF SOLOMON*

This collection of love songs has gotten into the canon only by means of a reinterpretation. It was understood allegorically, as the love of God for his people; in the Christian church as the love between Christ and his church or even the individual human soul. No book of the Bible has been allegorized in such detail as this one. One exegete says in this regard: "The history of the exegesis of the Song of Songs resembles far more a collection of theological curiosities than a meaningful history."

According to more recent interpretation the book has been understood as a continuous drama or as the reflection of cultic events. The interpretation that corresponds most nearly to the text itself continues to be the one that understands it as a collection of some 25-30 individual songs. As such they are of especial charm and originality, e.g., 2:8-14, which tells of a meeting between the lover and his beloved:

> The voice of my beloved!
> Behold he comes,
> leaping upon the mountains,
> bounding over the hills.
> My beloved is like a gazelle,
> or a young stag.
> Behold, there he stands
> behind our wall,
> gazing in at the windows,
> looking through the lattice.
> My beloved speaks and says to me:
> "Arise, my love, my fair one,
> and come away;
> for lo, the winter is past,
> the rain is over and gone.
> The flowers appear on the earth,
> the time of singing has come,
> and the voice of the turtledove
> is heard in our land.

---

*Translator's Note: The full title of the book, based on the Hebrew, is "The Song of Songs, which is Solomon's." The name for the book in German is "das Hohelied" (the sublime song). This free rendering of the Hebrew, first introduced by Luther, conveys the true meaning of the expression.

The fig tree puts forth its figs,
and the vines are in blossom;
they give forth fragrance.
Arise, my love, my fair one,
and come away. . . ."

The songs can also say much to us today. It is unnecessary to enumerate or classify them for biblical study.

*   *   *   *   *

ECCLESIASTES

This book is definitely on the periphery of the Bible. Its position in the canon was long contested. The New Testament never cites it. No biblical book is dominated by one leading theme as this one. "Vanity of vanities, says the Preacher, vanity of vanities! All is vanity" (1:2). The Hebrew word for "vanity" (*hebel*) occurs twenty-two times in Ecclesiastes and means actually "breath" or everything that is as fleeting as breath. Ps. 39:5, 11, for example, expresses the same idea. The term is used once as a proper name —Abel. At the beginning of the Old Testament there is an allusion to the transitory character of man in this name Abel; at the end, in the leading theme of Ecclesiastes.

The book belongs to the latest writings of the Old Testament. It originated in the second century B.C. The ascription of the book to Solomon implies that he was thought of as the father of wisdom— not as the author of the book. (This is true also of the Proverbs of Solomon and the Song of Solomon.) At the conclusion (12:9 f.) it is expressly stated that the author was a teacher of wisdom.

In this book wisdom suddenly changes into a world view that is skeptical. This skepticism of the Preacher can be rightly understood only as an objection voiced against an optimistic wisdom that thinks it knows all too well God's will as well as the way of the world.

There is no evidence that the book has been arranged systematically. The first part (chs. 1-6) contains predominantly longer poems; the second part (chs. 7-12), primarily simple proverbs and smaller clusters of epigrams.

A. THE POEMS (Eccles. 1-6)

1. The orbit of existence (1:2-11)

Wind and water surrounded by the stars in orbit encompass human existence. "All things are full of weariness" (v. 8), including mankind with his yearning and desire for knowledge. But where is there a limit? "There is nothing new under the sun" (v. 9) and at the end everything lapses into forgetfulness.

2. The spirit of investigation (1:12-18)

In the midst of all this, the human spirit strives to survey and to comprehend. But all this is a "striving after wind." Thus "in much wisdom is much vexation" (v. 18).

3. Testing life's pleasures (2:1-12) and finding satisfaction in resignation (2:13-26)

The poet has tested gross (v. 3) as well as refined intellectual pleasures (vv. 4-10), all to no avail (vv. 11-12). This is true also of the perception of wisdom and folly. He loses faith in everything. But then there is still the limited opportunity for the simple life in which daily bread is received thankfully.

4. Everything has its time (3:1-22)

At the beginning is a mature poem of distinct charm. The wise man of the Old Testament discloses here the temporal horizon of all existence. His glance then extends in a profound manner from this point to God: "God has made it so in order that men should fear before him" (v. 14). The great riddles of history, above all the riddle of injustice in the world (vv. 16-21), are a part of this temporal essence of existence.

5. The oppressed and lonely (4:1-12)

As an example, two grievous destinies in human existence are described: that of the oppressed (vv. 1-6) and that of the lonely (vv. 7-12). As so much in Ecclesiastes, these descriptions come very close to problems of our own time. In vv. 7-12 is one of the few passages in the Bible portraying the distress of lonely people—an existence without security (vv. 9, 10, 12) or warmth (v. 11).

6. A youth and a king (4:13-16)

7. Advice concerning public worship (5:1-7)

As to worship that is developing into mere activity and routine, the Preacher calls attention to one thing that is necessary: "But do you fear God" (v. 7). In other respects he advises reserve in matters pertaining to organized religion *(Institutionen)*. He warns against being too talkative (v. 2, cf. Matt. 6:7). He cautions against rash vows and idle gossip (vv. 4-7).

8. The poor man and his king (5:8-9)

9. The rich man and his wealth (5:10—6:12)

The rich man fails to find the very things for which he slaves and is envious. He does not really become satisfied, nor do his riches alter the fact that he must die.

B. PROVERBS AND EPIGRAMS (Eccles. 7-12)

The moribund state of existence, the futility of human endeavor to prevail over this condition, the frailty of human potentialities—all of this is portrayed here in the most somber hues, often with a slight tinge of grim humor. "Sorrow is better than laughter, for by sadness of countenance the heart is made glad" (7:3).

In the series of proverbs (7:1-8) that express an evaluation, beginning with the statement: "It is better . . . than," one can immediately perceive a typical example of pessimism.

In 9:1-2 one is reminded of the medieval dances of death. Again and again the fate of death is affirmed. Here fixed in reflexion is the somber emphasis of the psalms of lament, with which indeed also the lament concerning life's brevity is associated. The divine reply, anticipated by the laments in the Psalter, is no longer heard, and the Preacher waits forlorn in a stupefying world which he can no longer understand.

> That which is, is far off, and deep, very deep;
> who can find it out? (7:24).

And he can no longer understand God:

> Consider the work of God;
>   who can make straight what he has made crooked? (7:13).

An epoch of appeal and inquiry after God comes here to an end, replaced by the skepticism of the Preacher, crying out for a solution, for a change. He was not able as yet to renounce God, however. Laboriously he struggled through to a word such as this:

> Behold, this alone I found,
> that God made man upright,
> but they have sought out many devices (7:29).

This word extends even to the evening hymn of Matthaeus Claudius:

> Our airy cobwebs spinning
>   With erring and with sinning
> Far from the mark we stray.

*   *   *   *   *

THE LAMENTATIONS OF JEREMIAH

These five songs of lamentations arose after the destruction of Jerusalem (587 B.C.) and were sung during the ceremonies of lamentation that were observed by the remnant of those who remained in Judea. In the Hebrew Bible they are found in the Hagiographa under the title "Woe" *('ekāh).* * In the Septuagint, however, the songs were added to the Book of Jeremiah under the title "The Lamentations of Jeremiah."

The style of a dirge has been combined in a remarkable way with that of a lament in these songs. The death of Jerusalem is being mourned. Yet in spite of everything the people turn hopefully to God, anticipating something new when his wrath is turned away.

Songs 1, 2, and 4 begin with the woe of a funeral song, describing the misery at hand in contrast to what has passed.

---

*Translator's Note: "How" would be a more literal rendering of the Hebrew term *'ekāh.* It is an exclamation often used in lamentation (e.g., Isa. 1:21; Jer. 48:18; Lam. 1:1; 2:1; 4:1, 2).

A. THE FIRST SONG

This begins with a picture of a sorrowing widow.

1. Zion has become a widow. Forsaken by everyone, she is weeping (1:1-2)
2. Zion is laid waste; Judah is in exile. The enemies have robbed and plundered her. God has delivered up Judah to her sins (1:3-19)
3. A supplication for God's favor (1:20-22)

B. THE SECOND SONG

1. God has vented his wrath upon Zion and laid her in ruins (2:1-8)
2. The city is destroyed and has lost everything of value (2:9-13)
3. Her prophets prophesy falsely (2:14)
4. Her enemies triumph (2:15-17)
5. A summons to lamentation and a prayer to God (2:18-22)

C. THE THIRD SONG

1. God has afflicted me dreadfully (3:1-20)
2. A confession of confidence. A promise for those who trust (3:21-33)
3. An exhortation to return (3:34-41)
4. A fragment of a national lament (3:42-48, 51, 49 f.) *
5. A song of praise of one who had been saved (3:52-58)
6. A fragment of a personal lament (3:59-66)

D. THE FOURTH SONG

1. A lament concerning the sons of Zion (4:1-12)
2. The guilt and fate of the priests and prophets (4:13-16)
3. The conquest and fate of the king (4:17-20)
4. A final wish. Edom and Zion (4:21-22)

---

*Translator's Note: According to the author, in a communication from him, v. 51 should follow v. 48, as noted above.

E. THE FIFTH SONG

1. An introductory petition (5:1)
2. The lament of the defeated (5:2-18)
3. A glance at Yahweh (5:19)
4. Petition and inquiry (5:20-22)

The Book of Lamentations is a witness to the way in which the people submitted to the divine judgment carried out during the destruction of the land and city. It testifies to the fact that the prophets of judgment had really uttered God's word and that the false prophets had led Israel astray (4:13-16). Extending as a dominant theme throughout the songs is the confession of sin (1:5, 8 f., 14, 18, 20 f.; 2:14; 3:42; 4:6, 13-15; 5:7, 16) and the approval of God's judgment (1:14, 18; 2:17; 3:42; 4:11-16; 5:19). In these bitter laments a way has been found leading out of the devastation into the compassion of God, who again turns toward his people.

✳ ✳ ✳ ✳ ✳

THE BOOK OF ESTHER

The Book of Esther as the last of the five Megilloth was the text read for the festival of Purim,* whose origin it substantiates. It provides information concerning one of the severe persecutions threatening the Jews in the Persian empire, a persecution that was prevented at the last moment by the wise and beautiful queen Esther, whom King Ahasuerus (= Xerxes) had chosen as his consort. Haman, the king's favorite, who had initiated this pogrom, was executed, Mordecai, the guardian of Esther, taking his place. At the command of the king the Jews were permitted to take revenge on their adversaries. Thus 800 of the Jews' enemies were killed in Susa and 75,000 in the province of the empire.** To commemorate this deliverance, the feast of Purim was established.

---

*Based on the Akkadian word *pur,* meaning "lot."
**According to the Septuagint it was 15,000.

The book may be outlined, as follows:

1. The queen (Vashti) is divorced; Esther becomes queen (1:1—2:23)
2. Haman plots a pogrom against the Jews (3:1-14)
3. Mordecai's plan of rescue (4:1-17)
4. Esther makes preparation for the deliverance (5:1-14)
5. The honoring of Mordecai and the downfall of Haman (6:1—7:10)
6. Esther succeeds in preventing the persecution of the Jews (8:1-17)
7. The vengeance of the Jews on their adversaries. The day of the festival (9:1-19).
8. A supplement concerning the establishment of the feast of Purim (9:20—10:3)

The Book of Esther has come into the canon as a festival legend in connection with the feast of Purim. Its place in the canon has long been contested; even Luther rejected it vehemently. It can have no validity as a historical account* nor be retained uncritically in the Christian church. There is no reference to God in the entire book.

It should be understood in the light of a time of heavy oppression (not in the Persian period but in the time of the Diadochi, the successors to Alexander the Great). The desire for revenge on one's enemies may be heard frequently enough in the Psalms. There, however, the vengeance was expected at the hands of God. In this instance, it was assumed by men themselves.

---

*There is no historical record of Persian queens by the name of Vashti or Esther.

XXII

The Work of the Chronicler

Originally the work of the Chronicler was one book, consisting of two parts: the chronicle from David (Adam) up to the exile (1 and 2 Chr.) and the chronicle concerning the post-exilic period, from the first return up to Ezra's reform (Ezra and Neh.). To begin with, only the second section (Ezra and Neh.) was adopted into the canon; the first section 1 and 2 Chr. was then added. In the Hebrew Bible Ezra-Nehemiah therefore precedes Chronicles.

The work of the Chronicler belongs to the third division of the Hebrew canon called the Writings,* because it presents the history from viewpoints that are quite definitely devotional. It is a pious reflection on history rather than a historical account. It is important to bear this in mind in connection with the many details in which the Chronicler's exposition differs from that of the older history. The most important of these divergencies are indicated by the structure:

From Adam to Saul (1 Chron. 1-9)

David (1 Chron. 10-29)

Solomon (2 Chron. 1-9)

From the death of Solomon to the exile (2 Chron. 10-36)

A. THE CHRONICLE FROM DAVID TO THE EXILE
(1 and 2 Chron.)

1. From Adam to Saul (1 Chron. 1:1—9:44)

a. From Adam to the sons of Jacob (1:1—2:2)

---

*It was added only later to the historical books, as in our present Bible.

    b. Judah (David's family in ch. 3) and Simeon (2:3—4:43)
    c. Reuben, Gad, eastern Manasseh (5:1-26)
    d. Levi (6:1-81)
    e. The rest of the tribes (7:1—8:40)
    f. Lists of the Jerusalem families (9:1-44)

2. David (1 Chron. 10:1—29:30)

    a. The death of Saul (10:1-14)
    b. The kingship of David (11:1—21:30)
    c. The preparation for the building of the temple (22:1—29:30)
        (1) Advance preparations and the charge to Solomon (22:1-19)
        (2) The organization of the priests and the Levites (23:1—26:32)
        (3) The officials and the commanders of the army (27:1-34)
        (4) Solomon is presented as a successor and commissioned to build the temple (28:1—29:30)

3. Solomon (2 Chron. 1:1—9:31)

    a. The sacrifice and the appearance of God at Gibeon (1:1-17)
    b. The building of the temple and the transfer of the ark (2:1—5:14)
    c. The dedication of the temple (6:1—7:22)
    d. Solomon's rule (8:1—9:31)

4. From the death of Solomon to the exile (2 Chron. 10:1—36:23)

    a. Division of the kingdom. Rehoboam, Abijah, Asa, Jehoshaphat (10:1—20:37)
    b. Jehoram, Ahaziah, Athaliah, Jehoash, Amaziah (21:1—25:28)
    c. Uzziah, Jotham, Ahaz, Hezekiah (26:1—32:25)
    d. Manasseh, Amon, Josiah (33:1—35:27)
    e. Jehoahaz, Jehoiakim, Jehoiachin, Zedekiah (36:1-21)
    f. The edict of Cyrus (36:22-23)

    The first section of the four-part work consists only of genealogies, proceeding from Adam to the sons of Jacob, then continuing on to the tribes. The actual historical record does not begin until the death of Saul. There is no account of the deliverance from

Egypt, by which the nation was established, nor the wandering in the wilderness, nor the occupation of Palestine.

On the other hand, the kingship of David and Solomon stands unequivocally at the heart of the work in sections two and three. And at the center of this again is the account of the building of the temple and the establishment of the temple services. The focal point in Israel's history is thereby shifted from the act of deliverance at the time of the exodus to the inauguration of the temple worship.

After the death of Solomon, the Chronicler presents only the history of the Southern Kingdom. He does not consider the Northern Kingdom as belonging any longer to the people of God, after its separation from the Davidic kingship, which alone was legitimate. He gives information about it only as is necessary for the presentation of Judah's history. He does not, however, even mention the downfall of the Northern Kingdom. This radical depreciation of northern Israel is probably connected with a definite bias in the Chronicler's work. It intends to prove the legitimacy of the Davidic kingship and the temple cult in Jerusalem as over against the Samaritans, who had severed themselves from Judah and her public worship about the time of the Chronicler.

There is no parallel in the book of 1 Kings for 1 Chr. 22-29 with its account of the way in which David prepared for the building of the temple and its worship services. This section tells how he made advance preparations, even as to details. Then, before he died, he presented Solomon as his successor, entrusting him solemnly with the erection of the temple. In this section David is declared to be the one who really initiated the building of the temple. Its worship is also traced back ultimately to him.

In the work of the Chronicler the figure of David is not simply thrust into the very center but is also definitely idealized in comparison with the older account. Anything that could cast a shadow on the person of the king is as well as omitted, such as the entire history of David's accession to throne as well as that of the succession including the Bathsheba-Uriah episode. The idealization extends also over Solomon's kingship. Nothing is mentioned concerning the harsh measures he took to secure his throne at the outset, nothing about the external and internal difficulties that 1 Kings 11 reports. One detail might be mentioned—according to the Chronicler, it was not Solomon who relinquished twenty cities to Hiram of Tyre (1 Kings 9:11 f.) but rather Hiram who gave them to Solomon (2 Chr. 8:2).

This tendency toward idealization is not apparent in connection with the later kings of Judah. Instead, the account is profoundly influenced by the idea of retribution, which intends (as far as possible) to view the fate of each king as having been caused by his religious or irreligious conduct. Thus the premature death of Josiah at the battle of Megiddo is traced back to a failure on his part. The reason for the long reign of wicked Manasseh, however, is attributed to his change of heart while a prisoner among the Assyrians (2 Chr. 33:10-12). The leprosy of Uzziah was due to a divine judgment. It is reported, therefore, that he was buried *near** the royal cemetery (2 Chr. 26:23).

Throughout the entire account there is an emphasis on the cult as the real focal point of everything that occurred in Israel. The significance of the establishment of the temple worship is given greater emphasis by a remarkable manifestation. After Solomon's prayer of dedication, fire came down from heaven, consuming the sacrifice; and the glory of God filled the temple.

At every available opportunity, festivals and worship services are described. Importance, moreover, is attached to the willingness and readiness of people to participate in them. After the reestablishment of the ancient authentic Passover festival, the people were filled with such delight over this celebration that they immediately resolved to celebrate the festival once more (2 Chr. 30:23).

The Chronicler shows a special interest in the ones who attended to the worship—the priests and the Levites. Their importance is frequently emphasized. They even participate in warfare. The Chronicler felt it important above all to enhance the cultic significance of the Levites. He carefully distinguishes priests and Levites from the laity, altering all passages where a layman participates in a religious function or enters into a holy area. Thus, according to his account, Samuel was a Levite (1 Chr. 6:28); David's sons were

---

*"In the burial field which belonged to the kings, for they said, 'He is a leper.'" Note the difference in 2 Kings 15:7: "And Azariah (= Uzziah) slept with his fathers, and they buried him with his fathers in the city of David."

not priests but officials (1 Chr. 18:17). In the dethroning of Athaliah (2 Chr. 23) only priests could take part, because it took place in the temple.

B. THE CHRONICLE OF THE POST-EXILIC PERIOD
(Ezra and Neh.)

1. The return under Sheshbazzar and the rebuilding of the temple (Ezra 1:1–6:22)

    a. The edict of Cyrus (1:1-4, repeated in 5:12-15; 6:3-5)

    b. The freewill offering of temple vessels and the return under Sheshbazzar (1:5-11)

    c. The list of returning exiles (2:1-70)

    d. The rebuilding of the altar, and the feast of booths (3:1-6)

    e. The beginning of the temple construction (3:7-13)

    f. The hindering of the temple construction by the Samaritans who were rebuffed (4:1-5)

    g. The letter of complaint to Xerxes and Artaxerxes (4:6-16)

    h. The ban against building and the suspension of work (4:17-24)

    i. The resumption of building (Haggai and Zechariah) (5:1-2)

    j. New intervention and an inquiry addressed to Darius (5:3-17)

    k. The answer of Darius: a command to rebuild the temple on the basis of Cyrus' edict (6:1-12)

    l. The completion of the construction; the dedication of the temple (6:13-18)

    m. The celebration of the Passover (6:19-22)

2. The return under Ezra (Ezra 7-10; Neh. 8-10)

    a. Ezra returns to Jerusalem with a group of exiles (7:1-10)

    b. Artaxerxes gives Ezra full power of authority. (This section is in Aramaic) (7:11-26)

    c. A doxological conclusion (in Hebrew) (7:27-28)

    d. The list of those who returned home with Ezra (8:1-20) The Levites (vv. 15-20)

    e. Ezra's expedition to Jerusalem (8:21-36) The treasures of the temple (vv. 24-30)

(Neh. 8-10 should be inserted at this point in the following
sequence: Ezra 7-8; Neh. 8; Ezra 9-10; Neh. 9-10)

f. The oral reading of the law that Ezra brought along. The
   celebration of the Feast of Booths (Neh. 8:1-18)

g. The offense of mixed marriages is brought to Ezra's attention
   (Ezra 9:1-5)

h. Ezra's prayer of repentance (9:6-15)

i. Preventive measures are taken against mixed marriages
   (10:1-44)

j. The day of fasting. The adoption of preventive measures
   (Neh. 9:1-3, 38)

k. A prayer chanted by the Levites (9:4-37)
   (1) A summons to praise God (9:4-5)
   (2) A historical psalm (9:6-31)
   (3) A prayer for deliverance and a confession of sin (9:32-37)

l. An announcement of responsibilities (with a list of names)
   (10:1-39)

3. Nehemiah and the building of the city walls (Neh. 1-7; 11-13)

a. Nehemiah's first period of activity (1:1—12:47)
   (1) Nehemiah hears in Susa concerning the plight of Jeru-
       salem (1:1-4)
   (2) The prayer of Nehemiah, cupbearer of Artaxerxes
       (1:5-11)
   (3) Nehemiah receives a leave of absence and full power of
       authority (2:1-10)
   (4) The beginning of the construction of the walls after
       Nehemiah's tour of inspection and announcement. The
       derision and opposition of Sanballat and Tobiah (2:11-20)
   (5) The list of all those who participated in the building—
       from high priest to shopkeepers (3:1-32)
   (6) The derision of Sanballat and Tobiah. A prayer for
       revenge (4:1-5)
   (7) The attack of the hostile neighbors is frustrated (4:6-15)
   (8) The building of the walls, while armed and ready for
       attack (4:16-23)
   (9) The uprising of the poor in distress. The canceling of
       debts (5:1-13)
   (10) Nehemiah relinquishes his claim to an income as gover-
        nor (5:14-19)
   (11) The accusation and attack of Sanballat and Tobiah (6:1-9)
   (12) The attack by means of hired prophets (6:10-14, 17-19)

(13) The building of the walls is completed (6:15-16)
(14) Measures taken for the protection of the city (7:1-3)
(15) The increase in population (7:4-5)
(16) The list of returning exiles (7:6-69)
(17) The contributions (7:70-73)
(18) The listing of those who lived in Jerusalem and Judea (11:1-36)
(19) The lists of priests and Levites (12:1-26)
(20) The dedication of the walls (12:27-43)
(21) The regulation of the portions for the priests and Levites (12:44-47)

b. Nehemiah's second period of activity (13:1-30)
   (1) The eviction of Tobiah from a chamber in the temple (13:1-9)
   (2) Abuses in connection with taxes (13:10-14)
   (3) Desecrations of the Sabbath (13:15-22)
   (4) Abuses in connection with mixed marriages (13:23-29)
   (5) Conclusion (13:30-31)

It is unnecessary to add much more to this outline. A period of almost exactly a hundred years is depicted in Ezra-Nehemiah—from 538 to 432 B.C., i.e., from the first return out of Babylon up to the end of the period of Nehemiah's activity. For this period of one hundred years the second part of the Chronicler's work is our only historical source. It does not, however, present the history of Judah in a continuous and comprehensive fashion but describes the work of two men—Ezra and Nehemiah, the latter in the style of a personal memoir.

The fundamentally different character of this post-exilic historical account exhibits a plan that is similar for the three sections of Ezra-Nehemiah:

1. The permission to build the temple—
   The dedication of the temple (Ezra 1-6)

2. The endorsement of the law—
   Public service of penitence and commitment (Ezra 7-10; Neh. 8-10)

3. The permission to build the walls—
   The dedication of the walls (Neh. 1-7; 11-13)

At the beginning of each of the three sections is an authorization from the Persian king; at the end there is a religious observance that solemnly celebrates the performance of that which had been granted politically. The scheme includes the two factors that determined the events occurring in post-exilic Judah:

> (1) The decree of the Persian empire, which affected the environment of the Jewish religious community.

> (2) Public worship as the central feature of Jewish existence, around which their history thereafter revolved.

Everything in Ezra and Nehemiah revolves around these two factors. They provide an explanation also for the two basic tendencies that dominate the account:

> (1) On the one hand, there is complete as well as zealous loyalty over against the Persian sovereign.

> (2) On the other hand, there are ever-renewed efforts to maintain independence within the limits accorded them in relation to the Samaritans (Sec. 1), the question of mixed marriages (Sec. 2), hostile neighbors (Sec. 3).

In addition to these two dominant factors, a third emerges at the heart of the Book of Ezra-Nehemiah (Sect. 2). This is the oral reading of the law Ezra brought back with him and the commitment of the people to it (Neh. 8). Ezra had received express warrant for this from the Persian king (Ezra 7).

In the first section the temple is finished after many setbacks (6:13-18). With this the focal point for maintaining the life of the Jewish religious community was supposed to have been given.

The second section, however, begins by indicating the dismal situation in Jerusalem. Ezra started to put into effect an obviously necessary reform. He carried it out on the basis of the law he had brought back with him and had introduced in Jerusalem as binding. This law at the same time can hardly have been public or civic in scope. It can only have been a religious law.* If one assumes that the Old Testament includes the law of Ezra, then it can only have

---

*Cf. the expression "law of the God of heaven" (Ezra 7:12).

been the Priestly document (or the Priestly Code, the P source of the Pentateuch). Whether it was still a separate book or had already been fitted into the Pentateuch is not certain.

Public worship and the entire relationship to God as well had to be determined now by a comprehensive law, valid for the whole nation. Only in this way could the religious bond that held together the Jewish population be preserved, despite the numerous external and internal threats. Thus the religion of the law arose which later became ever more inflexible. That the work of the Chronicler, however, still contains a true vital piety is indicated by the many prayers that have been inserted in it over and over again.

XXIII

The Book of Daniel

The Book of Daniel consists of two quite different sections: the stories (chs. 1-6) and the visions (chs. 7-12). The two sections are linked together by the name Daniel, by the same period of time, and by the principal theme of steadfastness in faith at a time of severe distress.

A. THE STORIES (Dan. 1:1–6:28)

1. Daniel and his three companions remain faithful to their God, while serving at the Babylonian court (1:1-21)
   a. The exiles at court in the service of the king (1:3-7)
   b. They hesitate to partake of unclean food (1:8-17)
   c. Their obedience is rewarded (1:18-21)

2. The dreams of Nebuchadnezzar. The great image with feet of clay (2:1-49)
   a. The dream of the king and the refusal of the wise men (2:1-11)
   b. The threat of capital punishment. The solution is revealed to Daniel. A divine eulogy (2:12-23)
   c. Daniel tells the king his dream and its interpretation (2:24-45)
   d. The king promotes Daniel and extols his God (2:46-49)

3. The three men in the fiery furnace (3:1-43)
   a. The erection of the image and the command to worship it (3:1-7)
   b. The opposition of the three men and their confession of faith (3:8-18)

d. Nebuchadnezzar promotes them and extols their God (3:26-30; 4:1-3)

4. The dream concerning the tree and Daniel's interpretation (4:4-34)
   a. Nebuchadnezzar tells Daniel his dream (4:4-15)
   b. Daniel's interpretation: the king will be temporarily insane (4:16-24)
   c. The dream comes true. Nebuchadnezzar's recovery and praise of God (4:25-34)

5. The handwriting on the wall (5:1-31)
   a. A banquet in which the temple vessels were used. The handwriting on the wall (5:1-9)
   b. Daniel is questioned, and he explains the handwriting (5:10-28)
   c. Daniel receives honor. The king is slain (5:29-31)

6. Daniel in the lions' den (6:1-28)
   a. Daniel becomes the highest official. The attack against him, viz., the prohibition of all foreign cults for a month (6:1-9)
   b. Daniel prays and is thrown into the lions' den (6:10-18)
   c. Daniel is protected (6:19-24)
   d. The edict of the king, announcing that the God of Daniel should be recognized (6:25-28)

The stories once existed separately, all having the Babylonian court in the exilic period as their setting. Daniel and his three friends came with the exiles to Babylon and were selected and given training there for service as attendants at court. In the conflicts that they experienced at the Babylonian court, they remained loyal to their God and the faith of their fathers at the risk of their lives (chs. 1, 3, 6). Daniel's gift as a seer, moreover, held good in a foreign environment. More than once he alone was able to interpret dreams and visions that had to do with the destiny of the king (chs. 4, 5) and the empire (chs. 2, 5). He was accorded high honors because of this, even though he continued to hold on to his faith in stubborn loyalty.

264 THE WRITINGS

The principal part of the first section of the book is written in Aramaic (2:4b–6:28).

B. THE VISIONS OF DANIEL (Dan. 7:1–12:13)

1. The vision of the four beasts and the son of man (7:1-28)
   a. The four beasts of the sea, the ten horns, and the little horn (7:1-8)
   b. The Ancient of Days on the throne and the son of man (7:9-14)
   c. The explanation concerning the four kingdoms, given by the interpreting angel (7:15-25)
   d. The eternal kingdom (7:26-28)

2. The ram with the horns (8:1-27)
   a. The beasts, their battle, their horns (8:1-14)
   b. The explanation of the kingdoms by the angel Gabriel (8:15-27)

3. The interpretation of the seventy years of Jeremiah (9:1-27)

4. The events of the final age and the beginning of salvation (10:1–12:13)
   a. The vision of an angel. The struggles of the patron angels (10:1-21; 11:1)
   b. From the Persian empire to the kingdoms of the Diadochi (11:2-20)
   c. Antiochus Epiphanes, his downfall (11:21-45)
   d. The rise of Michael, the final battle, and the era of salvation. The sealed book (12:1-4)
   e. When will the end come? (12:5-13)

The visions (chs. 7-12) are accounts of Daniel in the first person. They belong to the large class of literature called apocalyptic, to which the little apocalypse of Isaiah (chs. 24-27), the visions of Zechariah (chs. 1-6) and Daniel (chs. 7-12) belong, along with various individual utterances in the Old Testament. In the New Testament the apocalypse of St. John is a representative.

The apocalypses are fundamentally different from the prophetic sayings. The apocalyptic writers belonged to the line of seers rather than prophets. The most important difference between them lies in the way the prophets point to *one coming event* in their announcements, whereas the apocalyptic writers sketch a *picture* of the future. This explains also the name given to them—they disclosed the future that was veiled to others.*

It is a characteristic of the visions that they could not be interpreted by the apocalyptic writers themselves. A heavenly intermediary had to explain them. (In Zechariah there was already an *angelus interpres*.)

The visions are dated: ch. 7, in the first year of Belshazzar; ch. 8, in the third; ch. 9, in the first year of Darius; and chs. 10-12, in the third year of Cyrus. All the visions (including that of Nebuchadnezzar in ch. 2) lead up to a definite point of time, viz., the final intensification of persecution against the people of God. This was then supposed to be immediately followed by the beginning of the kingdom of God, a fact that makes it possible to date these visions accurately. Thus they all relate to the time *after* Antiochus Epiphanes began his religious persecution in 167 B.C. but *before* this persecution came to an end, as manifest in the rededication of the temple in 164 B.C.

This reckoning of time, however, does not agree with the explicit assertion of the book, which purports to come from the first years of the Babylonian exile. Daniel himself, who had the visions, is represented as one of the exiles. The book, however, exhibits in every detail how far it is removed from that age. A whole series of statements are unprovable from a historical standpoint, e.g., the reference to Belshazzar as the last Babylonian king** who as far as we know was Nabonidus. On the other hand, the statements made in connection with the period of Antiochus IV (Epiphanes) are quite accurate.

The real significance of these visions in the Book of Daniel does not lie in their prediction of future events, but in the way the older

---

*Translator's Note: "Apocalypse" is derived from the Greek word *apocalyptein* "to disclose or uncover."

**Translator's Note: According to cuneiform records Belshazzar was crown prince.

concept of the history of God's people as a totality has been expanded into one of world history as a totality. In these visions for the
first time there is a grasp of world history—on the basis, that is, of
faith in Yahweh, the God of Israel, as Lord of history. The external
distress of Israel as a religious community cherishing God's promises, little Israel, who long since had been written off historically
speaking, laid bare this view of world history.

The concept of totality is represented by the statue (ch. 2), the
animals with the horns (chs. 7, 8), the numerical systems (ch. 9),
and the angels of the nations (ch. 10). This comprehensive view of
history that finds expression in the visions is sustained by the faith
that God is moving toward his destination, and that this destination
is the kingdom of God into which all history flows.

Index of Names and Subjects

Index of Scripture References

OLD TESTAMENT

NEW TESTAMENT